THE
EVERYTHING
GUIDE TO
BORDERLINE PERSONALITY
DISORDER

Dear Reader,

Borderline personality disorder is one of the most stigmatized and misunderstood mental health issues we have. It can create confusion and pain for the person suffering with it and for the loved ones who must deal with the symptoms.

I first encountered borderline personality disorder when I worked with substance abuse clients. The people I worked with exuded a distinct need and a fear of being alone. The families often felt the same way. It is a serious disorder with little in the way of information and reference for the people concerned. For some the world seems hopeless. They do not know where to turn or what to do.

But there is hope. Research has given new information on treatment options that can work. Many people with borderline personality disorder who seek and work within the guidelines of treatment see a large reduction in symptoms. There are people out there who care and who are ready to help. Have faith in your ability to make it through this and help your loved one live a happier life.

Constance M. Dolecki, MS, PhDc

Welcome to the EVERYTHING® Series!

These handy, accessible books give you all you need to tackle a difficult project, gain a new hobby, comprehend a fascinating topic, prepare for an exam, or even brush up on something you learned back in school but have since forgotten.

You can choose to read an Everything® book from cover to cover or just pick out the information you want from our four useful boxes: e-questions, e-facts, e-alerts, and e-ssentials.

We give you everything you need to know on the subject, but throw in a lot of fun stuff along the way, too.

We now have more than 400 Everything® books in print, spanning such wide-ranging categories as weddings, pregnancy, cooking, music instruction, foreign language, crafts, pets, New Age, and so much more. When you're done reading them all, you can finally say you know Everything®!

QUESTION

Answers to common questions

FACT

Important snippets of information

ALERT

Urgent warnings

ESSENTIAL

Quick handy tips

PUBLISHER Karen Cooper

DIRECTOR OF ACQUISITIONS AND INNOVATION Paula Munier

MANAGING EDITOR, EVERYTHING® SERIES Lisa Laing

COPY CHIEF Casey Ebert

ASSISTANT PRODUCTION EDITOR Melanie Cordova

ACQUISITIONS EDITOR Kate Powers

SENIOR DEVELOPMENT EDITOR Brett Palana-Shanahan

EDITORIAL ASSISTANT Ross Weisman

EVERYTHING® SERIES COVER DESIGNER Erin Alexander

LAYOUT DESIGNERS Erin Dawson, Michelle Roy Kelly, Elisabeth Lariviere, Denise Wallace

Visit the entire Everything® series at *www.everything.com*

THE EVERYTHING®

GUIDE TO

BORDERLINE PERSONALITY DISORDER

Professional, reassuring advice for coping with the
disorder and breaking the destructive cycle

Constance M. Dolecki, MS, PhDc

Adams Media
New York London Toronto Sydney New Delhi

*This book is dedicated to all who deal with a mental
health issue. The stigma eases each time people are
open to learning and growing.*

Adams media

Adams Media
An Imprint of Simon & Schuster, Inc.
100 Technology Center Drive
Stoughton, MA 02072

For information about special discounts for bulk purchases, please contact Simon &
Schuster Special Sales at 1-866-506-1949 or business@simonandschuster.com.

The Simon & Schuster Speakers Bureau can bring authors to your live event. For more
information or to book an event contact the Simon & Schuster Speakers Bureau at
1-866-248-3049 or visit our website at www.simonspeakers.com.

Manufactured in the United States of America

12 2022

Library of Congress Cataloging-in-Publication Data has been applied for.

ISBN 978-1-4405-2970-2
ISBN 978-1-4405-2994-8 (ebook)

Contents

Acknowledgments

I would like to thank my family for giving me the encouragement and support to complete this book. My husband, Bernie, kept me centered and motivated. I would also like to thank Kate Powers for giving me the opportunity to write this book and the patience to help me get through to the end. Last, but not least, I would like to thank the Cattaraugus County Council on Alcoholism and Substance Abuse, which gave me my start as a therapist and will always hold a place in my heart.

Top 10 Things You Can Do to Help
Your Loved One with BPD

1. Attend any therapy sessions you are invited to and learn about the treatment plan.

2. Stick to the instructions you are given by the therapist in order to keep your loved one on the treatment plan.

3. Learn and practice healthy ways of easing the pain and coping with the outbursts.

4. Avoid taking on responsibility that is not yours. That leads to enabling behaviors.

5. Do not accept blame or guilt when accusations fly. That leads to enabling behaviors.

6. Be consistent in your own behaviors. If something is unacceptable today, it is unacceptable tomorrow. Do not give in one day and stay firm the next.

7. Seek support and help for yourself.

8. Do not get embarrassed or isolate yourself because of what you live with.

9. Learn as much as you can about the disorder so you can recognize what is going on.

10. Keep hope and keep going. Do not give up.

Introduction

BORDERLINE PERSONALITY DISORDER (BPD) is a mental health disorder that affects how a person processes information and his or her ability to understand and cope with different social situations. People with borderline personality disorder have problems recognizing how they should and should not act, which makes it hard for others to be around them. Friends and family members can get caught up in the whirlwind of emotions and disorganization that are characteristic of people with this disorder. The symptoms often affect others almost as much as they affect the person dealing with the disorder itself, and the resulting hurt, frustration, and confusion leave many wondering what to do next.

Borderline personality disorder also affects how people see themselves and what they do as a result. People with this disorder are usually impulsive and do not always make thoughtful decisions. They often go through a series of unstable relationships and experience mood shifts that create emotional extremes. They will be in a loving relationship one moment and then ready to end it the next. This roller coaster of emotions often turns other people off.

Fortunately, there are things that can be done to help navigate borderline personality disorder. People who live with or are around this disorder on a continual basis can benefit from learning more about what borderline personality disorder is, what might cause it, and what works best in treating it. Managing this disorder is work, but it can be done, and all concerned can enjoy life. Research uncovers more helpful information every day, and new forms of treatment are having success in generating improvements. Personality disorders are not easy to live with or work with, but increased understanding helps create successful options.

Some Characteristics of BPD

CHAPTER 1

The Basics of Borderline Personality Disorder

Borderline personality disorder is an issue that affects how people process and express thoughts and behaviors. People with borderline personality disorder do not necessarily understand social events or the dynamics of relationships the same way people who are considered healthy do. It is hard for them to understand and work within proper social guidelines that allow for compromise and negotiation. They tend to see things in black and white, making situations either win or lose, with nothing in between. When things do not go the way they think they should, they do not feel good about themselves and they do not feel good about their interaction with other persons. This often leads to behaviors that go against social norms and the way most people would expect a person to react.

Some Characteristics of BPD

People suffering from borderline personality disorder find swinging from emotion to emotion very easy. They might overreact in a situation that calls for calm communication and clarification. They tend to act impulsively and jump to conclusions based on limited information that is not processed correctly. This impulsivity can lead to angry outbursts, emotional episodes that are above and beyond what the situation would normally call for, decisions and actions made with little or no thought, and problems with substance abuse and alcohol. People with borderline personality disorder are often overrepresented in the criminal justice system, as their impulsivity leads to problems with the law. They are more prone to fighting and substance abuse, which lead to illegal behaviors.

FACT

Borderline personality disorder is 50 percent more common than Alzheimer's disease. The American Psychiatric Association states that BPD affects 2 percent of the population directly, and countless family members, coworkers, and spouses live with those suffering from it.

People with borderline personality disorder often have low self-esteem, causing them to feel worthless and unlovable. This reaction makes them more prone to bad relationships. They feel a strong need to be in a relationship at all times, which leads to desperation and poor choices. People with borderline personality disorder often jump quickly into relationships and fall in love fast. Their friendships become very close very quickly, and often there is an attempt to make them exclusive. There is a strong need for love and approval from others that causes relationships to fall apart over small details that are interpreted as criticism or dislike. A minor disagreement can become a major blowup, as the potential explosiveness of the anger and emotion activate to counter some perceived rejection. Rejection is easily perceived and quickly acted upon.

Relationship issues are not limited to romantic partners. These behaviors are also evident in friendships, work relationships, family interactions, and interactions within groups or other social settings. The positive emotion and rush to commitment comes on strong in the beginning, providing comfort and belonging that the person believes will be lasting and perfect. People with borderline personality disorder jump from one "perfect" relationship or situation to another, and often see the achievement or attainment of something as the means to cure all of their problems.

ALERT

If you are in a relationship that you feel has progressed too quickly and your partner is demanding a fast and deep commitment, take a step back and evaluate it. Relationships are not races, and if someone cares about you and wishes to pursue a genuine relationship, that person should not mind taking it slowly at first if that makes you more comfortable.

In a person with BPD there is a tendency to move from one activity to another. Yet one activity could become a temporary obsession, with the person devoting a large amount of time to it, often at the expense of obligations and daily responsibilities. Commitments and promised acts are left undone, causing others to become upset and frustrated. When they say something to the person with borderline personality disorder, it is often taken as criticism. This engenders defensiveness in the relationship, causing it to be no longer perfect. Often it becomes the other person's fault that things did not get done. Due to issues with low self-esteem, it is very hard for someone with personality disorder to own up to mistakes or wrongdoings. She will go to great lengths to deny them and place them on someone else.

Borderline personality disorder is one of the most misunderstood mental health disorders and one of the most stigmatized. It is not a disorder that someone can deal with alone. This is a disorder that needs help and treatment. But people who have this disorder can learn to deal with the symptoms, and they can lead normal lives. New research and information have provided a lot of hope for those who need to cope with this disorder, either personally or in a loved one or friend. Borderline personality disorder has undergone a transformation from one of the most feared diagnoses to a condition that can be controlled with understanding, patience, and diligence.

Living with Someone with BPD

Most people who know someone diagnosed with borderline personality disorder have found themselves wondering what to do in different situations. They might find that they are the object of an angry outburst without provocation. They might also find themselves embarrassed from time to time, as their companion causes a scene or starts an argument over something seemingly trivial, like receiving a perceived dirty look from another person. The angry outbursts and strong emotional reactions are characteristic of the borderline personality disorder, but other personality disorders contain confusing or confused reactions to different situations too.

ESSENTIAL

People with BPD often invent, exaggerate, or imagine slights from other people. They might see someone in a store whisper something to their companion, and automatically assume this perfect stranger is mocking them. A genuine compliment can be perceived as a veiled insult. Ironically, it is usually the BPD's subsequent tantrum-like behavior that brings on people's negative feelings more than anything else!

The world as seen through the eyes of someone with borderline personality disorder is often somewhat distorted and focused on social practices that do not follow social norms. People who have borderline personality disorder were originally thought to be knowingly and intentionally self-centered and oppositional. For loved ones this led to much frustration and confusion. They did not know how to cope with the mood swings or the seemingly blatant unconcern for behaviors that caused embarrassment and conflict. People diagnosed with this disorder do not necessarily act to cause others pain, they are merely trying to navigate their world according to the way their brains process information and the way their environment shapes the processing of this information.

A person's biological makeup has a large influence on how perceptions and behaviors interact to create that individual's personality. When this is combined with problems within the living environment, like abuse or neglect, or some trauma, it can promote the development of personality disorders.

Personality disorders tend to have distortions in perceptions and information processing that lead to behaviors that do not go along with social norms for the person's community.

QUESTION

My spouse often gets angry at odd things, and seemingly out of nowhere. Is this a sign of BPD?
It might be. But getting angry is a completely human, natural, and normal emotion, so unless it happens frequently and intensely, and your spouse is blatantly unconcerned with these fits of rage, it may just be a case of letting off some steam. But if you ever feel unsafe or uncomfortable by your spouse's anger, leave at once and go somewhere safe.

Personality Disorder Basics

Personality disorders are some of the hardest disorders to recognize and understand, yet as a group, they are among the most common mental health disorders—about one in twenty individuals suffer from a personality disorder. Personality disorders are a group of disorders that focus on enduring thoughts and behaviors that are different from what would be considered "normal" thoughts and behaviors for a given situation in a given culture. A person dealing with a personality disorder has difficulty perceiving and relating to situations and people. People with personality disorders might see themselves as "normal" and look at others as the source of problems. They often have a narrower view of the world and have trouble navigating social events. Everyday stressors and problems are often amplified, causing greater hardship than they would for someone who did not work from this different perspective. Some mental health disorders classified as personality disorders include avoidant personality disorder, antisocial personality disorder, paranoid personality disorder, schizoid personality disorder, schizotypal personality disorder, borderline personality disorder, histrionic personality disorder, narcissistic personality disorder, dependent personality disorder, obsessive-compulsive personality disorder, and personality disorder not otherwise specified.

Personality disorders are grounded by the general personality traits a person has. Personality traits are the fairly consistent, enduring patterns of perceiving, relating to, and thinking about events that happen to and around a person. Some people react to or perceive situations more positively, while others have negative reactions and thoughts. Normal personality patterns adapt thoughts and behaviors to meet the situation. Thus, a person might be livelier after receiving a raise, and a little more serious when in an important meeting. A person with a personality disorder, on the other hand, might show emotions that are not expected for the situation, like anger at the raise, perhaps seeing it as an insult.

Personality disorders are normally recognized and diagnosed in adolescence or early adulthood, continue through adulthood, and might become less noticeable in middle age. The thought and behavior patterns are deeply ingrained and inflexible. The inability to recognize or react in culturally acceptable or "normal" ways presents challenges for family members and friends. They are often accompanied by other disorders, such as substance use disorders, mood disorders, eating disorders, and anxiety disorders. Since personality disorders are fairly common, it is likely that many people know someone who has been diagnosed with one.

Reaction to Social Situations

People with a personality disorder do not recognize social nuances the way other people do. They might see someone who walks slowly ahead of them as doing it on purpose to hold them up. They might see a dirty look from a stranger when there wasn't one. These perceptions tend to upset people with borderline personality disorder, and they tend to react angrily, often by making loud comments aimed at the person they feel did something to them. They are quick to find offense and retaliate. The impulsivity characteristic of the disorder usually prompts words and behaviors that bring negative attention to the person causing the scene and anyone who might be with that person.

Personality disorders are determined by the norms of each culture, so if the culture has a norm that would seem different to a person from another culture, that does not make it a disorder. The thoughts and behaviors have to be abnormal for that person's specific culture. It might be that a person is unfamiliar with a culture and needs to learn new ways of thinking and behaving, but that is a matter of acculturation and not a personality disorder. In one culture, talking to a tree might be a normal way of revering nature. In another culture, this same behavior might be considered abnormal.

Abnormal Thoughts and Behaviors

With a personality disorder, the pattern of abnormal thoughts and behaviors is stable and inflexible and cannot be attributed to the use of alcohol or drugs. People tend to lose their inhibitions when they take mind-altering substances or drink alcohol. Behaviors at that time would be impulsive, possibly erratic, and perhaps overly emotional. While these symptoms are similar to borderline personality disorder symptoms, they are the result of substance use rather than something more permanent.

FACT

According to BPD Central, almost 70 percent of people related to, in a relationship with, or otherwise associated with someone with BPD have sought the help of support groups or therapists to cope. You are not alone!

Personality Disorder Treatment

Personality disorders are best treated with the help of professionals. The potential harm of some of the symptoms should be taken seriously. People who have personality disorders can go on to lead relatively normal lives, but this comes as a result of hard work, awareness, and professional intervention. The person with a personality disorder needs the support of friends and family. Treatment goes more smoothly and is more effective when life outside of the treatment facility is consistent with what is covered within the facility. People with personality disorders often find themselves confused by adverse reactions from others. They need someone around them to help them learn to recognize and work within difficult situations. It is important to note that problems within the home and family can make symptoms of personality disorders worse. Treatment that involves the family helps everyone.

Is it something I say or do that sets my sister off? She seems to get very angry, very quickly!

The main problem with a personality disorder is the trouble someone has understanding social expectations and norms the way others do. Your sister might become confused and frustrated when others do not understand her, or when they do not behave the way she thinks they should. It is sometimes helpful to ask your sister how she understands what you just said or did and go from there.

What Are Some Causes of Personality Disorders?

Personality disorders seem to have both genetic and environmental influences. While some experts lean toward the influence of experiences in early childhood, others focus more on genetic predisposition. It is likely some combination of the two. People who have a genetic predisposition might fail to develop a personality disorder unless environmental circumstances prompt the development. In other cases people who do not have a genetic predisposition might develop a personality disorder without any specific explanation to be found. This is still an area open to research and speculation. While it is possible to narrow some causes down and provide some possible risks that make development of a personality disorder more likely, definitive causes have not yet been completely defined.

Possible Parental Origins

Personality disorders were originally thought to be the result of abuse or neglect by parents during early developmental years. Most of the focus was on mothering and consistency in providing a safe, nurturing, loving environment for the young child. This thought process placed a great deal of blame on mothers when their children developed personality disorders or related disorders such as schizophrenia. It became easier to scrutinize what the family environment looked like and what they did wrong than search further for other possible factors that could have been related to the onset of the disorder. Since Mom was the one most often home with the children, blame went directly to her.

The original theoretical model used for diagnosis and treatment of personality disorders was the psychoanalytic approach. The psychoanalytic approach places emphasis on subconscious thoughts that lead to behaviors contrary to what would normally be expected. It proposes that these subconscious thoughts are the result of conflict in family relationships, most often mothers conflicting with daughters and fathers conflicting with sons. In healthy family environments these conflicts are merely part of the developmental process. They do not amount to anything other than growth in negotiation of family roles.

In families where abuse and neglect do occur, fear and pain are being bred in the subconscious as the child is growing. As the child grows, the bad experiences from the early years would affect how the child looks at situations and reacts to them. Thus issues in personality disorders that create distortions in how situations are perceived and how people should behave and interact with others would be the result of that abuse and neglect. Using the psychoanalytical approach, it was thought that by uncovering these subconscious issues and exposing them to conscious thought, they would be able to deal with some of the symptoms of the disorder.

FACT

Psychoanalysis was first introduced by Sigmund Freud as a result of his own self-analysis in the early 1900s. Others before Freud spoke of the influence of unconscious processes, but Freud was the first to emphasize its importance in how people thought and behaved.

Time and technology have changed this line of thinking to some extent. There is still an element of environment to personality disorders, but they are not solely based on the experiences people have when they are young. There is also a biological component that seems to predispose certain people with sensitivity to personality disorders. Parts of the brain seemed to malfunction and cause some of the behavior and recognition issues that come about with personality disorders. There might be some issues with the levels of different hormones and brain chemicals. These issues would affect the message that is sent to the brain about a particular situation and how a person perceives that particular situation.

This combines with environmental issues like abuse or neglect to produce the conditions that create a disorder. There are other environmental issues, besides abuse and neglect, that can affect the formation of the symptoms of this disorder. Socioeconomic status can also be a problem. People who are born in lower income households seem to have a higher prevalence of personality disorders. This could be for a combination of reasons. First, households in poor neighborhoods are at higher risk for substance and alcohol abuse, which can also be linked to development of personality disorders. These issues are often also associated with higher risk of abuse and neglect. There are also environmental fears connected to higher crime rates and less availability to quality medical and mental health care. People who live in poor neighborhoods might also do so because they have a mental health issue that prevents them from getting a higher-paying job, or any job at all. This leaves them little choice but to move to a lower-cost neighborhood. If they do not get help for the issues they are experiencing, this adds to the problem and increases the risk for children. Socioeconomic status is actually a combination of both environmental and genetic factors, as the person with mental health issues living in the poorer neighborhood is more likely to pass on the predisposition or potential to children.

QUESTION

I believe that my mother suffered from BPD. Does that mean I will have it, and pass it on to my children?
The genetic link of BPD is being studied, and has shown some indication that there is an increased risk of developing BPD when a parent has the disorder. It should be noted, however, that it is not a given that someone will automatically inherit BPD. Environmental factors also influence its development.

There is a higher incidence of personality disorders in families with a history of personality disorders, but the genetic link does not seem to be enough. Some symptoms seem to be more biological, while others seem to be based on events in the person's life. The stronger the combination of negative factors in a person's life, the more likely an issue will develop. If someone with a personality disorder raises a child to think and behave as they do, the genetic and environmental issues might combine to cause more problems for the child. Some households, on the other hand, do not see the continuance of a personality disorder from parent to child. As stated earlier, causes are still under investigation, leaving everyone to speculate on which parts of an individual's life might increase risk, and what can be done to decrease risk.

General Symptoms of Personality Disorders

In order to be classified as a personality disorder, symptoms must be inflexible and maladaptive. They should not vary or waver from situation to situation but should remain consistent and stable for long periods of time. These patterns of behavior will be obviously different from the expectations of a person's culture. An individual with a personality disorder will have significant problems functioning within society, and this will create noticeable distress. Personality disorders have very strong symptoms that are easily noticeable because they greatly differ from how others in a given society act. While the patterns are consistent and stable, dealing with someone with a personality disorder often seems unpredictable and sometimes volatile. Strong reactions to minor issues, or issues that would normally seem minor to most in a given society, often create confusion and fear of what might come next.

ALERT

It's normal and healthy to get angry, as long as that anger is not violent, uncontrollable, or dangerous. If you or someone you love gets very angry, very quickly, and very often, sometimes at the most insignificant of events, it is possible BPD is present.

Although there are different personality disorders, most of them have some general symptoms that are the same. They include repeated mood swings, a series of frequent, unstable relationships, social isolation, tantrums and angry outbursts, general mistrust of others and expectation of wrongdoing, difficulty interacting with others and maintaining friendships, need for instant satisfaction of desires, impulsivity, and alcohol or substance abuse.

Mood Swings

Mood swings can also be attributed to mood disorders. With personality disorders, however, the mood swings are more persistent and seem more closely associated with personality traits. The swings in mood disorders are more transient, coming and going in cyclical patterns. However, in personality disorders the mood swings are consistent across time and occur regularly.

Unstable Relationships

People with personality disorders normally have a series of frequent unstable relationships due to many of the other issues associated with the disorder. The mood swings make it hard for another person to understand or anticipate what might happen next. The general mistrust aimed at another person makes it hard for that other person to get close and want to stay close. The impulsivity and substance abuse often lead to financial and legal issues that leave others reluctant to be close and risk responsibility or obligation for some of the behaviors and swings.

Substance Abuse

Substance abuse and alcohol abuse are two large issues that are often associated with personality disorders. These issues sometimes precede the disorder, meaning they are there before a diagnosis of a personality disorder, yet because the symptoms of a personality disorder need to be evident by adolescence or early adulthood, it is sometimes hard to determine which comes first. Most often, as the symptoms of the personality disorder begin to affect the individual, they begin to self-medicate by turning to alcohol or substances. Unfortunately, the use of these substances often increases the severity of the symptoms. There is more impulsivity because normal inhibitions are not in place due to the substance use. Anger or aggression can become more severe. And distrust can become paranoia as the perceptions are further warped by the substance interacting with the brain.

Personality Disorder Clusters

Different personality disorders fall into three main categories or clusters based on general behaviors and symptoms. The first category is Cluster A, which is characterized by odd or eccentric behavior. This cluster includes schizoid personality disorder, paranoid personality disorder, and schizotypal personality disorder. Symptoms typical of this cluster include problems thinking clearly and coherently, with possible distrust and paranoia. These disorders are actually closer to a link with schizophrenia that was originally attributed to borderline personality disorder.

ESSENTIAL

Personality disorders in Cluster B are usually defined by patterns of behavior that are repeated and do not waver in intensity. For example, narcissistic personality disorder, another Cluster B, is defined as a disorder in which the sufferer is inherently selfish, uncaring, and self-centered, but these behaviors must be consistent in order to make a full diagnosis.

In Cluster B, symptoms are characterized by emotional or dramatic behavior, and include antisocial personality disorder, borderline personality disorder, and narcissistic personality disorder. Symptoms typical of this cluster are normally more volatile, with frequent expressions of strong emotions. There is somewhat of a break with reality, and information from others has a tendency to be processed negatively.

Cluster C personality disorders focus on anxious or fearful behaviors and include avoidant personality disorder, dependent personality disorder, and obsessive-compulsive personality disorder. This cluster often contains symptoms of insecurity and anxiety. Obsessive-compulsive personality disorder should not be confused with the anxiety disorder, obsessive-compulsive disorder. The symptoms for borderline personality disorder are more pervasive and are not necessarily related to periods of anxiety.

In personality disorders, the individual usually does not consider her thoughts and behaviors to be unusual or problematic. This complicates matters for assessment and treatment. The professional involved in evaluation and treatment must sift through the thoughts and narratives of the person with the personality disorder to determine the truth of the matter and must also help this person recognize and be able to identify these problematic thoughts and behaviors on a daily basis. The inability to recognize their own thoughts and behaviors as wrong or abnormal makes it hard for family and loved ones to try to communicate pain or unhappiness with individuals with a personality disorder. Each particular personality disorder has its own consistent traits, thoughts, and behaviors.

Borderline Personality Disorder Facts

Borderline personality disorder was originally listed in the *Diagnostic and Statistical Manual of Mental Disorders, Third Edition* (DSM-III) in 1980. People with this disorder were thought to show considerable social contrariness and a pattern of using others for their own ends. This particular version of the DSM broke classifications into axes, separating Axis I disorders from Axis II disorders. Personality disorders were placed on Axis II as a means of separating them from the more widely known mood and anxiety disorders of Axis I. Axis II disorders were considered to be more pervasive, having a strong relationship to early-development issues caused by parent neglect, abuse, or inconsistency.

The term "borderline personality disorder" originally came about as a way to identify behaviors that were literally on the border between those identified as either psychotic or neurotic behavior. The original theory was that borderline personality disorder was related to schizophrenia because some of the symptoms were similar. Researchers thought that they were related biologically, and that borderline personality disorder was a milder, borderline form of schizophrenia. Over time, research indicated that while some symptoms with a biological basis were similar between schizophrenia and schizotypal personality disorder, borderline personality disorder did not share them, and therefore it was no longer regarded as a related disorder. Although the relationship between borderline personality disorder and schizophrenia was no longer accepted, the name remained, and the idea behind it stayed in the minds of health professionals.

BPD versus Bipolar Disorder

Borderline personality disorder has also been mistaken for bipolar mood disorder in both name and symptoms. Some confuse the two because the names are similar, while others are confused because many of the symptoms are similar and there is a lot more public attention and information available for bipolar mood disorder. The mood swings for borderline personality disorder are more consistent. The mood swings for bipolar mood disorder tend to occur in cycles, or can be the result of a certain situation or experience that has just occurred. With borderline personality disorder situations and cycles do not affect mood swings. They occur as part of the person's general pattern of behaviors.

The Stigma of BPD

The name borderline personality disorder itself has created stigma for those who have been diagnosed with the disorder, and the difficulty diagnosing the complex symptoms has caused some professionals to avoid working with people who have borderline personality disorder. It was originally categorized as an Axis II disorder in part because it was viewed as an incurable life sentence that became the person rather than something the person had to deal with. The identification with the person made it seem more like a personal fault rather than a condition the person had. This increased the stigma, especially as people with borderline personality disorder are already suffering from low self-esteem, and assuming others think negatively about them.

These assumptions make it hard for a people to communicate with individuals with borderline personality disorder because they often take the information personally. They see it as criticism and a personal attack, rather than a constructive suggestion. If someone disagrees with them, they become defensive and feel the need to prove they are right. There is a sensitivity to criticism that creates a negative thought process. If someone suggests another way of doing something, the person with borderline personality disorder might interpret it as meaning he is wrong in the way he is doing it. This then escalates, as it impacts his low self-esteem to create a situation where he sees himself as stupid or no good. He then feels the need to find some way to feel better. One way is through the use of substances.

There is a higher risk of drug and alcohol abuse in people with borderline personality disorder. Borderline personality disorder and substance or alcohol abuse disorders frequently go hand in hand. Many residents in treatment for substance abuse disorders have a borderline personality disorder diagnosis. The symptoms of borderline personality disorder do not go away easily, and they normally need treatment.

ESSENTIAL

Since those with BPD take even the most constructive criticism as a personal attack, sometimes the best approach is to use "I" statements rather than "you" statements. You're bound to have more luck with, "I get very upset when you get worked up over waiting in traffic" rather than "You need to stop yelling at every red light we get!"

Individuals with borderline personality disorder are often prone to episodes of anger and rage and severe depression, and they are a strong risk for self-inflicted wounds and suicide attempts. Substance abuse issues are often present and can contribute to thoughts and behaviors that are outside of the norm. The combination of borderline personality disorder symptoms and the mind-altering properties of the substance contribute to deviant behaviors. Over half of the people in the criminal justice system have symptoms of severe personality disorders, including antisocial personality disorder and borderline personality disorder.

Borderline personality disorder is difficult to treat, especially when other issues are combined with it. An extended length of time is usually necessary to properly work with this disorder, making insurance coverage difficult to get approval for. On the positive end, therapeutic advances have increased hope for recovery and provided various effective options for treatment and regulation of symptoms.

Borderline Personality Disorder in Different Forms

Borderline personality disorder can show itself in different ways. One of the main issues people who have borderline personality disorder often face is the intense fear of abandonment and need for close relationships at all times. This drive often results in a series of unstable relationships characterized by alternating extremes of both detestation and adoration. Feelings swing one way and then the other as minor issues within the relationship are taken out of context and exaggerated. The person with borderline personality disorder will swing from being deeply in love to feeling intense anger and dislike with minor provocation. This holds true for friendships and relationships with family members and coworkers and makes it difficult to navigate a relationship, as the person affected goes from one extreme to another without warning.

Separation Anxiety

The intense abandonment fears and angry behaviors can occur even in minor situations where there will be a limited amount of time of separation. It can also occur when there is a sudden change in plans, however minor that change might be. If someone is late, it could set off an excessive angry reaction. If an appointment with a therapist is canceled, it could lead to a strong panic reaction.

ALERT

If you are in a relationship with someone who always pushes for more—more time, more information, more involvement—never give more than you are comfortable sharing, and do not be afraid to say no. A healthy, loving partner will respect your wishes.

The individual with borderline personality disorder feels your abandonment so strongly in her intolerance of being alone that she will resort to many different types of behaviors. The need to prevent abandonment often results in poor decisions made as a result of impulsive behaviors and feelings of desperation.

Jumping into Relationships

This often sets people up for poorly matched relationships that are doomed before they begin. People with borderline personality disorder normally jump without thinking and become heavily involved, pushing for the same level of involvement from the other person. They become fast lovers or friends without allowing time for get to know each other first. They demand to spend a lot of time together and often share a bit of the most intimate details of their lives very early on. The other party in the relationship might be reluctant to take part in the sharing. This can be interpreted by the person with borderline personality disorder as rejection or as not being there enough. She expects that if she gives something in some way, whether it be information, time, or money, that the other person will reciprocate in some way they deem of equal value. When this does not happen in the expected way, it can lead to a switch from idealizing the other person to devaluing the other person. The impulsivity again comes into effect, as the relationship that started so quickly ends just as quickly, which affects the person's confidence about having a relationship.

Self-Esteem Issues and Risky Behaviors

People with borderline personality disorder often exhibit low self-esteem and self-damaging trends in behaviors, such as overspending, indiscriminate sexual encounters, substance abuse, and binge eating. They show extremes in behaviors that are almost obsessive or compulsive. These behaviors are meant to provide a high or a feeling of instant gratification. Unfortunately, this feeling does not last long, and the need for new feel-good options drives more self-damaging behaviors. The fallout from the behaviors often results in feeling worse in some way, further damaging self-esteem and creating more self-dislike. The end result can also bring on financial problems, sexually transmitted diseases, pregnancy, or other health problems resulting from the impulsive behaviors.

In addition, they might show signs of self-mutilation or suicidal thoughts and behaviors. Some behaviors are a ploy for attention, but others are very serious attempts to harm and end life. There is a great deal of self-harm and self-deprecation in thoughts and actions that prevent the person from thinking clearly. Impulsive behaviors are the norm, and those who live with someone with this disorder often find themselves trying to do damage control and act to anticipate and prevent tragedy.

Self-image is often unstable and highly guarded behind strong defense mechanisms that often lead to additional trouble. People who have borderline personality disorder have a high risk of substance use and abuse, and are overrepresented in prisons and counseling centers. The substance use increases the impulsive behaviors and the damaging results. It reduces inhibitions and can lead the way to aggression and fighting as the substance interacts with the parts of the brain that are already primed to override inhibitions.

ESSENTIAL

While some variants of self-harm are for attention only, you should always note and report any incidents of abuse in someone with BPD. It can be difficult to acknowledge this behavior and "reward" someone doing it for attention, but simply put, if someone is willing to cut herself for attention, you cannot be 100 percent sure of what else she may do.

An individual with borderline personality can present a compelling initial impression. They might be seen as fun-loving, ready for commitment, and eager to please. As time goes on and the behaviors show more intensity, the image changes and the individual might look a little more clingy and manipulating. These reactions are based on how the thought processes develop.

CHAPTER 2

Borderline Personality Disorder and the Brain

Borderline personality disorder, like most other disorders, has been studied for possible problems with the way the brain is functioning. Since people who have borderline personality disorder normally have trouble recognizing social norms and altering behaviors to reflect these norms, this has been an area of focus. There might be issues with the way messages are sent to and from the brain.

The Biology of BPD

The messaging system is made up of the central nervous system (CNS) and the peripheral nervous system (PNS). The central nervous system is made up of the brain and spinal cord, which extends down the back of the body. The brain and spinal cord are actually one continuous unit of connective tissue, rather than two separate structures. The peripheral nervous system branches out from the central nervous system. Messages are sent back and forth between the two systems. The peripheral nervous system contains the senses of the body, and is constantly bringing in input from the senses and sending this input to the brain. The brain is also sending feedback to the senses. If the eyes see something green, the brain identifies it as grass. If the nose smells smoke, the brain identifies it as such, and produces an alert reaction, readying to flee a dangerous situation if necessary.

The Role of Neurons

Messages are relayed from the nervous system to the brain by neurons. When a neuron receives an electrical signal from another neuron it releases a chemical messenger that impacts the next neuron, and so on down the line. This process occurs very quickly. Differing chemical messengers, called neurotransmitters, are sent for different reactions. As the message is sent, the neuron is placed on high alert, and is considered to be in the action stage. Once the message moves on to the next neuron, the neuron has the ability to go back to a resting stage. If all goes as it should, neurotransmitters are repackaged and ready for future use. If, however, the chemicals that spurred the message in the first place continue to come at that neuron, the message continues, and the neuron remains in an action stage.

If the process is not working the way it should, the neurotransmitters could continue to send messages to the next neuron, causing a chain reaction from neuron to neuron to continue that particular reaction. If, on the other hand, the neurotransmitters do not release as they should, the message does not relay the way it needs to. This again causes a chain reaction, only this time it is reaction of inactivity as the message stalls.

Different nerve transmitters are responsible for different aspects of brain function. For example, serotonin is involved in regulating mood. If the serotonin levels are not correct, mood could be affected. Someone might overreact or underreact to different situations. One way researchers have found to look into the messaging systems is through brain imaging. Brain imaging in its various forms can show different brain activity and potential areas of the brain that are not functioning as they should be.

ESSENTIAL

Human infants are born with thousands of neurons that increase as they begin to learn and do. The more an area of the body is used, the more neuron development occurs in that area. If there is little use in an area, neuron development slows. If someone is born blind, neuron development to sight organs will slow, while development to other, compensating sensory areas will increase.

Brain imaging is a recent addition to the research conducted on border-line personality disorder. Various forms of brain imaging have been used to learn more about which areas of the brain light up, or are active, when the person is faced with certain situations or problems. Different forms of brain imaging are able to pinpoint activity during different situations.

The electroencephalograph (EEG) records the electrical activity of the brain. Neurons are electrochemical information processors that produce an electrical current. Electrodes are placed on the scalp and are able to pick up the activity of the neurons through the electric current being generated. EEGs were one of the initial forms of brain imaging used, though they are not as exact as some of the newer methods.

Imaging Techniques

Functional imaging techniques have been able to pinpoint brain activity with more accuracy. These techniques measure changes in blood flow rather than neural activity, resulting in a map of brain activity showing where the blood flow goes during each task. One brain imaging technique is the positron emission tomography scan (PET scan). The PET scan is conducted by having the patient drink a liquid containing radioactive substances that are distributed in harmless amounts. The radioactive substance is able to gauge where the blood flow is occurring and convert it to a visual image using different colors. Red and yellow normally indicate increased activity in the brain, while blue and green normally indicate less activity.

The functional magnetic resonance imaging (fMRI) scan is similar to the PET scan. It measures brain activity through blood flow, but the fMRI uses magnetic detectors that can measure hemoglobin levels in the blood by measuring the differences in oxygenated and nonoxygenated hemoglobin. The oxygenated hemoglobin carries oxygen and the nonoxygenated does not. The greater the difference in these two, the more activity is occurring in that area. Like the PET scan, it shows activity using a color-coded map of the brain with red and yellow, and blue and green. The fMRI scan does not require ingesting a radioactive substance or electrodes placed on the skull and so it can be done more frequently.

FACT

The colors red and yellow are considered "hot colors" that indicate a great deal of activity, while blue and green are "cool colors" that indicate less activity. Researchers can study separate scans to see how these colors change in relation to different stimuli.

Measuring brain activity and tracing where it occurs allows professionals to see how personality development is affected by brain development. As will be discussed later, some areas of the brain have shown problems or lower levels of required chemicals that have influenced the symptoms of borderline personality disorder.

How Does the Brain Affect Personality?

Personality traits have a genetic connection. Traits are the inherited, consistent patterns of thought and behavior each person has. People process and react to information based on how their traits have been formed and how they have interacted with their environment. Two of the most identifiable personality traits using different forms of brain imaging are aggression and fearfulness. The region of the brain most often activated for these emotions in brain imaging is the amygdala.

The Amygdala

The amygdala shows differences in healthy brain function and brain function for those with borderline personality disorder. Imaging shows that the amygdala works with other areas of the brain to regulate anger and fear reactions. When this function is not as active, aggressive responses are higher. Other areas of the brain are more active at this same time—areas that control aggression and emotion. The area of the brain responsible for controlling or stopping anger responses does not seem to work as well in people with borderline personality disorder. This area does not light up with the red and yellow colors on a PET scan or fMRI to signal activation in response to situations that might be getting out of control. The brain functions act to help people decide how to react to situations. When areas of the brain are not reacting properly, overly emotional responses could result.

ALERT

If someone takes medication designed to calm down panic, it is possible to alter the firing sequence for neurons or prevent them from reuptake. This can cause problems thinking and performing certain actions like driving a vehicle or handling complicated tasks.

The tendency to misinterpret the words and actions of others could also be a part of the brain controls. Thus, people with borderline personality disorder do not seem to have a normal ability to cooperate with others. Other brain chemicals, including glutamate, have been implicated in the high incidence of impulsivity in this disorder. Higher levels of these brain chemicals seem to encourage the brain to act impulsively without the regulatory thoughts people normally use before acting. Glutamate has also been linked to major depression, which might explain why someone with borderline personality disorder has trouble regulating negative emotions. Thus, the glutamate neurotransmitters might be released more than they should be, and might not be taken back into the neurons as quickly as would normally happen.

These areas are all under careful study as researchers work to find the areas of the brain that seem to make it more likely someone will develop borderline personality disorder. As the chemicals and brain areas are identified, new forms of treatment can be found to help bring chemical levels back to a normal state. People who are able to think and control impulses and behaviors are better able to work through the issues that often get them in trouble. When the systems and chemicals responsible for this regulation are functioning properly, people with borderline personality disorder are able to learn to function more comfortably and make better, or at least more carefully thought-out decisions based on perceptions that are more in focus.

How Identity Develops

Identity develops as a result of the interaction of both biological and environmental influences. Identity is based on the distinct personality of an individual. As an individual progresses through life stages, an identity is formed and creates a reputation or recognition of that individual by others. It is a person's uniqueness. Identity development progresses based on how an individual perceives and integrates life experiences into his own unique characteristics. Thus, identity is a part of how a child interacts with his environment. One manner of interacting with the environment that seems to have a large impact on identity development is gender.

Gender Roles

Everyone is born a certain gender, and this affects how personality develops. Certain hormones are present in higher levels depending upon gender. Males normally have higher levels of testosterone, while females normally have higher levels of estrogen. Testosterone is a hormone that is linked with aggressive personalities. The higher the levels, the more likely the person will be aggressive or easily angered. This is reinforced by the environment in many cases, as males are socialized to be more aggressive in most societies.

Males learn about their roles from infancy. Most are dressed in certain colors considered to be masculine, and are given toys in these same colors to reinforce that they are males. Parents treat males and females differently as infants, providing gentler nurturing to females. As they become toddlers and young children, they are encouraged to play with toys that have a sporting or aggressive theme. When they go to school, their identity as males is further reinforced by how teachers treat them, and how they play with other males. As they get older, peers have a stronger influence and continue to promote certain traits expected in males.

QUESTION

My brother likes things that are traditionally feminine. Does this mean he has a lower level of testosterone?
Not necessarily. Personal tastes do not reflect the amount of testosterone in a human. The testosterone will be more influential in how your brother handles things when they do not go well or when he wants something.

Males are taught to keep emotions inside and be brave. They are given toys that encourage them to be rough and strong. These things translate into personality. They are often socialized to be more adventurous and follow the train of openness to experience. Males who fall into this pattern easily become aggressive and masculine, while those who do not have some trouble adjusting to society and what they should be. They become confused about their identity.

Females follow the same patterns of reinforcement, but are encouraged to be less aggressive and more nurturing. They are encouraged to have the trait of agreeableness. They are taught to obey and follow. The toys they are socialized with are more in line with nurturing tasks like taking care of babies and the house, waiting on others. The higher levels of estrogen play a part as this hormone is responsible for emotion regulation. Females with higher levels of estrogen tend to have a harder time regulating some emotions and might be more sensitive to the thoughts and behaviors of others. This stronger tie to emotion and trouble regulating emotion could be connected to the higher rate of borderline personality disorder in females as opposed to males.

Identity

Identity, however, goes beyond formation of gender expectations and gender roles. Identity is also determined through group associations, goals, and social interactions. People often define themselves by how they would like others to perceive them, or how they feel others perceive them. Social identity comes through group associations and social interactions. The groups people belong to provide information on the interests of the members of the group. Membership in certain groups creates an image of the members of the group. For example, membership in a country club might create the assumption that the members are rich. Membership in volunteer groups, on the other hand, might create an image of caring and giving on the part of the members. Members themselves tend to allow their own identity to reflect the message of the group. They tend to conform to the norms of the group, which affects identity formation.

As children grow older and age into adolescence, their identity is centered more on social events and peer groups than it is on home and family. Influence comes from who they hang around with and what their social groups do. If these groups are labeled in some negative way, the members of the group might conform to those negative ideas and begin to think and behave in that particular way. For example, if one member of a group is caught smoking a cigarette and the group is then labeled as a group of smokers, other members of the group might actually begin to smoke cigarettes. Their identity has been formed by what others have labeled.

Personality Disorders and the Brain

Chemical imbalances in the brain can lead to problems regulating emotions and behaviors. These emotions and behaviors are a part of how personality develops in a child. Each brain chemical is responsible for sending certain messages to and from the brain through the central and peripheral nervous systems. If the chemical levels are too low, it is possible that the person will have problems creating certain reactions, or stopping other reactions. For example, chemicals that are designed to help regulate the responses generated by the amygdala would help keep a person from overreacting to a situation with either anger or fear. If there is a low level of these chemicals in the system, the amygdala could create a larger response, or continue to create a response without regulation, or without as much regulation as would normally be there. Thus, if Bill went into a meeting and found that he did not agree with what was being said, he might become angry. If the levels of brain chemicals designed to regulate the expression of anger in social situations were low, Bill might show his anger to the rest of the room. He might speak loudly or become belligerent. If the chemicals designed to calm down an anger reaction, or to stop the anger reaction were low or not functioning properly, Bill might continue to show his anger on a prolonged basis, even if he notices that others are becoming upset with his reaction.

Social Behaviors

People who have personality disorders often have a hard time recognizing proper behaviors in social situations and cannot easily identify how their behaviors are affecting the thoughts and reactions of others. If the brain chemicals are not working to regulate the reactions, or identify the proper reactions for a particular situation, the behaviors go outside of the norms for that situation. The person's reactions are often impulsive or inappropriate for the situation, causing others to become embarrassed, confused, or frustrated. As they do, they tend to put distance between themselves and the person acting impulsively or inappropriately. When they do this, they project a sense of rejection, which the person could pick up on, further reinforcing inappropriate and impulsive reactions.

As the chemical balance in their brain is restored, people with personality disorders are able to assess social situations more accurately and respond as they should, or at least not overreact to the situation. They are able to regulate the excitement and calm down before emotions get out of control. Different centers of the brain are responsible for different processes. When a brain center malfunctions, it affects how a person is able to perceive a situation and how he reacts.

Case Study: Katie

Katie has borderline personality disorder. She is in treatment for BPD and substance abuse. She has trouble recognizing that she has a problem and often argues with her counselors and other group therapy members about things others would not even notice. One day another group member came in with a button that said, "Have a Nice Day." Katie did not like the button and picked on her group mate throughout the session rather than listening and learning. When the group leader called on her to respond to a question, she became angry and blamed the other group member for her inattention. She felt this group member was telling her what to do, and she did not like that. She got up and tried to take the button from him. Her thought processes became fixated on the button and the group member who wore it.

Thought Processes

In the previous scenario Katie had trouble regulating simple processes and often reacted with anger to minor incidents she viewed as directed at her. As chemical levels became regulated through medication and diet, Katie began to learn to identify the thought processes that she needed to work on to help her get through a normal day without picking a fight with someone. She realized that her own identification of different thoughts could be faulty and unreliable. This is a key element in treatment. In many cases, people who have borderline personality disorder have trouble recognizing faulty thought processes and distinguishing them from more accurate information.

They might see what others are saying and doing as wrong in comparison to their own thoughts. They are reluctant to work on or realign their own thoughts because they think they are right. The insecurities and low self-esteem combine to create a situation where it is harder for them to admit that they might have done something wrong or might be causing problems for themselves or others. They go back to thinking they are right and that external circumstances are at work.

Locus of Control

People with borderline personality disorder often use an external locus of control as part of their thought process. *Locus of control* is a concept that describes how people view their world and their ability to control it. Individuals who have an internal locus of control see their lives as theirs to determine. While they might recognize that there are circumstances they cannot control in life, they realize that in general they make the choices. With an internal locus of control people accept responsibility for their choices, learn from them, and move on. They understand that there are potential consequences to each decision and behavior. They also understand that they can make their own choices and create their own path in life. They believe that they have the ability to choose and control.

People with an internal locus of control are less likely to turn to negative forms of problem solving. They are able to accept and account for what they have done and do not need to find a means of hiding from it. They can accept mistakes and move on from them, learning and growing along the way.

People with an *external locus of control*, on the other hand, believe that much of what they encounter is out of their control or as done to them. They are the victims of wrongdoing, which absolves them from blame and responsibility. Responsibility for wrongdoing would mean that they have done something wrong and need to own up to it. Their low self-esteem prevents them from doing this. With the external locus of control, it is often someone else's fault when something goes wrong, either for the person with personality disorder or others around them. If a person with personality disorder fails to mow the lawn as promised, opting instead to sit inside and watch TV, it would be hard for this person to then take responsibility for not mowing the lawn. He might argue back that because someone had nagged him about it he no longer felt like doing it. Thus, ultimately, it was the fault of the other person that the lawn remained undone.

The line of thinking with an external locus of control often fosters the use of substances and alcohol, and provides an excuse for this use. By escaping accountability through blaming others, people with borderline personality disorder often cause more problems that need to be dealt with. These problems become more difficult with time, and the need to retreat from them increases. The thought process that things are out of their control becomes more firmly embedded in their daily lives. They learn to become more dependent on external aids, such as substances and alcohol, to make them feel better. As the use increases and more problems develop, they sink deeper into this thought process. Their lives truly become out of control, and they do not know how to get out of it.

Poor Reactions

When the faulty thought processes are in place, they combine with the insecurities and impulsivity to create poor reactions. They allow little things to seem more important and more negative than they really are. A person with borderline personality disorder sees someone who is nice to him and thinks that this person must like him if she is being nice to him. This thought process escalates to a point where he might believe this person is actually in love with him rather than simply thinking him a nice person. The faulty thought processes lead to some of the impulsive and destructive elements of the borderline personality behaviors, especially if the person makes any attempt to get out of the trouble he is in. Since the attempts are usually not well thought out and are more reactions created from fear and desperation, they often do little to help the matter.

The Role of Amygdala

The amygdala is thought to be responsible for identification and reaction to negative circumstances. Some brain imaging studies show that the amygdala might become hyperactive in people who have borderline personality disorder. When this happens, people tend to concentrate on the negatives and become hypersensitive to real or imagined criticism. This reinforces the out-of-control thought process. The person with borderline personality disorder does not know what to do and might begin to see little hope of ever resolving the problem. This can lead to more desperate thought processes that might include *suicidal ideation*, or thoughts about committing suicide, and how it might be done.

How Someone with BPD Thinks

People who have borderline personality disorder often process information with a negative slant. Information is scanned for potential threats and rejection. They often see the glass as half empty and have a hard time navigating the nuances of social relationships. The negative perceptions work in combination with the general sense of mistrust and the fear of abandonment that are characteristic of borderline personality disorder. Individuals have a hard time with their self-esteem, which leaves them open to processing what others say to them or about them as negative or rejecting. They hear comments and dwell on the negative aspects of them, often interpreting them as a sign of disapproval. Constructive criticism becomes criticism that is taken personally and negatively.

Distrust

Distrust is constantly at work in the thought process. The words and behaviors of others might be overanalyzed and twisted to become purposeful putdowns or negative interactions. Someone who cuts ahead in the supermarket might simply be busy getting groceries and not noticing that another person was next in line. But a person with borderline personality disorder might interpret it a little differently. She might see the person as trying to annoy her or get the better of her. This simple incident could cause anger and frustration for the rest of the day. The person with borderline personality disorder might dwell on it and discuss what she might do to the offender if they were to meet again.

Fear of Abandonment

Distrust and fear of abandonment also become issues in relationships. If someone is late or forgets plans, the person with borderline personality disorder could take this as a sign that the person no longer loves her or wants to be with her. Such an incident often makes for more problems in the relationship, causing anything that the person later says or does to be scrutinized and analyzed with a negative outlook. If the person tries to explain what happened, the information might be seen as lies or some form of manipulation. If instead the person turns around and expresses affection, he might find he is met with resistance and disbelief. Individuals with borderline personality disorder easily fixate on the fear of an upcoming rejection. They begin to anticipate the rejection, which gives rise to thoughts and behaviors that tend to make rejection more likely.

The Need to Be Right All the Time

In most cases someone with borderline personality disorder has difficulty recognizing that what she is doing is not normal. If someone were to suggest this to her, she might see it as a way for the person to put her down and make her feel bad.

ALERT

A person with borderline personality disorder will instantly key in on negatives and stop listening to the rest of the feedback. It is helpful to begin with strengths and show how these strengths can become even better by doing something else, rather than pointing out what the person did wrong.

The need to be right is often associated with low self-esteem. A cycle of thought can occur in which people with borderline personality disorder feel that they need to be right in order to be liked. They often experience thoughts where they see themselves as unlovable. They then get the idea that if they are right or seem smart, others will like them. If they are wrong about something, they become very embarrassed and tend to think of themselves as no good or stupid and react accordingly. They become angry and defensive because they fear it is proof they are no good. This feeling of worthlessness is something they feel they need to avoid at all costs. They lose reason and begin to focus on avoiding the issue rather than dealing with their mistake. Thus they build up a general sense of mistrust of others, which provides them with insulation from being wrong.

Case Study: Mike

Mike was in an individual session on cognitive behavior therapy. He was learning about faulty thought processes and how they have affected his behaviors. He was diagnosed with borderline personality disorder, generalized anxiety disorder, and substance abuse disorder. He became angry with himself and his counselor when the counselor pointed out that one of his examples was in the wrong category on his worksheet for therapy. The counselor tried to explain why so that Mike would understand how this affected his thinking, but he became fixated on the fact that it was in the wrong category. He blamed his counselor, telling her that she had not explained the worksheet correctly. He then refused to do any more on the sheet and stormed out of her office.

Possible Brain Connections

The National Institute of Mental Health reported a study that showed how the part of the brain that is responsible for responses to unfairness and violation of social norms, the bilateral interior insula, did not show as much activity in study participants who had been diagnosed with borderline personality disorder. The study looked at how situations involving violating trust activated the insula in healthy participant brains, causing levels of activity to rise during these times and then return to a lower level when the situation was more trusting. Participants with borderline personality disorder, on the other hand, did not seem to show a difference in activity from situation to situation.

Two aspects of borderline personality disorder might have a bearing on this study. People who have been diagnosed with borderline personality disorder have a hard time trusting others as a matter of course. The participants in this study who had been diagnosed with borderline personality disorder were more likely to be distrustful naturally without distinguishing between trust and nontrust situations. Additionally, the participants with borderline personality disorder might have had trouble differentiating between the social situations. Since they have trouble recognizing social norms, they would not be able to identify if others are violating these norms or not. This means they are also more likely to violate social norms themselves, because the violation does not register as such to them.

FACT

It is not unusual for people with borderline personality disorder to be distrustful of others without reason. They seek to avoid disappointment and do not take fear of rejection well—although they expect others to reject them. If someone with BPD does not trust what you say, ask him how you can make him more comfortable with your answers, either through extensive proof or more evidence.

Trust Problems

People with borderline personality disorder might trust quickly as they begin a relationship, but then drop back as the relationship does not work out as perfectly as originally imagined. No relationship is perfect, and people with borderline personality disorder are set up for failure, as their quick closeness leads to subsequent disappointment. When friends and significant others are chosen indiscriminately there is also a higher likelihood of finding someone who is untrustworthy to begin with. Someone with borderline personality disorder might see a violation of trust in some form as normal for the situation.

This thought process might be a result of the brain not activating correctly in areas that allow people to recognize instances where trust or any other social norm has been violated. The different areas of the brain responsible for this recognition might need extra help to function correctly. People with borderline personality disorder must be able to properly recognize social rules and norms in order to begin to function within them.

CHAPTER 3

How Do I Know If Someone Has BPD?

You may be related to, in a relationship with, or work with someone that you suspect is suffering from BPD. You may even wonder if you have BPD yourself. You should view this situation as objectively as possible and see if there is a pattern in your behavior, or the behavior of your loved one or coworker, that may be indicative of a BPD diagnosis. BPD, like all personality disorders, depends heavily on patterns of repeated behaviors, so if you know what to look for, it can be easier for you to classify symptoms as those of BPD or as simply normal behavior.

Mistaking Borderline Personality Disorder for "Normal"

It is important to note that in order to be diagnosed as borderline personality disorder, the symptoms must be pervasive, contrary to cultural norms, and cause noticeable distress. While it is hard to recognize symptoms when dealing personally with someone with borderline personality disorder, because the symptoms can confuse and frustrate, the symptoms are noticeable. Identifying the difference between normal and borderline personality disorder is often difficult because those who are around the disorder are so busy they do not necessarily see the symptoms as they really are.

FACT

The National Alliance on Mental Illness (NAMI) has a helpline available to call Monday through Friday, 10:00 A.M. to 6:00 P.M. EST. NAMI staff members can give you nonprofessional information on various mental health topics and issues, provide referrals to professionals close to you, and offer support from people who have been there. The website has additional information: *www.nami.org.*

The defense mechanisms in place for borderline personality disorder often push the issue back on the other person. Someone with borderline personality disorder in college might get back a paper with two questions marked wrong out of twenty. When this happens, the two questions will become a sign of his failure, despite the fact that he still received a very respectable grade. He might go up to the instructor and argue these two questions, perhaps telling her that she had not covered the material properly, or that the questions were wrong or unfair in some way. This places the other person on the defensive and keeps her off guard, so busy responding to the latest accusation that she does not see what is really going on. Normal behavior might result in the student being disappointed in his results, perhaps questioning the instructor, but ultimately knowing that he too played a part in his final grade, perhaps by not studying or not fully understanding the material. Someone with BPD, however, would not even acknowledge that he might be at fault.

People who have borderline personality disorder believe they are right and do not see other perspectives. This makes it hard to reason with or identify the disorder. The focus is on others, who must now prove they were not doing something wrong. This keeps them from thinking clearly about what is going on.

Symptoms of BPD

While it can be hard to identify symptoms of borderline personality disorder from brief encounters or close proximity, it is possible to see some signs that will help. In general, if the signs are specific, repeated, and consistent over a period of time, they are likely the result of something more persistent than a passing problem. The symptoms will occur through different situations, both good and bad, and will not be dependent on the use of drugs or alcohol.

Discussion will likely lead nowhere, as the person with borderline personality disorder will fail to hear or think about what is being said in a rational manner. There will be no recognition of behavior problems. Compromise will not be brought into the conversation because the person with borderline personality disorder does not see or understand the wrongdoing that is being presented to him. It is not merely denial; with borderline personality disorder there is an inability to recognize or understand. This inability to understand is often one of the best indicators that things are not normal. Behaviors might or might not be able to be explained away with current environmental situations, but the inability to understand remains.

Everyone goes through one or more relationships in his or her lifetime, whether they be friendships, work relationships, or romantic relationships. People with borderline personality disorder tend to experience this more often. The quick onset of adoration and the need for complete closeness right from the start are usually signs that something is not normal. They are part of the insecurities and fear of abandonment. They are also part of the need to have someone around at all times. Since relationships do not start out on solid ground to begin with, and the person with borderline personality disorder has trouble recognizing proper social behaviors, the relationships normally do not last very long. When someone with borderline personality disorder is out of one relationship, he is looking quickly to be in another. This next relationship follows the same pattern.

Self-Harm

Serious symptoms such as self-harm and suicidal ideation are strong signs that a person is experiencing issues that are not normal. Most people do not cut themselves or think about committing suicide. These behaviors normally occur when there are strong feelings of psychological pain. These more harmful symptoms must be dealt with quickly in order to prevent additional problems or even tragedy. While all signs that show that things are not quite normal should be dealt with, the ones dealing with harm to self or another can be some of the most serious.

ALERT

It is very important to take threats and comments about self-harm or suicide very seriously. There is a strong risk of attempts for someone with borderline personality disorder. If you hear a threat, or suspect that someone might be thinking that way, contact help immediately and let the professionals figure out what is going on and what needs to be done.

General Warning Signs

Each warning sign when taken individually might not seem as pertinent to borderline personality disorder as the entire package of warning signs that are presented when someone is aware of them and looking for them. People with borderline personality disorder do not usually recognize that something is wrong with them. They often see problems in others, but not themselves. This can be seen as a general warning sign of a personality disorder. The inability to recognize that thoughts and behaviors are not quite right is a symptom of the processing errors normally present.

According to the American Psychiatric Association, personality disorders are normally characterized by the following general symptoms:

- Enduring pattern of thoughts and behaviors that deviate markedly from cultural norms and expectations in at least two areas that include cognition, affectivity, interpersonal functioning, and impulse control.
- Thoughts and behaviors are inflexible and pervasive across a wide range of situations.
- Significant distress and/or impairment occur as a result of the symptoms.
- The pattern is stable and occurs over a long period of time, with onset tracked back to adolescence or early adulthood.
- The symptoms are not better explained by another mental disorder.
- The pattern is not directly due to substance or alcohol use, or a general medical condition.

Thoughts and Behaviors

Thoughts and behaviors that remain generally consistent over time, and do not seem in line with the standards of that particular society could indicate a problem. A person might express anger when someone pulls out in front of her and then drives slowly on the road. It would not be unusual. Someone with borderline personality disorder, however, might not only become angry but also might harp on this situation and continue to complain about it for a period of time afterward. She might then also complain when someone walking with a shopping cart takes longer than she would like to get out of her way. This, too, would result in a period of complaints and anger. The person might then get stuck at a red light at leaving the parking lot and again become angry at what is being done to her. The thoughts and behaviors are consistent from one situation to the next whether the person was stressed, in a hurry, turning soon after encountering the car, or merely spending some quiet time.

The thought would remain that someone is intentionally doing something to her and that she is entitled to better treatment. There would be no recognition of someone else's perspective in these encounters. She would not see that someone else might be in a hurry, or might have some emergency to take care of quickly. She would only see that someone has inconvenienced her. She would see things only through her own irritation and would not be able to see the perspective of another. The incidents would be blown out of proportion.

Embarrassment

This type of thought process sticks. Someone who is around this person often enough would be able to anticipate the potential for angry words or rude comments in social places. Trips to the grocery store could result in embarrassment or exchange of angry words as the person with borderline personality disorder impulsively makes comments others can hear and take offense with.

QUESTION

My wife constantly speaks out and makes rude comments to others in the grocery store when I am with her. What can I do when this happens?
The best thing to do is point out that what just happened is unacceptable and leave the store immediately. When you get home, create a list of dos and don'ts for the supermarket, making sure she understands that you will leave the store every time she violates the list.

Behaviors often indicate a disregard for others unless there is a conscious effort to think about things. She might eat in front of others without thinking about whether or not someone else is hungry. She is also likely to engage in the same behaviors that upset her, such as cutting someone else off in line or driving with no regard for other cars. She does not see how the two are related. She feels she is entitled to do these kinds of things and gets upset when someone points out that she has done so. She may have trouble understanding why it is a problem. She can then turn right around and make angry comments when someone else does the same thing to her. The thought process goes one way, centering on what she is thinking and feeling, rather than on what she might be causing someone else to think or feel. She has a right to do these things, but someone else does not. She has a great deal of trouble seeing this distinction or understanding that she does this.

Self-Perception

People with borderline personality disorder often think of themselves as kind and generous. If their actions are good for them they think that they are good for everyone. Again this is because they do not have the ability to see someone else's perspective, they only see good and bad from their own perspective and that is it. There is a double standard at work, where they feel that something is being done to them, whereas others bring it on themselves. If someone with borderline personality disorder doesn't get a job, it's because the boss's friend or relative was chosen instead, whereas if someone else does not get the job, it is because another applicant had better qualifications.

The impulsivity of the behaviors often provides for trouble and misunderstanding. The brain seems to switch to action mode with little thought. When this happens, others might become insulted or offended by what is said or done. Since anger is also a possibility, the impulsive behaviors could lead to fighting or damage to others. The behaviors seem to be quick reactions that most people would not make because they are able to understand and follow the norms for that particular society. This impulsivity can be confused with impulsive behaviors in other disorders, especially disorders that often include angry outbursts or trouble controlling aggression.

Symptoms That Confuse

Borderline personality disorder symptoms can sometimes be confused with symptoms of other disorders. Even though BPD is a comorbid condition with other disorders, it is important to distinguish which symptoms are rooted where. For example, impulsivity is also a symptom of attention deficit/hyperactivity disorder (ADHD). With ADHD, the impulsivity would be relatively the same, but the other symptoms of borderline personality disorder would not be present. The impulsivity would include interrupting others, difficulty waiting until someone is finished speaking, intruding in conversations, and making decisions with little thought about the outcome beforehand. On the other hand, people with borderline personality disorder do not necessarily have trouble concentrating on something for a period of time, as with ADHD, although there might be some disorganization and attempts to avoid tasks that require heavy concentration and mental effort. The behaviors with borderline personality disorder include impulsivity but also include multiple other symptoms that point to this particular disorder.

BPD and Bipolar Disorder

Borderline personality disorder could also present with mood swings that might seem similar to those of bipolar mood disorder. There could be intense episodes of irritability or anxiety, but they do not cycle in a pattern from one extreme to the other. The moods also normally last only a few hours or possibly a few days, while mood disorder swings can last for months. Unlike the swings in mood disorders, which are not easily or consciously controlled by circumstances, in BPD moods such as anger, panic, or despair would more likely be a result of a reaction to stressors pertaining to relationships or social interactions.

BPD and Anxiety

The anxiety in borderline personality disorder seems more closely associated with fear of abandonment and problems with social interactions than a generalized fear or anxious feeling based on chronic anxiety issues. The fear is often based on something in the moment and can gravitate easily and quickly to anger rather than remaining fear. The fear is pervasive only as it pertains to thoughts of abandonment and being left alone. There are no panic attacks or instances of fear that do not have a basis in some social situation. If panic attacks or other fears are present, it could be that the person with borderline personality disorder also has an anxiety disorder. It is not uncommon and will be discussed later in the book.

Substance Abuse

Borderline personality disorder might also be masked by substance or alcohol use. Some might believe that the impulsive, angry, aggressive, moody behaviors are the result of the drug or alcohol use. Substance abuse can act in tandem with the natural symptoms of borderline personality disorder to create stronger reactions, but the symptoms of borderline personality itself are not dependent upon substance use. The symptoms are present whether the person is using at the time or not. Since people with borderline personality disorder often turn to substance use or alcohol use to self-medicate, it is sometimes hard to separate the symptoms of the two.

Can It Be More Than One?

Borderline personality has a very high rate of *comorbidity*. This means it often coexits with or is accompanied by other mental health issues. Since symptoms start in adolescence, some earlier disorders such as conduct disorder might precede the diagnosis for borderline personality disorder. As has already been stated, borderline personality disorders are often accompanied by anxiety, mood, and substance abuse disorders.

Determining Differences

The nature of borderline personality disorder symptoms brings to mind other disorders. Symptoms are similar and can cause confusion, as certain behaviors can have more than one cause. Many treatment methods for borderline personality disorder are similar to those for other disorders that it might be confused with, but there are certain biochemical features that indicate possible differences between one disorder and another. Symptoms themselves are not the only means of identifying which disorder is which. It is also important to look at how many symptoms are present and in what combination. A professional will look at how severe the symptoms are, how often they appear, whether or not they disappear at certain times, and what might be happening in the environment to influence the symptoms.

ALERT

It is important to let a professional decide what symptoms mean. Symptoms might be noticeable to a layperson, but professionals are specially trained to ask questions that will be able to get to the bottom of what is going on. Borderline personality disorder has severe symptoms and needs the help of a professional.

The questions asked are designed to determine which mental health issue is present, or if more than one is present. Borderline personality disorder has symptoms that are noticeable and can be severe. They are consistent and are not based on what is going on in the person's life. If there are symptoms that seem to come and go in relation to a cycle of outside issues, it might be a different disorder. On the other hand, if the symptoms of borderline personality disorder are present and remain fairly steady and consistent, and other symptoms also seem to be present, it could be that more than one disorder is present.

For example, the anxiety created from fear of abandonment, which is common with borderline personality disorder, could also reflect anxiety generated by an anxiety disorder. Yet the anxiety with borderline personality disorder is more specific to that perceived circumstance of abandonment and does not generally include other anxieties or chronic fears. Thus, if the anxiety seems to be more generalized or persistent outside of abandonment issues, it could be the result of an accompanying anxiety disorder. An anxiety disorder could add more insecurity and dependency to the borderline personality disorder thought and behavior process, and additional fears would likely be evident too. Excessive worry that causes distress or impairment in the ability to function normally in some area of daily life would be more closely related to an anxiety disorder than borderline personality disorder.

Source of Some Similarities

Disorders with similar symptoms normally present with specific symptoms, but do not have the entire package of symptoms present in borderline personality disorder. Anxiety disorder would present with symptoms of fear and anxiety, but would not present with impulsivity. The brain processes that malfunction to create the problems with borderline personality disorder might not be the only parts of the brain that are not working properly, or they might be causing different problems that create other disorders.

The amygdala, which has been implicated in the anger and fear responses of borderline personality disorder, has also been implicated in anxiety disorders. The fight-or-flight reaction that is centered in the amygdala normally comes into play in traumatic or dangerous situations. In anxiety disorders, this function seems to activate without the presence of an obvious threat, causing neurochemicals to be released that put the body on high alert. This often causes panic attacks that are characteristic of anxiety disorders. If panic attacks are present, an anxiety disorder is likely present, as the issues in the amygdala affect the body in a way that adds to symptoms of both disorders.

QUESTION

How can a person have more than one personality disorder?
Personality disorders are not the same and cover different parts of personality, which are affected by different parts of the brain. As different parts of the brain send or receive the wrong messages, or fail to get proper messages, different areas of thought and behavior can be affected.

Borderline personality disorder also shares symptoms and similarities with other personality disorders, so it is important to be sure that the specific set of symptoms match up with the personality disorder in question. Some personality disorders might have fewer symptoms in common with borderline personality disorder. It is possible to have other personality disorders, usually from a different cluster, occurring at the same time as borderline personality disorder.

CHAPTER 4

Comparing BPD to Other Personality Disorders

In addition to borderline personality disorder, there are several other personality disorders that focus on a certain specified set of symptoms. It is easy to get two or more mixed up, and to see similarities without the distinguishing differences. Each cluster of personality disorders has some general issues that are characteristic of that particular cluster, with individual differences between each disorder within that cluster. Disorders in Cluster A are clustered around eccentric thoughts and behaviors. Those based on emotional and dramatic behaviors are classified within Cluster B. Others are based on strong fearful behaviors and are assigned to Cluster C.

Schizoid Personality Disorder

Schizoid personality disorder is a Cluster A personality disorder characterized by its seeming lack of interest in socializing or dealing with interpersonal relationships. People with this disorder do not normally appear close to friends or relatives, and do not tend to join in many social groups. They tend to prefer to spend time by themselves rather than with others, and are seen as loners. When given the choice, they often choose activities completed individually and hobbies that do not require contact with others. They would opt for stamp collecting over joining a baseball team. They do not tend to show a great deal of interest in sexual experiences, and they do not seem to be able to develop pleasure from sensory input. A walk along the beach with a beautiful sunset would do little to pique their interest.

Expression of Feelings

People who have schizoid personality disorder often have little regard for the approval or criticism of others. They do not seem to care what others think of them or their behaviors. They do not necessarily even recognize other people. There is little emotional reaction to situations, and strong emotions like anger and happiness are rare. They tend to have trouble recognizing and responding to nonverbal forms of communication such as head nods or smiles. Outward signs of emotion seem bland and lifeless. Expressions are normally blank and do not portray upset.

ALERT

The emotionally blank exterior presented by people with schizoid personality disorder does not necessarily present a true picture of what lies beneath. When people with schizoid personality disorder get to the point where they can trust someone and open up, they have been known to reveal feelings of pain and discomfort with social interactions.

Individuals with schizoid personality disorder seem to have a great deal of trouble expressing anger in particular, especially in response to direct provocation. They might react passively to adverse circumstances and be unable to provide expected responses to different events and occurrences. This makes them seem to lack emotion and be directionless.

Specific Features of Schizoid Personality Disorder

People with schizoid personality disorder normally have few friendships and work better under conditions where they work alone. They seem uncomfortable or unable to function properly when they need to interact with others. This feature, however, should be based on the cultural norms for a given society. Some cultures are more aloof than others as a normal method of social interaction. This type of behavior might also occur as someone moves from a rural area to a more heavily populated urban area. They might experience a form of emotional freezing as they adjust to the new environment that would include engaging in solitary activities and less frequent communication. Immigrants moving from heavily rural countries could be mistakenly perceived as having schizoid personality disorder as they adjust to the larger metropolitan areas and new cultural norms.

Schizoid personality disorder might first be noticed in school. Older children and adolescents might exhibit poor peer relationships forming and tend to stay by themselves. They are often underachievers in school. These behaviors can and usually do mark these children as different and leave them open to teasing and bullying by other students.

Distinguishing Schizoid Personality Disorder from BPD

The differences between schizoid personality disorder and borderline personality disorder are a little more obvious than the differences with other personality disorders. Whereas a person with schizoid personality disorder shows a lack of emotion and there is a lack of desire to interact with others, a person with borderline personality disorder swings the other way. In some ways, they are almost opposite. Schizoid personality disorder is characterized by a lack of desire for close relationships. Borderline personality desire is characterized by a strong need for constant close relationships. Schizoid personality disorder often shows a lack of strong emotions, while borderline personality disorder is characterized by overly strong reactions to situations. Someone with schizoid personality disorder might seem indifferent to the criticism or comments of another, while someone with borderline personality disorder would likely overreact to perceived slights.

ESSENTIAL

There is a higher risk of developing schizoid personality disorder when relatives have been diagnosed with schizophrenia or schizotypal personality disorder. Schizoid personality disorder is relatively rare and is uncommon even in clinical settings.

Histrionic Personality Disorder

Histrionic personality disorder is an attention-seeking disorder from Cluster B. People with this disorder can become overly emotional and exhibit this emotion for all to see. There is a distinct need for attention and they often do not wish to share this attention with others. People with histrionic personality disorder seek attention through dramatic means. They feel uncomfortable or unappreciated when they are not the center of attention, which leads to many erratic and possibly irrational behaviors designed to return to the center of attention. Attention does not necessarily need to be positive, and people with histrionic personality disorder can often be found at the center of controversy or conflict in groups of people or social interactions. They normally present with a charming and lively initial impression, usually seeming open to new experiences and ready to be the life of the party.

Attention-Seeking Behaviors

This persona normally wears thin fairly quickly as others catch on to the need to be the constant center of attention. When they are not the center of attention they often do something dramatic, and sometimes detrimental to others, in order to return to that position. They might make up a story or tell a lie in order to once again have all eyes on them. They are prone to interrupting others in order to remove the focus from them. In other cases, people with histrionic personality disorder might bring attention upon themselves by being overly flirtatious, using obvious flattery, or providing a description of a recent traumatic illness or event. The illness or event is often either false or overblown. The story of the illness or event might change from telling to telling, especially if it seems that there is a need for greater attention from others.

Someone with histrionic personality disorder is usually overly concerned with appearance. In keeping with the need for attention, the person might dress and behave in a sexually provocative or seductive manner. This occurs as a part of the behavior package, and is not limited to someone this person has a romantic interest in. It occurs in a wide variety of social, occupational, and professional relationships, and it is often inappropriate for the social context of a given situation.

According to the American Psychological Association, about 2–3 percent of the general population has histrionic personality disorder. It is diagnosed more often in females in clinical settings, but since females are more numerous in clinical settings, it could be due to the larger sampling.

The Carefully Orchestrated Look

People with histrionic personality disorder often use their appearance as a way to draw attention so that it focuses on them. In addition to seductive dress, they normally spend a great deal of time, energy, and money on clothes, hair, and other grooming methods. They wear clothes and often make statements that are designed to bring about comments. They might fish for a compliment by mentioning how long it took them to get ready or by commenting themselves that they just do not think they look very good. They are actually priming others to disagree with them and tell them that they look very nice. They can become easily upset and overreact to comments that are deemed unflattering in some way.

Communication and Social Patterns

Speech is often dramatic and vague. Histrionic personalities might make sweeping comments with little to back these comments up. They are upset if someone calls them on this and asks them to explain further, as they are often unable to do so. They are easily influenced by others or by current trends, adopting new patterns of communicating and catchwords based on what they see others doing. They follow quickly with someone else's train of thought and seek to have others solve their problems without regard for their ability to do so.

People with histrionic personality disorder often have a high opinion of their popularity. They tend to describe people they have met only once or have only a brief acquaintance with as good or best friends. They see these relationships as closer and more intimate than they truly are. They often interpret looks and attention by others as romantic interest in them. People with histrionic personality disorder believe that the focus of attention of others is mainly on them.

Case Study: Jenna

Jenna was at a college football game with her friends. She had previously dated two of the football players on the team. Whenever one of these players would look back toward the crowd of thousands, she would proclaim to her friends that they were looking for her and then were watching her. She also pointed out three other males in the audience who were interested in her because they had been watching her.

Her friends were unable to discern any special attention, and when the two football players were later asked, they replied that they had not even known she was at the game. When Jenna found this out, she became angry and said they were lying. She was firmly convinced that they had been watching her and could not understand why anyone would think they had not been.

How Histrionic Personality Disorder Relates to BPD

Highly emotional attention-seeking and manipulative behaviors characterize histrionic personality disorder. There is a strong need to associate with others and to be in relationships. While borderline personality disorder can also be characterized by the attention-seeking behaviors, there is a greater element of self-destructiveness and angry disruptions in close relationships with borderline personality disorder. Whereas people with histrionic personality disorder have an overblown sense of popularity, someone with borderline personality disorder would be more likely to experience feelings of deep emptiness. In both cases there is a need to be in relationships and a desire for attention; the attention is the primary objective of someone with histrionic personality disorder, while someone with borderline personality disorder is more focused on not being alone.

ALERT

In most cases it does little good to directly contradict the observances of someone with histrionic personality disorder, especially as they relate to perceived attention. Such contradiction often results in angry responses and efforts to disprove your observances through manipulation and possibly lies. It is better to try to refocus the conversation and the topics of attention to something else. If the person with histrionic personality disorder receives no attention with this topic, she will move on to one where she might get the attention she needs.

Avoidant Personality Disorder

Avoidant personality disorder is in the Cluster C category of personality disorders and is characterized by a pervasive pattern of social discomfort. People with avoidant personality disorder normally experience feelings of inadequacy and project this onto others as they feel they are being judged negatively. They are hypersensitive to negative evaluations in most contexts.

Social Fears

People with avoidant personality disorder tend to avoid social situations, including work and school activities that involve a great deal of social interaction. They fear that their thoughts and behaviors will be met with criticism, disapproval, and rejection. They might think that others are watching them eat in judging what they eat and how they eat it. They become self-conscious and avoid situations where this might happen.

Individuals who have avoidant personality disorder often seek to avoid leadership positions as much as possible. They fear that their decisions will be met with scorn or disapproval by those underneath them. They tend to focus more on what others are thinking of them and their decisions than getting the job done. They do not want to be in a position where others can scrutinize and judge them.

Relationships

The fear of rejection characteristic of avoidant personality disorder makes it hard for a person with this disorder to form both friendships and romantic relationships. He avoids forming new friendships because he fears criticism and rejection. Someone with avoidant personality disorder often presents stringent tests to would-be friends in order to prove that they will be supportive and nurturing. Relationship intimacy is often difficult, as there is an assumption of criticism. People with this disorder often act with restraint in a new relationship and have difficulty revealing information about themselves.

ALERT

It is very important to carefully phrase information and feedback when speaking to someone with avoidant personality disorder. If the person did the dishes without asking, but missed some spots on some of the plates, it would be better to praise him and thank him for doing the dishes without asking. As you are praising the person and thanking him, you could point out that he they did a great job, the results would be even better if next time he tried a different approach.

Group activities are often avoided as much as possible, and participation usually comes only after there are repeated and generous offers of help and friendship. People with avoidant personality disorder might tend to cling to someone else within the group for support and insulation from others. They tend to be shy and inhibited, especially at first, and share very little of their thoughts or personal information.

Handling Criticism

Individuals with avoidant personality disorder are hypersensitive to criticism. Their threshold is very low. Mild criticism is interpreted as an extreme circumstance. They become hurt easily. Since they fear negative attention and often see negative attention where there is none, they tend to be shy, quiet, and inhibited. This is especially true when they are unsure of the task or the subject at hand.

While they fade into the background to avoid criticism, many actually long to be active participants in social activities. They do not feel competent and are especially shy with strangers as they are not sure of reactions. They believe themselves to be socially inept and concentrate more on what they think others think of them than what they are doing. They fear any situation that might prove embarrassing to them. They dwell on minor mistakes and think that everyone is watching them and thinking negatively of them.

Features of Avoidant Personality Disorder

Avoidant personality is relatively rare, occurring in between .5 percent and 1 percent of the general population, according to the American Psychological Association. It occurs in about 10 percent of the population in treatment for diagnosed mental health disorders. Avoidant personality disorder symptoms normally begin in infancy or childhood with symptoms of shyness, isolation, and fear of strangers. Young children might remain close to their mother and avoid playing with other children. If pressed to play with other children, they might do so for a short period of time but are often excluded or exclude themselves from interactive play. They might do better with play that involves each child working individually, but there is still the persistent fear of criticism. If criticized by another child, they will likely return to their mother and remain there.

While these symptoms are normal at various stages of child development, most children begin to outgrow them as they get older. Toddlers who have trouble separating from their mothers often lose this fear partway through preschool or kindergarten. They become more preoccupied with making friends and playing. With avoidant personality disorder, these symptoms remain and likely increase throughout adolescence and early adulthood as new social relationships become important. Adolescents are likely to remain isolated and not join any groups or activities in high school. They tend to eat alone in the cafeteria and leave right after school ends. They do not raise their hands in class or offer to participate and normally look very uncomfortable answering questions or speaking out in class. They might also avoid days where they need to do an oral report.

Older adults might outgrow or exhibit reduced symptoms of avoidant personality disorder. Some evidence suggests that this disorder does not present with symptoms that are as strong in older age. This could be due to changes in hormone levels, differences in social relationships, or a combination of both.

Comparison with BPD

Avoidant personality disorder is not often closely associated with borderline personality disorder. The symptoms do not seem to intersect, and while there is sensitivity to negative feedback with borderline personality disorder, it is not a strong symptom and does not prevent the attempts to form personal relationships. Avoidant personality disorder seeks to remove the possibility of humiliation and rejection and accepts that this could prevent interpersonal relationships. Borderline personality disorder, on the other hand, seeks those interpersonal relationships above all else and fears potential abandonment and isolation. They are not normally diagnosed together.

Obsessive-Compulsive Personality Disorder

Obsessive-compulsive personality disorder is a cluster C disorder. It is characterized by a preoccupation with orderliness, perfectionism, and mental and interpersonal control. There is little flexibility, openness, or efficiency in the behaviors. This disorder often begins in early adulthood.

Characteristics of Obsessive-Compulsive Personality Disorder

Individuals with this disorder act to maintain a sense of control by creating and following extensive rules, attending to trivial details and procedures, and compiling comprehensive lists and schedules that go beyond the original purpose. Thoughts and behaviors are excessive and often result in rituals or repetition that must be conducted in certain circumstances.

Projects are often left unfinished as the individual becomes too enmeshed in perfecting each minute detail. They are often unable to step away from their project or work and might decline vacations or time away, thinking they cannot take the time away from what they are doing. Hobbies and leisure time activities are approached as tasks rather than side activities for enjoyment. The perfectionism and rigid rules remain in effect even during these normally fun activities.

Behaviors

Individuals with obsessive-compulsive personality disorder are overly critical of themselves and mercilessly rigid in dealing with others. They have extreme black and white thinking with high standards to meet in order to pass self-assessments. Dealings with others are based on rules and procedures rather than humanity. If something is against a rule, even if it is necessary, it will not happen no matter how much another person might need the help.

This also translates to moral rules and values, with the individual seeing it as their duty to follow rules and help others do so too. If someone asked to borrow a dollar to buy a gallon of milk, the individual might think it would be bad for the borrower's character to simply give them the money. In their line of thinking it would be better to go without the nutrition rather than borrow money from another. They often impose their own thoughts on others.

No Arguing

Individuals with this disorder see themselves as right and feel their way of doing something is not only the right way to do it, it is the only way to do it. They steadfastly insist on their own views and do not delegate well, thinking no one else could do as good a job as they can. In their minds there is only one way to do a job, and they know this way. They are rarely open to the ideas of others.

Decisions can be painstaking and time-consuming, which again results in nothing getting done. Authority figures they respect are given undue deference, while those they do not respect are resisted. Affection is stingy and stiff. They have difficulty expressing feelings or paying compliments.

Where It Stands

Obsessive-compulsive personality disorder is not often diagnosed with other personality disorders and should not be confused with obsessive-compulsive disorder (OCD). The presence of true obsessions and compulsions is more in line with obsessive-compulsive disorder. While those with obsessive-compulsive personality disorder tend to have trouble getting rid of things, they are more likely to do so because they do not want to get rid of things that might have use later on. They do not want to replace them or spend money on something like it at a later date. With obsessive-compulsive disorder the hoarding is extreme and overpowering.

Obsessive-compulsive personality disorder is not often diagnosed with borderline personality disorder. Relationships are almost opposite as those with obsessive-compulsive personality disorder are not as eager to enter into intimate relationships and do not express the emotion in the same extremes.

Dependent Personality Disorder

Dependent personality disorder is another cluster C disorder. It is characterized by a pervasive and excessive need to be taken care of by another. People with dependent personality disorder are normally submissive and clingy in relationships. These behaviors are designed to find a more dominant personality to take care of them and take responsibility for them.

Characteristics of Dependent Personality Disorder

People with dependent personality disorder often exhibit difficulty making day-to-day decisions like what to have for breakfast or what to wear. They seek a great deal of advice and reassurance from others, and will often change their own thoughts and choices based on the input of others. They normally choose one person to refer to for most decisions and place responsibility for these decisions on that person. They tend to be passive and are most comfortable when decisions are made for them.

When adolescents with dependent personality disorder need to make large decisions like what career they should choose or where to go to school, they rely on a parent or close friend to do it for them. As they age, the decisions they need made for them might change, for example, needing someone to decide where they should live. The need for help with decisions goes beyond what would normally be expected. It would be normal for an adolescent to turn to her parents for input on which college to go to in order to best complete her goals. It would not be normal for the adolescent to need her mother to decide what she wanted to do and how she should go about doing it.

ALERT

Dependent tendencies often occur as the result of a medical condition that reduces a person's ability to function normally. Someone who is paralyzed would naturally be more dependent upon others for many functions of daily life. This thought pattern could extend to other decisions as this person becomes used to the dependency. In this case the dependency is situational and not part of a personality disorder.

Relationships

Since people with dependent personality disorder are dependent on others for decisions, there is a strong need for at least one close relationship with someone who is more dominant. They often agree to things they might not normally go along with so they do not lose the person they are looking up to. They fear alienating others and withhold anger and harsh words in order to keep the peace.

People with dependent personality disorder lack self-initiative and are more likely to follow than lead. They want someone else to make the decisions and they wait for this to happen rather than doing so themselves. They are followers when in large group settings. They believe others can do a better job making decisions. They do not think they are able to function independently and project that persona to others. Once they are assured that someone else is supervising, they are able to function. It is their belief that they are incapable that makes them dependent, rather than a true inability to function.

Emotional Issues

People who have dependent personality disorder will go to great lengths to avoid responsibility and decision-making activities and gain nurturance and care. They will go along with decisions they do not like and that are against their own moral beliefs and values, and even the law if need be. If Ted sees himself as dependent upon Mary, he will do what he needs to do to remain in this position, including doing her schoolwork for her and stealing a ring for her. Even demands that are unreasonable are completed in order to maintain the dependent relationship.

People with dependent personality disorder will endure physical, psychological, and sexual abuse even when choices are available. They will put up with nasty and demeaning comments to remain with the person they are dependent upon, tagging along to places and events when they are not invited or not wanted.

Facts and Comparison to BPD

Dependent personality disorder is one of the most frequently diagnosed personality disorders in mental health clinics. It is similar to borderline personality disorder with strong fear of abandonment issues. With borderline personality disorder, however, the reaction is more severe and potentially more intense. The pattern of unstable relationships is similar, but the ends sought in the relationships are different as dependent personality disorder seeks someone to take care of and be responsible for them.

CHAPTER 5

Some Causes Related to Borderline Personality Disorder

Borderline personality disorder has more than one cause, and in most cases is the result of a combination of issues. Some look at it as an illness that is the result of biological and genetic differences. A person with borderline personality disorder has often suffered negative personal experiences, notably while growing up. There might be some trauma in the person's history that caused severe problems and insecurities. Some have even suggested that borderline personality disorder is in some way related to posttraumatic stress disorder. Borderline personality disorder also has a high genetic link. There are brain mechanisms that do not seem to be functioning correctly, and this seems to be present from one generation to the next.

Personal Experiences

Strong evidence from research supports the link between negative childhood experiences and the development of borderline personality disorder. This link seems to be especially strong when the experiences involve close caregivers. The experiences linked to development of borderline personality disorder are often traumatic in nature and might include physical abuse, sexual abuse, emotional abuse, emotional or physical neglect, early separation from close caregivers, and parent practices or insensitivity. The more traumatic these experiences are, or the greater the number of these experiences, the higher the risk of developing borderline personality disorder, especially when a genetic predisposition might be present.

ESSENTIAL

As high as 40–71 percent of those diagnosed with borderline personality disorder have reported a history of some form of sexual abuse by a noncaregiver as a young child.

Childhood Experiences

It is important to note that while these traumatic experiences happen to a child, the presence of caregivers who have BPD or some other type of mental health disorder that prevents them from coping properly can affect thought and behavior development simply by modeling poor behaviors on a daily basis. Children learn how to deal with anger and cope with problems by watching the adults they grow up with. If caregivers anger easily and do not handle it well or are aggressive either with the child or others, it could affect how the child learns to handle these situations. If parents have poor parenting skills, they are more likely to show poor coping or problem-solving skills too.

Children who grow up in a world of violence learn to handle things through anger and aggression. If they are sexually abused, they become confused about how normal relationships progress. If they are abandoned by their parents or primary caregivers in some way, they become distrustful and insecure. In addition to extreme experiences, the general parenting style exhibited by the primary caregivers affects how the child sees the world and learns to interact within it.

Parenting Style and Attachment

Theories on parenting style and childhood attachment show a large relationship between abusive or neglectful experiences in young childhood and how the child's thought and behavior processes develop. Parents who are nurturing yet firm often raise children who feel secure and able to face problems. Parents who are abusive or neglectful, on the other hand, often raise children who are fearful, angry, and easily frustrated. These children do not view the world in the same way, and they often develop a survivor mentality. They will do what it takes to get by in the way they feel they need to live. If they are raised with these insecurities, they are more likely to have issues with abandonment. For them, abandonment is a very real state.

QUESTION

I think I use more than one parenting style at different times, is this possible?
Yes it is. Parents are actually a combination of most of the styles. At some times they are more permissive, such as perhaps on a vacation, while at other times they might be more authoritarian, such as in times of potential danger. If you are authoritative most of the time, you are doing well.

There are four different types of parenting styles. The authoritative style is the preferable style. It is characterized by high support and high attention. The parents supervise their children, set limits, and show love. The authoritarian style is a rigid style. It is characterized by high attention and low support. The parents supervise their children heavily, set strong limits, but have trouble showing love or approval. The permissive style is almost the opposite of the authoritarian style. It is characterized by low attention and high support. The parents do not supervise or set limits on their children, but are willing to provide them with whatever they want and allow them to do what they want. The neglectful style is the least desired style and is characterized by low attention and support. The parents are either not present or are pre-occupied and do not supervise or support their children. The children are left on their own.

Trauma

Trauma seems to play a large factor in the development of borderline personality disorders. Negative events in early life can create situations where a child becomes mistrustful or overly dependent on others. The need to survive creates different reactions based on how the child learns to feel comfortable and which actions they can take in order to be able to survive. The different components of trauma begin to form different survival mechanisms.

Abuse

The various forms of abuse suffered in early childhood set the stage for some of the symptoms of borderline personality disorder. Children learn that they cannot trust adults when they are abused by them. They grow to expect bad things and disappointment. They are unable to afford secure bonds with the abusers. Children of abuse might cope by retreating from others.

They might decide that if they cannot trust others they are better off in care of themselves. This often makes it harder for them to identify with others or feel responsibility for what they do. They expect others to do wrong so they do not see a large problem with doing wrong to others. They have trouble understanding the proper give-and-take in a healthy relationship. This can lead to problems interacting with others in society. In their perception, they are not doing anything wrong and are going by what they expect out of relationships based on their own early experiences.

Others might become clingier due to the insecurity involved in the abusive relationships. They might not feel that they are worthy of love or that others will be interested in them. This causes them to form abandonment issues. They fear that others do not want to be around them and do whatever they can to keep people from leaving. They might perceive that once someone leaves they will not come back. This is often the result of psychological or emotional abuse. If primary caregivers, who should be the most nurturing and supportive influences in the child's life, are putting the child down and telling them that they are unlovable or bad, the child begins to believe that they truly are.

ALERT

While most states recognize physical abuse and take strong measures to deal with it, few are equipped to make determinations on psychological and emotional abuse. Psychological and emotional abuse, while they do not cause observable physical scars, can be just as serious and as painful as the physical ones. The danger is that because they are not observed, they are sometimes left for the child to deal with alone.

Neglect

Neglect in early childhood can result in problems forming attachment. The child has a hard time forming a secure attachment to caregivers who are not there either physically or emotionally. In cases of neglect, the child does not learn about proper loving relationships. They do not see the work involved in relationships, because what was modeled for them did not show any work or concern.

FACT

In extreme cases of neglect the child might develop reactive attachment disorder. Reactive attachment disorder occurs when the child is unable to form any type of attachment to any caregivers while growing up. These children often become antisocial and have a great deal of trouble with authority.

Children who are neglected often have trouble with authority. They are impulsive because they have not learned how to reason things out, and they do not like others to tell them what to do. They are not raised in a supportive environment, so they do not have a high level of self-esteem based on caregivers' feedback. They might be sensitive to criticism and become defensive rather quickly.

Abandonment

Children who are abandoned in some way and left to the care of others often have problems adjusting and developing. They must try to form new bonds with new people. The natural attachment from parent to child is broken and must be rebuilt with someone else. Children who are fortunate enough to find loving and caring people to raise them have a better chance of adjusting to the issues that come with abandonment.

Unfortunately, many children who are abandoned end up in various public care systems that might provide physical care but do not necessarily help with the emotional instability caused by the abandonment. Without a loving, nurturing environment, the children fail to form the proper attachment to the new caregivers. The situation reinforces negative thoughts in the child's mind. The child might believe he is unlovable, or that it is his fault he was abandoned. He might feel he was bad in some way and think that others are blaming him for what has happened. In some way he looks at what is happening to him as punishment for something he did.

Children in these circumstances are then unable to form healthy, positive self-esteem and might feel like they cannot do anything right or that there is no reason for anyone to like them. They have trouble forming relationships because they do not believe they are worthy of anyone's affection. In children who also have a genetic predisposition toward these types of thoughts and behaviors the environmental reinforcement will cause thoughts to spiral downward.

Heredity

There is a high incidence of borderline personality disorder within families, indicating a hereditary element. Early information indicated a strong biological connection between schizophrenia and borderline personality disorder. This has since been scaled back, however, as new research seems to point to the interaction of both environmental and biological issues. But borderline personality disorder does tend to run in families, though the environmental circumstances discussed earlier also have a large influence.

Recent studies have discovered a possible variation in the gene that controls the function of the neurochemical serotonin. Those who have this variation of the serotonin gene seem to be at higher risk for developing borderline personality disorder if it is also shown that they have experienced dramatic childhood experiences. In other words symptoms have the ability to develop through genetic means, but need to be activated by poor environmental circumstances. If the environmental circumstances are not present, the gene does not seem to have the same effect.

FACT

Borderline personality disorder is as high as five times more common in close family situations. The risk is also higher in families with other mental health conditions.

Serotonin

Serotonin is involved in the regulation of mood and has been linked to different psychological conditions, such as mood and anxiety disorders, and antisocial behaviors. Serotonin is found throughout the body, but only in a small quantity within the brain itself. It is not able to cross into the brain through the blood flow process, so serotonin present in the brain must be produced in the brain. When serotonin interacts with norepinephrine a few different circumstances can occur. When both these neurotransmitters have reduced reactions, a person normally experiences inward-directed anger and reduced responsiveness. When serotonin has reduced reactions and norepinephrine has overreactions, there is external aggression and impulsivity. When serotonin has overreactions and norepinephrine is underreactive, a person is normally withdrawn. When both are overreactive, there is an increase in symptoms of anxiety, phobia, avoidance, and anxiety-related personality traits.

The Limbic System

Other studies have indicated differences in the structure of the brain and the way the brain functions for people who have borderline personality disorder. The limbic system, which includes the amygdala, seems to be most closely related to the emotional instability symptoms normally exhibited by someone with borderline personality disorder. The amygdala seems to play a key role in some of the stronger symptoms.

The brain's limbic system becomes overactive during puberty, which is about the time many believe borderline personality disorder begins, again lending more credence to the connection with this particular system. The limbic system is a set of brain structures located just under the cortex. It is sometimes considered part of the evolutionary primitive brain because many of the emotions and motivations regulated by it relate to survival. In addition to fear and anger, it also regulates feelings of pleasure, such as those received during eating and sex.

The two largest structures in the limbic system are the amygdala and hippocampus. Both are involved in emotional regulation. Emotional regulation often becomes a problem due to hormonal changes in puberty, which might indicate that people developing borderline personality disorder are having problems with the regulation of neurotransmitters most involved with emotion, such as serotonin and dopamine.

FACT

According to *Borderline Personality Today*, there is a greater number of severe headaches and migraines reported in patients with borderline personality disorder as compared to the general population.

Neuroimaging

Neuroimaging studies have shown differences in the volume and activity of brain structures related to emotion and impulsivity. Recent research indicates that the hippocampus and amygdala region could be as much as 16 percent smaller in people who have borderline personality disorder. Another study found that the size of the hippocampus within the brain was reduced in people with borderline personality disorder who seemed to exhibit stronger related symptoms.

Impulsiveness and aggression are thought to be the symptoms that are most often considered heritable. These are also symptoms most closely related to the amygdala and the limbic system. This has prompted some to speculate that the genetic link has more to do with certain specific symptoms than the entire disorder, especially since the symptoms considered most heritable are also prevalent in other health disorders. Other mental health disorders also have a genetic component, many of which are also linked to this same area of the brain.

ESSENTIAL

While dopamine's role in borderline personality disorder is still somewhat questionable, hyperactive dopamine function has been linked to overactivity in the amygdala, which would lead to problems regulating emotion and creating proper reactions to social situations.

Presence of Other Disorders

Since borderline personality disorder can be described as a complex disorder with a collection of symptoms, there are many symptoms that cross over to other disorders.

Research on the limbic system and its functions shows a connection to some other disorders. Mood disorders and anxiety disorders are connected to areas of the limbic system that are similar to those that seem to be causing symptoms in borderline personality disorder.

Problems with Comorbidity and Determining Causes

Researchers have stated that it is difficult to conduct neuroimaging studies that are able to separate comorbid disorders. Since the amygdala and other areas in the limbic system are implicated in both borderline personality disorder and disorders often found to accompany borderline personality disorder, such as mood and anxiety disorders, it is hard to determine which functions are causing problems related to each disorder.

Neuroimaging studies have not yet been able to distinguish between two different disorders when there is a symptom overlap. The National Center for Biotechnology Information (NCBI) has reported research on neuroimaging studies that have used participants with borderline personality disorder and other disorders combined. The NCBI presented an analogy that might describe how the brain functions in borderline personality disorder patients.

They use an analogy of a horse and rider. In borderline personality disorder patients, the affected brain structures (the horse) run wild, while the cognitive areas (the rider) are asleep or unable to regulate or inhibit impulsive behaviors. Since this same can be true for the symptoms of impulsivity related to antisocial personality disorder, it would be hard to determine which problem is related to which disorder.

FACT

Mood disorders are the most common disorders to co-occur with borderline personality disorder. Anxiety disorders are almost as prevalent, and eating and substance abuse disorders show significant relationships. Posttraumatic stress disorder has a large risk of comorbidity with borderline personality disorder—and is believed by some to be the true nature of borderline personality disorder.

A Combination of Causes

The age-old debate on nature versus nurture comes into question when looking at some possible causes of borderline personality disorder. It is safe to say that a large range of symptoms present in borderline personality disorder might speak more fully for the argument that it is a combination of both. Emotion regulation and the brain systems responsible for this are at the root of more than one disorder, yet the genetic potential is not enough.

Predisposition and Environment

Many people talk about the genetic component as a given. If a child is born to a parent who has borderline personality disorder, or another personality disorder, there are those who think that this means the child will also have borderline personality disorder. This is not necessarily the case. Children who have close biological relatives with borderline personality disorder have a higher risk of inheriting the genetic issues that might be responsible for the disorder. The problems already discussed about gene variation in brain chemical levels can be passed on from one generation to the next. This does not mean they will, but the risk is there.

The environment has a great deal to do with whether or not the symptoms develop fully. The extreme circumstances discussed earlier, such as abuse and neglect, create the maladaptive thought processes that give rise to the symptoms. When thought processes occur, different brain chemicals are interacting. The parts of the brain responsible for more negative emotions are the parts of the brain that have been implicated in causing symptoms of borderline personality disorder. If a child begins a thought process that overuses these negative emotions early on, this can set off a chain reaction.

ALERT

Borderline personality disorder has a strong environmental component, especially when there is the presence of a traumatic or abusive situation in early childhood. Thus, it is important to refrain from stressing the genetic potential as a given conclusion. This can often create a situation where the person believes that she has borderline personality disorder whether she does or not. They she begins to exhibit the symptoms and it can become a self-fulfilling prophecy.

A poor environment, or traumatic childhood experiences can often lead to these negative thoughts. Unfortunately, they can also often be tied to a chain of negative experiences that continue to occur during childhood and beyond. This sets the child up for behaviors that fall into line with borderline personality disorder.

Parenting

Parenting practices can often set the stage for good or bad development. The behaviors parents model and how they teach their children to behave can have a lot to do with how the children learn to perceive situations and develop problem-solving skills. If parents show positive ways to deal with disappointment and anger, the child has a better chance of learning to use similar ways.

In addition to showing the right types of thoughts and behaviors, parents play a very large function in showing unconditional love, nurturing, support, and unconditional positive regard. The word *unconditional* is very important. Children need to feel love no matter what they do. Often in cases of abuse and neglect love is provided grudgingly, conditionally, or sometimes not at all. The child feels that she must do something in order to earn the love. If she does not accomplish something in the right way, she is shown negative feedback.

The insecurities that are produced when a parent relies on conditional love often lead to low self-esteem and fears of abandonment in the child. When children are provided with a secure upbringing, even when a trauma or abandonment has occurred, they are more likely to develop better self-esteem and feel more secure. Unfortunately, this is not a given, and sometimes the trauma from the abuse or abandonment is too deep-seated to go away simply through the exhibition of positive regard and unconditional love.

QUESTION

Does this mean that children can be prevented from developing borderline personality disorder if they are provided with unconditional love and support?
Unfortunately, the answer is no. A large variety of different factors weigh into the development of the symptoms of borderline personality disorder. They must all be taken into account, and the way the child perceives the world will have a lot to do with how they relate to good and bad circumstances.

It is important to recognize both biological and environmental issues that could combine to create a situation where borderline personality disorder develops. It is not a given that someone will develop this disorder simply because a parent or close relative has it. It is also not a given that someone will develop this disorder simply because she has suffered traumatic or abusive events in her childhood. Not all children who are abandoned by their parents go on to develop this disorder. Yet the risk increases with all of these things. It is always good to be aware of the different aspects of a person's life that might combine and aid in development, but it is also important to remain open-minded and try to look at what is happening as objectively as possible.

CHAPTER 6

Who Has Borderline Personality Disorder?

Borderline personality disorder is not a disorder people like to announce that they have. The array of symptoms and the historical stigmatization of the disorder make it less likely someone will go public with this diagnosis. Some people are more likely to get this disorder based on heredity or traumatic events in their lives. Other demographics might also increase risk, such as gender and age. It is sometimes helpful to look at who has the disorder in order to determine who might have or develop the disorder. Also because much of the information on this disorder makes it seem insurmountable and debilitating, a look at people who have or might have the disorder might provide a different perception of people with borderline personality disorder.

Important Factors

Borderline personality disorder is most often diagnosed in females. About 75 percent of those diagnosed with the disorder are female. Most people diagnosed with borderline personality disorder are or have been in some form of inpatient treatment. Symptoms are often so severe they need professional treatment around the clock to stabilize with initial diagnosis, or when other disorders are present to complicate matters. Inpatient status is usually initiated as a result of substance abuse issues that have caused problems with the law.

Most treatment studies that have been conducted so far on borderline personality disorder have included only women.

Many people with borderline personality disorder also meet criteria for clinical depression. About 25 percent also meet the criteria for posttraumatic stress disorder. Of those who are dually diagnosed, or diagnosed with more than one disorder, about 50–67 percent are diagnosed with borderline personality disorder. This complicates treatment as the symptoms of more than one disorder interact.

Borderline personality disorder is actually more prevalent than schizophrenia or bipolar disorder, both of which have received more attention. Until fairly recently in history, borderline personality disorder did not hold a very hopeful prognosis for treatment and recovery.

Statistics

Some of the statistics for borderline personality disorder provide a good indication of how serious this disorder can be. Nearly 70 percent of people diagnosed with this disorder will make at least one suicide attempt. About 8–10 percent of those diagnosed with this disorder will successfully complete a suicide attempt, often because they are unable to control impulses during depressive episodes. This rate doubles when a person has a history of self-destructive behaviors and/or suicide attempts. This rate is more than

50 times the rate of the general population. This underscores the danger of these symptoms.

ESSENTIAL

Statistics for borderline personality disorder are dependent upon a diagnosis. Since many people do not seek treatment, many people are not diagnosed. The actual incidence of this disorder is likely higher.

Outlook

Borderline personality disorder, along with other mental health disorders, are underdiagnosed as people do not seek treatment. The stigma attached to having a mental health issue causes many to avoid admitting to a problem. For those who do seek treatment, there is a good prognosis. Treatment can include various forms of psychoeducation, medication, support groups, and psychotherapy. Some research suggests that symptoms can decrease as an individual ages, especially with treatment. It is important to seek diagnosis and subsequent treatment.

Famous People Who Have BPD

Some reports have linked certain famous people with this disorder based on how they have behaved in public, what is known about their families, and information on how they grew up. It should be noted that the people mentioned have not been given confirmed diagnoses of the disorder, but the descriptions and symptoms present a possibility that shows how behaviors can be overlooked due to other circumstances—such as celebrity, when making a determination.

Some people have speculated that Princess Diana suffered from borderline personality disorder based on some of her childhood information and the behaviors she showed in public. Princess Diana suffered the loss of her mother at an early age as her parents divorced and her mother left her. Her father was described as emotionally withdrawn after the divorce, which would have left Diana with little in comfort or support. Others point out that she had large problems with her self-esteem and feared abandonment, which was why she remained in her marriage as long as she did.

ALERT

Each person listed fits more than one symptom of borderline personality disorder, but the symptoms themselves do not guarantee a diagnosis. Assessment professionals are trained to look at the symptoms as part of a larger picture presented by each individual and decide from there. Even though a famous person might exhibit some of the symptoms it does not mean she has the disorder.

Another celebrity who seemed to show abandonment fears, and who went through a series of turbulent, chaotic relationships, along with mood swings and anxiety was Marilyn Monroe. Marilyn Monroe also presented with more than one suicide attempt, lending itself to speculation about borderline personality disorder.

QUESTION

Could these people have a different disorder?
Yes, it is possible that another disorder is present, or that no disorder is present. It would be up to a professional to do a lengthy evaluation to determine what the symptoms mean in each individual case.

One famous person who might seem to fit the general impression of what someone with borderline personality disorder might look like is Adolf Hitler. Hitler's mood swings and strong emotional outbursts were legendary. He moved from erratic behavior to insecure behavior quickly and repeatedly. He showed both antisocial and narcissistic tendencies and had trouble controlling emotions.

Confirmed Case

While most cases do not have a public confirmation, one person did speak out. Author Susanna Kaysen wrote the book *Girl, Interrupted* about her experiences in a psychiatric hospital after she had been diagnosed for borderline personality disorder at the age of eighteen. She spent two years in the hospital and documented her stay, her treatment, and her own perceptions of what was happening to her and around her. The book was made into a movie with the same title. Susanna detailed her problems with fear of abandonment, mood swings, and problems focusing and grasping reality at times.

Patterns

While the only case listed that is confirmed as an actual diagnosis is Susanna Kaysen, the others mentioned do show symptoms that have led to speculation. One common pattern seems to be an abundance of creativity and intelligence. The stigma attached seems to overshadow the personal attributes of those who might have borderline personality disorder. It is important to give credit for the accomplishments and abilities of the people who have this disorder. They are not simply bored, empty individuals who have little to show for their lives.

Another pattern that seems to be emerging is a link with posttraumatic stress disorder, and with eating disorders. It is unclear how these links are working, but it could provide a deeper understanding of the severity of the symptoms, and the thoughts behind the symptoms. People who are diagnosed with borderline personality disorder are dealing with psychological pain and insecurity and might feel that their lives are out of control.

Aren't We All a Little Different?

It is easy to begin to see symptoms in others after reading the details of a certain disorder. Many people exhibit one symptom or possibly two, or have an explosive episode. The truth is that at one point or another everyone will likely show some symptom of some disorder. Only about one-third of the people who could be diagnosed with a mental health disorder are. Most do not seek treatment.

Everyone is unique in some way, and everyone has his or her own thought patterns. Each person processes information in a way that is different from everyone else. This makes each person different in some way that might seem unusual to someone else.

When Similar Symptoms Might Arise

People also exhibit one or two symptoms when they are in the midst of a crisis, have had a bad day, or are simply not processing things correctly on a given day. When someone is coming down with an illness, they do not necessarily perceive things positively. They might also be more likely to become angry quicker or to cry quicker. They might explode or become clingy. These symptoms would then disappear as the illness abates. Someone might simply feel blue for no discernible reason. This can cause others to look for a reason, which often leads to speculation.

ALERT

Diagnosis should be based on how the symptoms affect the person exhibiting them rather than how someone else views the symptoms. Different values and beliefs can lead to misdiagnosis so it is important to look at how the symptoms relate to the individual rather than your own beliefs of what should be.

Keep Empathy in Mind

Borderline personality disorder is a disorder that can cause severe feelings of discomfort and negativity in the person experiencing it. Yet this person should not be treated as an outcast. She is not contagious, and she is not crazy. She is trying to work through different ways of perceiving and feeling.

Borderline personality disorder is an issue that does need to be addressed with professional help. The array of symptoms exhibited by one single person often provides a clear indication that there is a problem and not simply the unique nature of that person. Although there is no single person without some form of issues they must deal with, mental health issues remain a source of stigma today.

It is important to recognize the potential differences in the thought processes of people with borderline personality disorder, but it is also important to recognize that they are human beings. The differences created by borderline personality disorder can be treated. People can live healthy, happy lives.

ESSENTIAL

Some personality profiles show that people with borderline personality disorder often show personality traits that combine histrionic personality disorder, narcissistic personality disorder, and antisocial personality disorder. This causes a wide range of symptoms and behaviors.

It is also important to be sure that what you are looking at is actually borderline personality disorder. Other personality disorders have similar symptoms to some extent. Some people can exhibit symptoms when they are on drugs or alcohol. There is also the possibility of environmental problems that can overwhelm a person and cause her to make poor decisions that mirror those of someone with borderline personality disorder.

When Parents Have the Disorder

CHAPTER 7

Facing the Disorder

Up to this point, the focus of this book has been on identifying and learning more about what happens to people
with borderline personality disorder. This disorder, however,
affects how others relate and interact with BPD people. The
various people who come in contact with people with borderline personality disorder face challenges communicating and
relating to them. This is especially true in close relationships.

When Parents Have the Disorder

The disturbances of the person with borderline personality disorder spread outward to envelop all members of the family. A spouse must deal with the constant accusations, mistrust, and fear of rejection. Children who have a parent with borderline personality disorder often find themselves facing the impulsivity, mood swings, neediness, and fear of abandonment of a parent. This can be very disconcerting for a child. The child often grows up early, as family focus is normally on the parent and the needs of the parent.

Child as Caretaker

The child is often placed in the position of caretaker or expected to fulfill emotional needs of someone who cannot meet these needs on their own. This sets the child up for failure, as she cannot meet these needs. The parent often becomes angry and belligerent, perhaps resorting to insults and statements designed to hurt.

ESSENTIAL

> Parentification is a process in which parents turn to their children to parent them. The parent or parents confide in the children and turn to them for comfort and advice on matters that are above the child and should not involve the child. They also look to the child to take care of them—plan meals, clean, cook, keep them on schedule, etc.

These children grow up in uncertainty and have no consistency in parenting to rely on for support, safety, and rules. They do not know how the parent will react from one situation to the next, and could face a seemingly endless harangue of complaints and imagined slights or days of stony silence as punishment for a perceived wrongdoing by the child. The child is often more mature and better able to handle the situation than the adult.

Problems That Develop

Unfortunately, children who are raised to be caretakers tend to grow up with low self-esteem. Since they were not raised in an environment where they did anything right, they do not feel they can. The parent with borderline personality disorder is often putting them down or is disappointed because the child cannot make them feel better. The child takes this to heart and feels that it is her fault.

The child might become an overachiever who is never satisfied with any accomplishments. This type of child often develops black-and-white thinking. They either succeed or they fail, there is no middle ground. They become angry with themselves when they do not succeed and can become easily frustrated. They might give up quickly when they see that they are not going to win or do well based on their standards. They do not take criticism well and are often easily discouraged. These particular behaviors and thoughts run themselves to the development of borderline personality disorder in the child.

These children might also become loners. They might feel reluctant to form relationships based on the feedback they are given by the parent with borderline personality disorder. They might feel they are not worthy of it, or that they are going to do something to ruin it. They might also see it as a time where they will open themselves up to more pain. They withdraw from society in general and have a part-time interaction with others. They are mistrustful and expect to be hurt.

Some children who are parentified begin to see themselves as the head of the household and start to make more and more decisions with less input from parents. They begin to see themselves as more mature and more capable of taking care of younger siblings and become defiant of parent decisions. They are left to cover so many responsibilities in the house that they become resentful when the parent tries to step in and take over again.

Similarities to the Disorder Itself

Children who are parentified, or who live in homes with a borderline personality disorder parent, present with similarities to some of the symptoms of borderline personality disorder, causing others to assume the child is developing borderline personality disorder as a result of genetic inheritance. This is not necessarily true and the symptoms must be seen as part of a total package of thoughts and behaviors that persist beyond the home circumstance. While the child is reacting to the environment, it is not a given that the disorder will develop, especially if help is provided.

QUESTION

Social Relationships

Social relationships with someone with borderline personality disorder can often be characterized as chaotic, intense, and emotionally charged. Someone with borderline personality disorder often has serious problems with interpersonal relationships and can move from clinginess to withdrawal quickly and frequently. Many of the symptoms introduce additional stress into the relationship. The constant up-and-down and conflicts can cause someone to feel frustrated and out of control. This can occur in romantic relationships, professional relationships, and friendships.

The Beginning

Relationships often start out on a very positive note. People with borderline personality disorder begin each relationship happily and with high hopes. They tend to be more giving and show a very caring side. Their positive qualities come out quickly. Due to the high impulsivity of the disorder, they tend to seem fun and exciting to begin with. They are often willing to do new things and keep things lively.

This occurs because in the mind of the person with borderline personality disorder this relationship is perfect. People with this disorder very quickly see the relationship has something that will make them feel better and keep them from feeling alone. These strong positive feelings often cause them to be more giving and solicitous. They might shower their new friend or lover with gifts and make this person the center of their attention for a period of time.

The other person usually feels very flattered to begin with and overwhelmed with the care and devotion provided to her. If she is insecure herself or has trouble finding relationships, she might be just as willing to jump into the quick closeness characteristic of someone with borderline personality disorder. Unfortunately this does not last and certain issues seem common.

ALERT

Many relationships start with an initial feeling of euphoria. There is that early connection that allows people to feel that there is someone else in their life, whether it be romantically or in other relationship forms. This feeling however, is an initial feeling that does not last. Any relationship is work and requires give-and-take. If someone comes on too hard too fast and showers you with gifts and praise right from the start it is wise to be leery of that person.

Friendships

Friendships often come and go with someone who has borderline personality disorder. The ups and downs can send others out the door, especially early in the friendship when there is little invested in the relationship. They find themselves the target of the symptoms and see the relationship as too stressful to continue to work at. After the initial burst of attention and care, the friends often find themselves more on the giving side of the relationship. They tend to get the brunt of angry outbursts and often find themselves comforting the other through any number of emotional episodes.

The high impulsivity of borderline personality disorder makes it likely that individuals with the disorder will want to have fun without worrying about responsibility at times. This tends to create a situation where the friends are left to take care of responsibilities and deal with the bad times while others get to go have fun. Friends often find themselves brushed aside while the person with borderline personality disorder goes off to play with someone she either does not know or does not know well.

It is also painful to be a friend and feel out of control in situations where someone with borderline personality disorder acts destructively. Friends might find themselves trying to help the person work through episodes of self-harm, overdoses, or even suicide attempts. They are torn between the need to stand by their friend and the constant stress and need for hypervigilance.

FACT

Once in treatment, the prognosis for borderline personality disorder is relatively positive. Many people are able to control and reduce symptoms quickly and might present with few or no symptoms within the first couple of years of treatment.

How Someone with Borderline Personality Disorder Feels

People with borderline personality disorder greatly want to be liked. They do not like the fact that they go through so many friendships and often feel very insecure. They feel like others want more from them than they have to give and do not feel that others support them when they are in need of help. They also believe they have put an image out there of being strong and self-sufficient, which might actually come across to others as moody and aloof. They are seeking love and acceptance, but the desperate nature of their thoughts often conveys other impressions to those around them. This can become a challenge in professional relationships.

Professional Relationships

Many people with borderline personality disorder have successful careers and are able to get along at work. Unfortunately, others have trouble and are unemployed, underemployed, or unhappy. The high impulsivity and problems with self-esteem and identity often cause people to move from job to job and career to career. They often have a hard time settling down in just one field and remaining there. They also have a hard time maintaining the same type of work day in and day out.

Job Hopping

The inability to stay in one job or one field for any period of time often leads to job hopping. The person with borderline personality disorder will move from one job or duty to the next, often without completing the first. As with any other relationship, the job relationship starts out idyllic and fades from there. It is hard to form a professional relationship with people with BPD when they are constantly moving about and often complaining about what is happening.

ESSENTIAL

Certain fields seem to reinforce the black-and-white thinking of borderline personality disorder. Some of these fields are in human industries such as social work and clinical therapy, while others are in criminal justice fields such as police officers, prison guards, or military officers. In each of these cases the field provides for power and control over others, and working in the "good guy" role in either caring for others or putting bad guys in their place.

The Work Environment

Workers with BPD often have trouble focusing on what they are supposed to be doing and do not always get the work done. This leaves coworkers to pick up their slack, which often causes resentment and coworkers avoiding them. When people with borderline personality disorder feel like they are being avoided they become even more defensive and perhaps begin to generate conflict. This makes for an uncertain work environment.

Boundaries are often disturbed in professional relationships, as people with borderline personality disorder might come to rely too much on others to help them through. They might also perceive that they are doing more than their fair share of the work and begin to pick battles with other employees as a result. If it is a high-stress field, they might become even more unstable, and emotional outbursts could result. If it is a field that has direct contact with customers, there could be problems maintaining contracts and keeping customers satisfied.

Because people with borderline personality disorder often move from job to job rather frequently, professional relationships do not develop to any great extent in many of these cases. The emotional investment does not have time to develop, and if they don't do their share of the work, it actually seems more a relief when they move on.

Romantic Relationships

Romantic relationships can be especially trying, since both parties normally invest so much of themselves into this type of relationship. Often that initial burst of love, caring, and attention provided by the person with borderline personality disorder can sweep someone off his feet, preventing him from thinking as clearly as he should. By the time he realizes something is not quite right, he is already emotionally invested in the relationship and finds it harder to end it. The constant ups and downs of the relationship also cause someone to have a hard time thinking clearly. Romantic relationships are normally characterized by extreme highs and lows that tend to lead to some similar patterns and trends.

QUESTION

Why would anyone want to start a relationship with someone with borderline personality disorder?
These relationships are certainly challenging, but that does not mean that good, lasting relationships cannot occur. People with borderline personality disorder are often kind and caring individuals who are having trouble learning to deal with the symptoms of their disorder. Treatment can be very effective at helping increase relationship function.

Trends Within Romantic Relationships

Romantic relationships with someone with borderline personality disorder are normally difficult to navigate, and tend to have certain common features. Since a larger percentage of those diagnosed with borderline personality disorder are female, some of these features tend to relate to females. Studies seem to indicate that relationship stress has a greater chronic effect on females, although this might be due to the thought processes of the disorder itself. There are also a greater number of romantic relationships over the course of time, and a greater number of unplanned pregnancies.

People with borderline personality disorder tend to have more former partners, and relationships, especially romantic relationships, are more likely to end in a breakup. Women with borderline personality disorder tend to exhibit more negative attitudes about sex, and are more likely to feel pressured into having sex rather than willingly taking part. The high impulsivity in borderline personality disorder makes it more likely that sexual relationships could be indiscriminate. The additional potential complication of childhood sexual abuse can also complicate this aspect of a romantic relationship. People with borderline personality disorder who were sexually abused as children are already predisposed to having trouble with sexual relationships and often need therapy to work through the experiences of childhood in the symptoms of borderline personality disorder.

Making a Romantic Relationship Last

One of the largest problems with any romantic relationship is the work it takes to keep it going healthy and strong. Every relationship has pitfalls and problems that cause disagreement and conflict. The main component in making a relationship last is learning how to handle conflict and work out the difficult times. This is where someone with borderline personality disorder can run into problems.

She begins with such high hopes and puts her new partner on a pedestal he cannot live up to. The overattention and gift giving can be overwhelming for the other person, and if his responses are not what she had in mind, she might feel like she is giving much more than her new partner. This is likely the case, as people with BPD come on so hard so quickly that the other person does not have a chance to reciprocate as expected.

Once the honeymoon period ends and reality sets in, the person with borderline personality disorder learns that this new perfect relationship isn't quite as perfect as expected. The black-and-white thinking can get in the way and cause the withdrawal process to begin. It is important at this point to help the person recognize that it is okay to make mistakes and still be in love. It is also important to find ways to cope with these mood swings and learn to work together through them. It is possible to do, and even likely to achieve success if professional help is involved. The person with borderline personality disorder needs to seek treatment to help with the symptoms, and the couple can seek help with therapy together in order to establish ways of getting through the hard times.

Breaking Up

Unfortunately, many relationships involving someone with borderline personality disorder do dissolve eventually. But the intense fear of abandonment can cause some problems in the breakup process. The person with BPD might become distraught at the thought of abandonment and have trouble letting go. Sometimes the thought of breaking up with someone with borderline personality disorder can be so uncomfortable that the partner avoids it, hoping that the relationship will just die on its own. Since the person with borderline personality disorder has intense fears of abandonment, this rarely happens. The best that can be hoped for is that she finds someone else and breaks it off herself. It is better to be honest and upfront about the issue.

Being Honest

An honest break from someone with borderline personality disorder will likely be an uncomfortable occurrence. The direct confrontation could result in an angry outburst or lengthy episode of emotion by the person with borderline personality disorder. She might also become severely depressed or engage in self-destructive behaviors, such as cutting, overindulging in drugs or alcohol, or, worse yet, attempting suicide.

ALERT

It is important to remain calm and try to keep the breakup situation from getting out of hand. Do not attack or threaten; rather, listen to what the person has to say and do not interrupt. Be sensitive to what she is feeling and acknowledge her pain. Try to be gentle and patient.

It is important to do this in a calm manner and choose words carefully in order to minimize the negative feelings it will create. It is also a good idea to contact family members or other friends of the person with borderline personality disorder and let them know what is about to occur. They will then be able to watch for any self-destructive behaviors and head them off.

While the honest approach certainly seems to have its pitfalls, it does tend to provide for closure and give greater potential for a clean break. If done correctly, the person with borderline personality disorder will have other supportive members near her to help get her through it.

Becoming Unavailable

Some people will try to end the relationship by simply becoming unavailable to the person with borderline personality disorder. They will stop taking or returning phone calls, avoid places where they might run into each other, not answer the door, and use any other method of avoiding the person with borderline personality disorder. This is done in the hopes that the person will simply give up and move on to someone else, leaving them alone and able to avoid a potentially emotional and turbulent scene.

Unfortunately, this scenario feeds into the fear of abandonment. Unlike the clean break where there is at least an explanation and a warning of intent, this leaves the door open and prevents closure. The person with borderline personality disorder can interpret this in many different ways, all of which are negative and self-destructive. Her fears of abandonment and being alone are realized when the breakup is done this way.

Why Are You in This Relationship?

Since relationships with people with borderline personality disorder can be so volatile, it is important to look at why someone would choose to be in such a relationship. It is easy to become swept off of your feet with the over-attention, flattery, and gifts that are presented by this person. Yet this does not last long, and the relationship can become unstable.

There is often something that keeps a person in a relationship with so many ups and downs. People with borderline personality disorder are often very caring, sensitive people who really want to be in a good relationship. They want a relationship to work, but they have a great deal of trouble admitting their faults even to themselves. This causes them to blame others, and in a relationship this includes their partner. The partner thus takes the brunt of the blame for any relationship problems. When the partner with borderline personality disorder is not in treatment, it is not normally a good, healthy relationship. Why do people remain in this type of relationship?

Why This Relationship?

When someone is in the midst of the symptoms of borderline personality disorder they are not presenting themselves as an ideal partner. So the question is: why stay in this type of relationship? Often people who enter into this type of relationship are happily overwhelmed with the attention and gifts. They are vulnerable because they themselves do not have high self-esteem or feel that they can easily get another partner. They worry that if they let this relationship end, they will not be able to get into another one.

There are some issues that create insecurity. They might have to do with finances, looks, self-esteem, or any number of other issues that might manifest as a result of childhood baggage or past poor relationship experiences. A male in a relationship with a female with borderline personality disorder might be looking to save her, like a knight in shining armor.

The initial appeal of the relationship plays into some part of that person's own needs. Some part of that initial thrust in the relationship makes the other person feel good. Then, when reality starts to hit, problems begin and many turn away from this type of relationship. When someone stays in this type of relationship, there are usually other issues at work. This is especially true if the relationship becomes abusive in some way.

ALERT

Rage reactions can occur with little provocation, and without notice. They are unpredictable, unexpected, and can be very dangerous.

Can It Ever Work?

Relationships can work in this type of situation. The most likely success occurs when a person with borderline personality disorder is in counseling and is actively working on the symptoms. Couples therapy can also work to help both partners learn to interact positively with each other and to work through when the symptoms occur.

This takes a commitment on both parts, and work is required. It is important to note that if abuse is present, it must be dealt with. If it is not addressed, the relationship remains unhealthy and unstable, and can be very dangerous. Basically if the positives outnumber the negatives, and abuse is not present, it is possible to work through the issues and develop a healthy relationship.

CHAPTER 8

The Family and Borderline Personality Disorder

Family members cope with the uncertainty from day to day, worrying about how their loved one will react to something. When someone with borderline personality disorder is not in treatment, it can cause havoc within the family system. Family members need to seek treatment themselves in order to learn how to deal with the symptoms and move on with their own lives in a healthy manner. Family members often avoid bringing others around the person with borderline personality disorder, and are not always eager to go on family outings with this person. Each family system is unique, but there are certain similarities in how the disorder affects the system.

Characteristics of the Family System

The family system can become unstable when someone in the family has borderline personality disorder. Family members often feel helpless to control the situation or minimize the damage done during strong emotional episodes. They live day-to-day and have a hard time making plans for simple family outings. They also feel helpless to prevent the self-destructive behaviors that often occur with someone with borderline personality disorder. The family members are often the ones dealing with the behaviors and driving the person to the emergency room. This can cause feelings of guilt, as the family members can become resentful of this added burden.

Guilt

Family members deal with many conflicting feelings and emotions. They want to help, but they feel helpless. In many cases, they just want the problem to go away. Different members of the family feel guilt for different reasons. In every case, a part of each family member's life is affected by the disorder and each one must deal with it in some way. They want to be supportive, but they also want their own lives. This often leads to inner conflict and tough decisions.

ESSENTIAL

Family treatments have become a new form of therapy in working with borderline personality disorder patterns as they affect family. It is designed to provide family members with a deeper understanding of what is going on, and developing positive interactions with the issues that are causing problems.

As discussed earlier, romantic relationships can suffer greatly when borderline personality disorder symptoms are out of control. A spouse might feel trapped in a relationship and want out. The spouse might want to end it and get on with her own life. This leaves her feeling guilty because she knows her partner needs her, and if children are involved, she wants the family system to be okay.

Spouses either remain in a marriage where they do not feel love or commitment or they leave and feel like they are deserting someone who needs them. If the children are also torn, it makes the decision that much harder. They might also feel guilty because they resent the burden that has been placed on them.

Even when love remains and both partners remain committed, there is guilt. The partner might not feel she is doing enough to help, or that she cannot deal with some of the problems that arise as a result of the symptoms. The partner of the person with BPD becomes frustrated and sometimes take out those frustrations on the children or spouse, then feels bad for doing so.

Guilt of the Young Child

Children often feel guilty because they wonder if they have done something wrong to make the situation worse. This might be a result of various behaviors by the person with borderline personality disorder. The attention-seeking behaviors often present in someone with borderline personality disorder could affect how the children see what is going on. If the person is acting out in some way that the child believes is overdramatic, or that the child does not understand, the child might not react. If the behavior escalates or the person is harmed, the child might believe that it is his fault.

The children also feel guilty for wishing the person would go away or leave them alone. They might wish for another parent or that they were the child of some friend's parents so they can have what they perceive to be a normal life. This would likely cause some guilt in and of itself, but if something did then happen to the parent, they might feel like they wished it into being. If the parent is abusive in some way, children may have trouble attaching to that parent in the first place.

Family Interactions

Family interactions are often characterized by the ups and downs of the person with borderline personality disorder. There could be bouts of intense, controlling anger that alternate with intense fears of abandonment.

Family members, especially children, do not know what to do in situations like this. They often react defensively by fighting back, or retreat as quickly as possible. The constant uncertainty leaves family members unable to trust their own perceptions of reality.

Older adolescent children who might be developing borderline personality disorder could be involved in substance abuse, eating or starvation, and highly impulsive behaviors such as driving recklessly. Family members are often left wondering when they'll get a call saying that the adolescent has been arrested or is in the hospital. The unpredictability of this one child often takes the bulk of the parents' time and energy. This leaves the rest of the children to fend for themselves in many cases. Their accomplishments are overshadowed by the sibling's dangerous behaviors.

QUESTION

Can the family ever have normal time together?
With borderline personality disorder, the symptoms normally are at their worst when there is a stressor. The larger the stressor they are experiencing in their perception, the greater the symptoms. When the stress subsides, the symptoms usually subside too. This gives the family times when they can be together under normal circumstances.

The person with borderline personality disorder might also try to divide and conquer. One other family member might become the target for a period of time. During this period of time a campaign might be waged against that person to other siblings and parents. The target is left wondering what he has done to deserve this, and other members of the family are trying to figure out what is truth and what is not.

It is also very difficult to deal with the continual threat of suicide or self-harm. This leaves the other family members on constant alert. Blame tends to go around the family as they all try to figure out what is happening and what to do about it. One aim each member must have is to set boundaries that allow him or her to interact with all members of the family, including the member with borderline personality disorder.

Setting Boundaries

Setting boundaries is a very important activity. The family members will need to be gentle but firm in this endeavor as they might be met with anger and/or emotional outbursts. It is important to use a calm voice and maintain the boundaries that are set. Boundaries and limits need to be clearly defined and remain the same throughout. It is often necessary to repeat the same boundaries over and over again from one situation to the next.

Lack of Boundaries

People with borderline personality disorder often have a very hard time respecting the boundaries of others. They might treat a family member as an extension of themselves rather than a unique separate being. Their fear of abandonment and rejection cause them to overreact when boundaries are set. Since they themselves do not have solid boundaries, they may move quickly into a relationship that is not agreeable, over the boundaries of friends and people connected to other family members.

Those with BPD often interfere in other people's lives where they do not belong. This can cause resentment and often causes problems with other people's interactions. People with borderline personality disorder enter into interactions where they do not belong, become combative, and often end up with a sense of rejection before it is all over. This sense of rejection often causes them to attempt to turn a family member against those they see as having rejected them.

Case Study: Casey

Casey's mother was diagnosed with borderline personality disorder. Casey had a hard time making close friends because she did not like bringing anyone over to her house. She also did not like to go to other children's houses because her mother wanted to talk to the parents, and this often caused trouble. Casey wanted to go to Samantha's party, so she took the chance and showed her mother the invitation. Her mother was excited because she had thought all along that Casey just could not make friends. She did not realize that it had anything to do with her. Casey's mother called Samantha's mother and had a nice ten-minute conversation. Casey's mother then called Samantha's mother back and had another nice conversation. Later that evening, Casey's mother called Samantha's mother again. It was late and Samantha's mother had been sleeping. Samantha's mother asked her to please call back in the morning. Casey's mother took this as rejection, and when Casey woke up the next morning she was told she could not go to Samantha's party because Samantha's mother was rude and she did not like her.

FACT

Since most people who have been diagnosed with borderline personality disorder are female, the family dyad that seems to be affected most by the symptoms is the mother/daughter dyad. If the relationship is abusive, it increases the risk of the daughter developing symptoms of this disorder.

Boundary-Setting Process

When setting boundaries a person needs to be firm but sensitive. People with borderline personality disorder do not recognize that they are overstepping boundaries or even that other people would want the boundaries. Acknowledge their feelings but firmly point out limits. The manner of presentation is important. If the person with borderline personality disorder becomes offended or feels rejected, he will focus on that emotion and it will get out of control.

It is important to use "I" statements when explaining and setting up boundaries with people with borderline personality disorder. The discussion should not become centered on what a person with borderline personality disorder has done. The person becomes defensive and focuses on what he needs to do to remove blame from himself. He does not see that he has done something wrong and has a very hard time accepting the blame. The original intention of the meeting gets lost.

Use a calm voice and explain with patience. Acknowledge that you realize he is trying to help, or mean well in some way. Then explain the boundary you are setting up and why. Keep it as simple as possible and try not to involve others if possible. The more people involved the more likely it is that blame will begin.

Once boundaries have been established, they must remain consistent. This sometimes means having to take extra time for an explanation, or risk an emotional episode. If the boundaries are breached and nothing comes of it, the boundaries will continue to be breached. By remaining firm, yet gentle, the person with borderline personality disorder does not feel threatened and can continue to work on recognizing these boundaries. This is one of the ways trust can develop.

Trust

Borderline personality disorder is often the result of child abuse or abandonment. Child sexual abuse is common in this disorder. These are not situations that create a great deal of trust. Children who have these experiences learned that trust is often broken and they need to rely on themselves. They are often fearful of others and do not want the attention that has been given to them.

Issues of Mistrust

Unfortunately, in the family situation this trust often comes at the hands of a family member. While statistics tend to indicate that sexual abuse is more often at the hands of a nonrelative, physical abuse seems to be higher with a parent. This leaves a child with few to turn to for trust and security. The child grows to dread and avoid the attention of the people who should be there to protect him. As a result, he also develops a mistrust of other adults and authority figures.

Abusers are often unpredictable. They can be fun and supportive one minute, and angry and abusive the next. Children do not know what to expect at any time. They cannot establish any kind of pattern to go by and become mistrustful even of the good times because they are often followed by bad times. It makes them distrustful of good times in general and they are wary of others who treat them kindly. They are often waiting for the other shoe to drop. If they are subsequently placed in another home, this mistrust carries over.

Issues from Abandonment

Children who are abandoned or threatened with abandonment also develop trust issues. They begin to feel that no matter what they do someone is going to leave them. Words of reassurance are met with mistrust. If the person is late or does not make it into some preplanned event for whatever reason, it is viewed as abandonment. Any reason or excuse given is ignored or discounted as a lie. Trust never develops, because any little deviation is seen as proof that rejection and abandonment are coming soon.

How Trust Is Perceived

Borderline personality disorder is characterized by emotional outbursts and constantly changing moods. It is likely that most people who deal with this disorder have been through a series of relationships, either romantic or otherwise. They might also have experienced some form of rejection within the family system. If they were abused as children they have also experienced that form of negative interaction. All of these negative interactions combine to reinforce the negative perceptions that are often there.

People with borderline personality disorder are often hypersensitive to nonverbal forms of communication. They interpret gestures and facial expressions negatively and look for signs they are right.

As a result of these negative interactions, trust is perceived in a different way. Trust is looked at as vulnerability. People who trust leave themselves open to hurt and more problems. Trust is a risk that many are not willing to take, as it often builds them up for a larger disappointment and fall. They have already gone through this and have been hurt. They might also feel that they do not deserve love or positive attention and are wary when they receive it. These feelings of unworthiness set up an expectancy of disappointment and rejection.

Defenses are built up over time and supersede trust. Trust becomes a liability and leaves the family member vulnerable to new pain and disappointment. Trust is a risk that can occur only when conditions seem safe and accepting. This often happens after the person has been put through multiple tests that prove he or she will not leave or abuse that trust. Even when the trust is given to some extent it is normally reserved in some way, and defenses are ready to go up at the first sign of trouble. This is an issue that can be worked on and lessened to some extent, but trust comes hard and there is usually a little bit of mistrust that remains and affects relationships at some level. This is an issue that might need to be acknowledged and attended to on a regular basis. The issues that cause the mistrust in the first place need to be dealt with on some level. Other issues could be accepted as part of the thought and behavior package for that individual.

QUESTION

If they cannot trust, how do people with borderline personality disorder have healthy relationships?
This is one of the reasons relationships come and go so often. They cannot let down their guard enough to have a complete sharing relationship. It is possible to develop a trusting relationship, but it takes work.

Acceptance

One of the largest tasks for all members a family system to accomplish is getting to a point of acceptance on issues that remain. Each member has his or her own personal issues and perceptions to work through, along with how the thoughts and behaviors of the family member with borderline personality disorder affect those issues. Everyone must come to a point where he or she is able to function through the issues that cannot be resolved. There will be some issues that cannot be completely resolved in any family system, and some symptoms of borderline personality disorder will likely cause some problems that will be harder to work through or live with.

Recognizing the Issues

With treatment, many of the symptoms of borderline personality disorder will be reduced or removed to a great extent. As the family member with borderline personality disorder begins to recognize and take control of many symptoms, it will be easier to communicate and work through differences and needs, including setting boundaries. One of the largest stressors for someone with borderline personality disorder is fear of abandonment and the resulting issues that are created.

It is also important to remember that someone with borderline personality disorder has a hard time understanding and practicing proper social skills. There will likely be frustrating and embarrassing moments within the family itself and in public. This decreased understanding can sometimes cause her to act in a way that will turn others off, forcing family members to scramble to make things right again. Family members might lose friends, get into trouble in school, lose romantic relationships, and even have trouble at work if there is interference. These are issues that are best handled by creating firm boundaries. Yet there is also a need to accept that this reduced understanding is likely going to remain. The family member with BPD will often need reminders, and it is also a good idea to anticipate potential problems before they occur.

ALERT

It is important to take the feelings and goals of all members of the family system into account when trying to decide what a plan of action can be in any circumstance. Children can feel they are lost in the shuffle when their sibling with borderline personality disorder receives all the attention. This can cause resentment and resistance.

Each person exhibits different symptoms, and the symptoms that cause the most problems for a given family will be unique. It is up to family members to recognize which symptoms cause the most problems and create plans for what to do about them as they occur. Acceptance does not mean just living with symptoms. Acceptance means recognizing that circumstances can occur where the symptoms might affect the lives of other members of the family system. With acceptance comes an acknowledgment that there are issues that need to be dealt with. Once this acknowledgment occurs, the family system is able to move forward in detail in their own positive ways of dealing with the situations. This is often best handled with the help of a professional therapist.

Dealing with the Stigma

The stigma associated with borderline personality disorder affects more than just the person who has the disorder. Family members must also deal with how others look at them as individuals and the family itself. Since the research that is available today does indicate that borderline personality disorder develops in association with child abuse, child sexual abuse, and abandonment issues, the family tends to be scrutinized.

QUESTION

Where can I find accurate information on borderline personality disorder on the Internet?
As with any topic, some websites are more accurate than others. Government websites normally provide more accurate, credible information. The NIMH provides information that is both current and well researched. Educational sites from various universities will also provide more accurate information but might not go into as much depth or be specific to people trying to deal with the effects of this disorder. The American Psychological Association (*www.apa.org*) is another scholarly resource with good information for general knowledge and up-to-date research.

It is not a well-known or widely publicized disorder, which means that the information that comes out on it to the general public is often sketchy and not completely accurate. The inaccuracies and errors in reporting become misconceptions about the disorder and affect the family dealing with it. Some avenues meant to help might actually hurt the public image. Unfortunately, some online support groups have become forums for people to vent their frustration after negative encounters with someone with borderline personality disorder. When people read the negative, angry posts, they begin to believe that people with borderline personality disorder are unmanageable, manipulative, and often violent. While those symptoms are out there, they do not explain the entire person, and when they become the focus of some public discussions people get the wrong impression. Once they get this wrong impression it is much harder to deal with them in social or business situations. The family becomes as ostracized and stigmatized as the person with the disorder.

Understanding

With acceptance comes a form of understanding. Family members cannot heal someone with borderline personality disorder, and they cannot understand everything this person is going through, but they can accept that this disorder does cause issues that everyone needs to work on together. As the family members accept that there are issues, they can learn to work on understanding them by listening carefully to what their loved one is telling them. While it might not immediately make sense based on family members' own thoughts and perceptions, it is important to realize that the thought process is different for those with borderline personality disorder and their perceptions and fears are very real to them.

People with borderline personality disorder often need help. Since they do not recognize social situations correctly, they do make mistakes. They also feel pain and fear. It is important to be there for them and to support them, but not to let things get out of hand. Understanding does not mean being taken advantage of. If someone does not want to get help or work on the issues they are experiencing, that is their choice. It is not a question of deciding whether or not to live with this situation.

Decision Making

Choices are made on a daily basis within any family system. When a family member has borderline personality disorder, there is an additional need for care in the decision-making process. Issues are not as easily defined, and solutions might be nonexistent in some cases. Additionally, the person with borderline personality disorder might have trouble understanding the various aspects of a given decision. It is sometimes tempting to just make the decision without his input and be done.

Creating a Decision-Making Process

The best way to work around the uncertainties is to create a process the family can use for larger or more important decisions. This creates a sense of routine to the process and allows everyone to know what to expect. The process would be designed to allow everyone the opportunity to speak and be heard. In some cases this might mean setting time limits on how long any one family member can speak, and developing consequences for speaking out of turn or becoming belligerent.

It is best to begin with a family meeting on how to conduct a family meeting. This is going to be up to the individual family to develop something that works for them. The most important thing is to be open to what works for everyone. This can actually be a tricky process as family dynamics get in the way and the family member with borderline personality disorder might push for more control or attention during the process. Again, guidelines should be set up ahead of time for how to conduct even this first meeting.

Who Should Be Included

Every person in the family needs to be able to have a say in the decision that is being made. This does not, however, mean that every person should have an equal say or an equal influence over the decision. Decisions that affect the entire family as a unit should be discussed more evenly among the members of the family. Decisions that affect just one or two of the family members might not be open to equal say from all parties. Everyone in the family feels important to the family unit and wants to have some say in what occurs within the family. Yet some decisions are not appropriate for all members.

ESSENTIAL

Someone with borderline personality disorder is not always able to get out the words she actually means. The misunderstandings can escalate a disagreement or cause a meeting to go awry. It is important to listen to what she is trying to say, not necessarily what comes out of her mouth. Look at body language and think about what she might be trying to get across before reacting.

Younger members of the family would not have the ability to understand or weigh in on more complex decisions, such as divorce or taking a new job. At the same time, however, it would be important to let them know how a new job would affect their lives too. When making decisions pertaining to the family member with borderline personality disorder and possible treatment options, it is important to include all family members to some extent.

While all family members cannot make each treatment decision, they should all be kept informed as much as possible, as they are a large part of this person's support network.

Guidelines

Family meetings should be set up with some level of structure, especially when someone within the family has borderline personality disorder. If the rules are set right from the start, it is easier to remain within the boundaries. One person should be chosen as the leader or moderator who keeps things moving and reminds people when they are stepping out of bounds. Of course, this person should not be the family member with borderline personality disorder.

As the rules are agreed upon, they should be put in writing. This document of rules would be best used in poster form as a visual reminder to everyone in the family during each decision meeting. This helps the younger members of the family remember what the rules are, and the family member with borderline personality disorder has a visual to look at to keep him on track with the boundaries that have been set forth for these meetings.

It is important that the person with borderline personality disorder understand the purpose of these rules and be part of creating these rules. This does not mean that there will not be lapses and he will not fight with some of these rules when he becomes heated during a meeting, but it does help to show him what he agreed to earlier, and to keep others in line too.

Guidelines should include who can speak, how long the person can speak, and how often the person can speak. There should be consequences for speaking out of turn, insulting someone, or starting a fight. Consequences might be to lose a turn speaking or have a reduction in speaking time, or, if the behavior is more extreme, to have to leave the meeting altogether. Other guidelines might include how long the meeting can last, whether or not there will be a vote, or if there will be some other way of making a decision, and how often these meetings can be called.

How This Process Helps

A structured decision-making process allows all participants to feel they have a say in what is being accomplished within the family system.

Oftentimes when a family has a member with borderline personality disorder much of the family members' lives feels out of control. Family members do not feel they have a say in things, as they are focused more often on the behaviors of the one family member. This can cause resentment and feelings of worthlessness. When all members are given the ability to speak as part of the family, they identify more fully with the family system and feel like they have some level of control.

It also helps the family learn how to interact with each other and decide how to solve problems as a unit. They take back some level of control into the family system, even if the meetings do not all go well—and chances are they will not all go well. Even in normal family systems members disagree on a daily basis, so this is to be expected. The structure of the meetings helps to establish limits and boundaries for all. As long as the family meetings remain within the structure they have set up, they have the ability to fall back on the rules and consequences and regroup. If this means that the meeting must be postponed to a later date when everybody is feeling calmer, that is what should be done.

It is not likely that every meeting will be a success. The insecurity and strong emotional reactions characterized by borderline personality disorder will likely cause some problems. The main goal of this meeting process, however, is to allow everyone to speak and be heard. This is very important. Each family member's feelings must be validated in some way. This meeting allows that. It also helps to some extent with learning to communicate with the member with borderline personality disorder and might even help that person work through some of his stronger fears, including rejection and abandonment.

CHAPTER 9

Why Is Abandonment an Issue?

Human beings are social creatures. As such, most human beings thrive on the comfort and presence of others in their lives. Humans are not wired to live in isolation. For many, the fear of being alone or being abandoned is minimal. Most people come from households where they have family members they can turn to, friends, and possibly even romantic interests. They feel connected to other people, and are confident in the concern others have for them. People with borderline personality disorder, on the other hand, have a different take on real and perceived abandonment. They feel that they can never rely on others, and the fear of abandonment is very real and at times all-consuming.

What Fear of Abandonment Means to Relationships

For people with borderline personality disorder the fear of abandonment is very real and can be overpowering. They will do anything to prevent the abandonment. They often feel that there is nothing beyond that abandonment. If someone leaves them, it is like the end of the world for them. They become clingy, needy, and helpless. They might become hysterical and they might threaten self-harm.

Brain Involvement

While much of what people with borderline personality disorder will do to avoid abandonment will be manipulative in nature, the fear is very real to them. They feel it as a physical fear reaction. It is like a panic attack that they will do anything to avoid. In some manner, the brain switches to a hyperalert status designed to deal with a strong threat. It is like the fear someone might feel if they were trapped in a burning building. The brain goes into a fight-or-flight mode, and the reactions involved are driven by the need to survive. This is not something that should cause such severe reactions, and in most people it would not. In someone with borderline personality disorder, however, the brain mechanisms and the thought processes behind those brain mechanisms are almost instantaneous.

FACT

Panic attacks are intense fear reactions to some initially unknown stimulus. The person experiencing a panic attack might feel like he is having a heart attack, cannot breathe, or is going to faint or throw up. The reaction is extreme and comes on quickly. In most cases, the initial reaction is unexpected and cannot be tied to anything. Once a panic attack has occurred, however, the fear of having a panic attack will be the catalyst for avoidance and future attacks.

Someone with borderline personality disorder has such a deep-seated fear of abandonment that the reaction occurs without thought. It is like they self-destruct. Fear of abandonment is one of the largest stressors they face, and until they learn to deal with it, it will create a strong reaction whether they wish it to or not. The fear center of the brain, the amygdala, causes the quick reaction and can set off additional emotional reactions.

How Distrust Affects This Fear

In addition to the instant brain reaction, there is the ever-present generalized mistrust of what others say that will affect how this person perceives potential abandonment. Since the brain is on hyper-alert, it is hard for this person to calm down. Gentle reassurances by others might not help, especially since these reassurances would be suspect.

Unfortunately, most relationships have a hard time making it through mistrust and fear. The overreactions that ensue when fear of abandonment comes to the surface often push people away. In the end, a self-fulfilling prophecy could come into being, as people with borderline personality disorder actually push others to abandon them.

Manipulation

When people with BPD feel abandonment is imminent, they often attempt to manipulate the situation in order to avoid this rejection. This manipulation can occur in many different ways. It can occur as threats to leave the other person, to harm themselves, or some other overt behavior. Some might become very angry, flying into an unmanageable rage. In each of these cases the behavior is aggressive, threatening, and designed to avoid abandonment. The other person in the relationship might hesitate to do anything that would be connected with abandonment in order to avoid these types of behaviors.

Most manipulation, however, is less aggressive in nature. They might become very clingy, saying that they cannot function without this other person even for a very short time. They might try to induce feelings of guilt, pointing out all the things they have done for the person. They very often will beg the other person not to leave, usually in tears. They will agree to anything, and promise anything they think will help them with their case.

They might make up a story or a lie that will bring sympathy or provide them with some sort of leverage to keep the person there. When this happens they will often play dirty, bringing up any information they think can be used against the other person or used to make the other person feel guilty. They will play on emotions trying to ensure that future abandonment will not occur.

Case Study: Jennifer and Craig

Jennifer and Craig got into an argument on Mother's Day. Jennifer has borderline personality disorder and was very disappointed in the breakfast Craig and the kids gave her. She felt that she deserved better. She became sullen and began picking on the kids. When Craig stepped in, Jennifer blew up and started screaming at him. Craig knew that this was not a good situation for the children and decided he would take them to his mother's. He would allow Jennifer to calm down and would then come back for her in another hour or so.

Jennifer perceived this as abandonment and panicked. She grabbed on to Craig's arm and would not let him leave. She began crying and got down on her knees and begged him not to leave. She promised she would make a great lunch and that she would stop picking at the kids. She then switched tactics and started in on how Craig was ruining her Mother's Day. She cried harder and talked about how she had tried so hard to be a good mother all year. When she saw that this did not work either, she threatened to hurt herself while they were gone, stating that they would be sorry they had rejected her. Deep inside she felt unworthy of their love and did not think they would come back to her because she was not important enough. This is the heart of abandonment.

Dealing with Self-Image

When someone fears abandonment, it usually stems from several different reasons. One very real reason is that they have already been abandoned before. For individuals who have faced abandonment, especially as children by primary caregivers, the fear is very real and very present. They have already experienced it, they know that it can happen, and they do not want it to happen again. This kind of abandonment damages the person's self-image. They do not see themselves as lovable or worthy of a relationship.

The other reasons someone fears abandonment come down to feelings about self-image. When people have a poor self-image, they do not feel worthy of the love of others. They do not think they are important enough to be cared for by another person. They also believe that once a person leaves there is no reason for them to come back. This causes a thought process where they think they need to keep the person from leaving in the first place.

FACT

Self-image is the perception each person forms of him- or herself. This image develops based on how the person wants to be perceived by others and how the person thinks others do perceive him or her. Feedback by others contributes to its development.

Where It Comes From

Poor self-image often begins in early childhood. Children need love and support, and positive encouragement during childhood. When they do not receive this, they often wonder why. Other children receive negative feedback from parents and other caregivers. Some children, unfortunately, develop a poor self-image as a result of real abandonment. In each case the thought process begins with perceived disapproval or rejection.

Children who are provided with love and support often form positive attachments and learn to move securely away from their caregivers as they grow. They understand that they are loved unconditionally and they are able to experiment and fail without fear. They are able to take these failures as learning experiences and grow from them, eventually succeeding and finding things they are good at. When this occurs, a positive self-image is formed along the way. The child is comfortable and feels capable. This continues through adolescence and adulthood.

When circumstances in some way prevent the child from receiving this positive love and support attachments are not as securely formed. Children who were constantly criticized or who face negative reactions when they do something wrong tend to hesitate to try to do other things. They become more fearful of failure and less willing to try new things. Their thought process becomes more black-and-white and they view any minor mistake as a large issue with their entire being. Rather than being able to compartmentalize or keep certain things in certain categories, the child sees one entire negative package. If for example a child is not good in math and does not do well on a test, he might see that he needs to work harder in that one area. If a child has a poor self-image, he might see that he is no good as a whole. It is a matter of perspective. This perspective increases the negative self-image.

How Self-Image Relates to Abandonment

This black-and-white image that prevents compartmentalization causes the self-image to remain negative. There is little leeway for imperfections. Since feedback at a young age was not good, there is an expectancy that this will continue. The self-fulfilling prophecy comes into play as the child believes he is no good and begins to act in the manner others have been pushing him into. He begins to feel worthless and lose sight of any good qualities or strengths he has.

QUESTION

Is there any way to change a person's self-image?
Yes, a person's self-image can change throughout the course of her life. As she learns that she is capable of things, and others focus on her strengths, she can begin to create a better self-image.

When children lose sight of their strengths and become more set in their perceived bad points, they feel less and less lovable. They do not understand why anyone would want to be with them, and if someone does come to be with them they are wary of the situation. This wariness in turn begins to push the person away, causing the abandonment. The lower self-image also makes them feel uncomfortable when they are the focus of positive attention. They do not know how to handle it, and since they do not believe it, they are not sure how to react. This can create an inappropriate reaction that again turns people off and pushes them away. As this cycle continues, they grow to expect abandonment more and more and develop survival techniques devoted to preventing it.

Behaviors That Follow Fear of Abandonment

When people fear rejection, they naturally become leery and afraid. This is a normal reaction to some form of rejection. If they experience a rejection of some sort, they might get emotional and feel some pain. They might beg the person not to leave, or try to maintain contact for a while until natural healing processes kick in. They will likely feel less self-assured and their self-image will decrease a bit for a period of time. For someone with borderline personality disorder, these fears and behaviors are magnified.

What Is Abandonment?

Abandonment is an extreme form of rejection that involves a physical or emotional absence created by the words or behaviors of another. Physical abandonment is an active process in which a person physically leaves another. Emotional abandonment occurs as a person becomes unavailable for support or attention. In each case someone is left feeling deserted and disconnected with little hope of closure.

For people with borderline personality disorder, abandonment is a devastating experience they do not feel they can climb out of. They see it as an ending with no hope beyond. They are unable to function because it is a process they cannot think through. There might be some form of control and regulation for some symptoms, but if abandonment is perceived in some way, function is lost.

While many of the behaviors that accompany the fear of abandonment in someone with borderline personality disorder are more in line with the manipulation of others, there are oftentimes other elements at work. People with borderline personality disorder are impulsive in choosing relationships. This means they do not always choose good mates. They are not always the ones who are abusive or acting negatively. They often choose mates who are abusive themselves. Unfortunately, that fear of abandonment is so pervasive that they will choose to remain with someone who is abusive rather than be alone.

Case Study: Elise and Paul

Elise and her husband, Paul, met at a bar and became instant soul mates. They were together three months before they decided to get married.

Elise was struggling with the symptoms of borderline personality disorder and was happy with how supportive he was. This changed shortly after they got married. Paul had a problem with drugs and alcohol, and often became violent when he was high. He threatened to leave many times and each time Elise begged him to stay. Each time he beat her, she put up with it. She also found out he had been having an affair and wanted to move in with another woman. Even then she did not want him to leave her. It reminded her too much of when her dad left when she was five years old.

Her friends warned her that eventually he would kill her with the abuse he leveled at her. On some level Elise knew this and was very worried, but the fear of abandonment was stronger than the fear of his fists. When he finally did leave, she was unable to function for a period of time and had to move back in with her parents. After some time had passed she admitted that she was glad the relationship had ended, but during the time she was in the relationship the fear of abandonment overshadowed all reason. She did not think anyone else would love her.

When Will I Be Loved?

People with borderline personality disorder often fear that they will make a mess of their relationships. They are not walking blindly through their relationship satisfying their own selfish needs, although it might sometimes seem that way. They often spend hours wondering what they can do and say to keep a relationship going. They need constant reassurance that everything is okay. They do not believe that they are capable of having a good relationship. Unfortunately many of the symptoms they exhibit with borderline personality disorder make it hard for them to have a good relationship.

Fear of Love

There is a love-hate relationship that goes on in the mind of someone with borderline personality disorder. On the one hand they very much want to be in a relationship and want to be loved. On the other hand they worry that if they open themselves up to love they open themselves up to abandonment. They overanalyze every interaction and look for things they have done wrong. When they find them they seek reassurance from the other person that things are okay. If they do not get this reassurance they are lost.

Often the other person does not even understand what the problem is, let alone know how to reassure the person with BPD that it is okay. This confusion is often misinterpreted as anger or distancing. The resulting reaction creates a situation where the other person begins to distance himself.

FACT

According to the NIMH, adults with borderline personality disorder showed stronger overemotional reactions when looking at words with unpleasant meanings compared to healthy people. They believe there might be an overactive startle reflex that responds to negative input.

People with borderline personality disorder are often struggling with feelings of depression, loneliness, and isolation. They do not have a good self-image and are distrustful of positive feedback from others. They constantly seek reassurance, but they have a hard time believing this reassurance.

This can lead them to seek tangible, material methods of reinforcing self. This can come in the form of overspending on material goods, buying friendships, or engaging in a series of sexual encounters designed to prove desirability. In any case, their behaviors end up causing more harm than good and do not bring about a safe loving relationship. They become oversensitive to what others want from them and model themselves to meet those perceived needs. They lose themselves and present a false front.

The False Image

People suffering from the insecurity of borderline personality disorder often present a strong, competent front. They want to show the world that they can do anything. On the inside however, they are a mess. The outward confidence belies a shaky self-image and low self-esteem.

In order to try to improve self-image, or at least what they see as others' perception of them, they will often look for cues from others for what they would approve of. They then mold themselves after that. They can become a chameleon, changing from one relationship to the next. If they become interested in someone who likes skiing, they will tend to take up skiing and immerse themselves in it. If the next relationship likes motorcycles, skiing will be completely abandoned and motorcycles will be the new obsession.

What Happens to the True Self

Their true self remains buried beneath the fake images presented to get people to like them. They are afraid to bring this true self out because they do not think they are lovable as they are. They feel that if people saw the real person inside, they would not want to be with them. If they do what others like, then others will like them.

QUESTION

How do I know I am looking at the true self?
This is not easy, because there are so many layers of defenses and subterfuge created to avoid rejection and abandonment. The true self will not be a reflection of what others want or expect. The true self will emerge when the person feels it is safe for it to emerge. One way to encourage this is to simply ask questions such as: What sounds good to you? What would you like to do?

Unfortunately the true self that is buried does not remain silent. Everyone has his or her own individual likes, wants, and needs and there is often a drive to meet these. When a person is busy meeting everybody else's likes, wants, and needs, she is not tending to her own. This can cause disharmony and resentment. The resentment is often directed at the person she is giving up her own wants and needs for, even though that person does not know that this is happening in many cases.

Where the Anger Comes From

Much of the anger reaction in abandonment situations is actually a fear reaction. Since people with borderline personality disorder are overemotional with strong reactions to different stimuli, this fear might come out as anger. Explosive anger episodes are also characteristic of borderline personality disorder and could be a natural reflex reaction to certain situations. Interactions can be misinterpreted, causing confusion or fear, and resulting in anger. While this anger is often directed at someone else, it can also manifest as self-harm.

Anger at Self

The fear of abandonment often drives someone with borderline personality disorder to go to a great deal of extremes. They might do things they would not normally do, say things they would not normally say and embarrass themselves in order to avoid this rejection. When they do this type of thing they become angry with themselves. They do not want to show people their weakness. They have often learned that showing weakness results in further hurt.

They also see themselves sinking to new lows and doing things they would not normally do. They do not want to do these things, but the fear of abandonment overrides all else. This causes them to become angry with themselves for giving in and doing these things. They often feel ashamed of themselves for being so weak. This goes against the image they want to portray to others of being strong and confident.

ESSENTIAL

The inability to recognize some aspects of social situations can cause someone with borderline personality disorder to act in a way he perceives to be strong and confident, yet comes across as confusing and irrational.

As the inner conflict wages, the strong self they want to portray to others actually gives way and reveals that weaker, fearful inner self. Since the anger of borderline personality disorder can be so explosive and dangerous, when it is directed inwardly, at the sufferer, it can often result in self-harm. The person might feel she needs to punish herself for this weakness. This can come in the form of cutting, burning, or other activities that create damage to self. The rage itself might cause the person to punch a wall or put a fist through glass in order to release the inner tension that has been building up. Remember that the true self is hidden and is building up tension within as the person strives to meet what she feels are the expectations of others.

Anger at Others

When people with borderline personality disorder suppress their own wants, needs, and self, they often become angry and resentful at the people they are trying to impress. They do not feel they can have a relationship with another person without doing these things, but they feel that it is something they are doing and putting into the relationship above and beyond what they are getting from the other person.

Unfortunately, the other person normally does not have any idea that this is going on. The partner does not understand that the person with borderline personality disorder feels she is in an unequal relationship in that she is doing more. The partner also does not realize that the activities he is joining in are really more one-sided and his BPD partner's needs are not being met.

ALERT

The strong anger reaction can occur without warning. This anger can become rage, and needs to be taken as a serious threat of harm to self and others.

When the anger hits, the partners of people with BPD become confused. They do not know what to do because they do not know what is wrong. If it is not explained to them properly, and it often is not, they become frustrated and often feel the need to step away from the drama that is unfolding. These explosive anger episodes can leave partners in shock. The natural reaction is to begin to withdraw emotionally. When the explosive episode ends and they realize that their partner is withdrawing from them they tend to become clingy, which only increases the likelihood of abandonment.

Biological Basis for the Reaction

As stated earlier, the fear of abandonment can set off a strong, automatic biological reaction. While the initial reaction is fear, the fight-or-flight response often kicks in as anger. They are often angry with themselves for failing again. They are also angry with their partner for not fulfilling the idealized image they had of them. Since the fear reaction is in effect, emotions are on heightened alert. The adrenaline pumps through the system and if they have not learned to regulate their emotions, the adrenaline often finds dispersal in an angry reaction. The brain chemicals push for release. Once the release has occurred, the person might swing the other way and become overly calm.

CHAPTER 10

Borderline Personality Disorder and Instability

Instability in borderline personality disorder manifests itself in a few different ways. Emotional instability is characterized by the strong emotional changes that can be dramatic and severe. There is a high impulsivity, and there are problems with self-harm and suicidal thoughts. The instability is most dangerous because it is unpredictable and there is the potential for harm at any given point. Since it is so unpredictable, it is important to seek treatment to manage the thoughts and behaviors that might bring the reactions on.

Why Is There Instability?

Instability is a key element of borderline personality disorder. This instability is, at its root, a part of the loss of control and inability to properly recognize social norms. Perceptions that go awry or situations that seem out of control for someone with borderline personality disorder can lead to strong emotional reactions without notice.

In Females

As previously discussed, certain brain chemicals have been implicated in the symptom process. Certain hormones might also be involved, including hormones that increase during premenstrual development stages in females. These hormones might prime a female to be more sensitive to interactions, causing stronger reactions than a situation might call for.

Females are also more likely to be abused sexually as children, which adds to the emotions that are bottled up and left to simmer, including fear, shame, and anger. They are unable to express these emotions during times of abuse, and are often reluctant to tell others what has happened. This leads to emotions that simmer under the surface, ready to explode at any time.

It is important to note that borderline personality disorder might be diagnosed more often in females because the symptoms that are listed pertain more often to how a female reacts with this disorder. Males might exhibit different symptoms but still have this disorder.

Self-Control

As discussed earlier, the centers of the brain responsible for inhibitions and self-control do not seem to work in the same way in people with borderline personality disorder. Although some of the impulsive behaviors and mood swings are intentional attention-seeking manipulation, many are not. The thought or action occurs before reason comes into play.

Self-control occurs as someone recognizes the situation and thinks through what should be done in order to prevent certain consequences or to achieve a certain end. Someone with borderline personality disorder has trouble thinking through what might happen. The actions occur responsively. In cases where they recognize that what they did was not right, they tend to regret it after they have calmed down. In other cases, they do not recognize that what they did was wrong according to social expectations.

QUESTION

Do people with borderline personality disorder have any self-control?
Yes, they do. Although the instability is fairly common and there is a good deal of unpredictability, there are also certain situations that will likely set this problem off more than others. When you can figure out things that might be more likely to trigger the problem, you can try to prepare the person beforehand.

The thought process behind self-control is not regulated in the same way in those with BPD, and the areas of the brain that trigger excitement and anger often override them before they can even come into play. The reaction spurs on emotion and the emotion triggers more emotion.

Perceptions

Perceptions and social situations can bring out a good deal of instability. Situations that would not normally cause problems for people who use normal thought processes can cause strong outbursts in someone with borderline personality disorder. The increased fear of and focus on the potential abandonment and rejection cause a hypersensitivity to what others say and do. A seemingly innocent statement can set the person off, as some form of threat is perceived in it.

There are also problems with the accuracy of perceptions, as people with BPD do not recognize the way to behave in certain social situations. If they make mistakes in social situations, they are likely to key in on the reactions of others and be confused as to why they are occurring. Since they do not know that they have done something wrong, and have a very hard time admitting to or recognizing this, they see the reactions of others as rejection. Rejection and fear of abandonment are the strongest impulses for instability and out-of-control thinking.

Case Study: Kelsey

Kelsey was out with friends at a new restaurant. The restaurant was very busy and the waitresses were moving very quickly. Their waitress looked hurried and stressed when she got to them. Kelsey asked for something that was not on the menu and became angry with the waitress when she said they didn't have that. The waitress had another person asking her for something from another table and turned to him for one minute to tell him she would be right with him. When she turned back to Kelsey, Kelsey interpreted her actions and the look on her face as a sign that the waitress did not like her and wanted her to leave. She began yelling at the waitress that she had as much right to be there as everyone else and made a scene.

Her friends tried to calm her down, but she was yelling too loudly. The next thing they knew the manager was there and they were asked to leave. This infuriated Kelsey more and she resisted all the way out. When they got outside, her friends were angry with her and she did not know why. She blamed the poor service and the fact that the waitress did not like her. She said the waitress was obviously against her from minute one and had set that whole scene up just to frustrate her.

Kelsey became even more upset when her friends did not want to go with her to get something to eat someplace else. They all wanted to go home because they were so embarrassed. Kelsey accused them of making plans to go someplace else without her the minute she left. She was sure they wanted to go talk about her behind her back.

The next day she tried to call her friends and see if they wanted to go to the movies. She couldn't understand why none of them answered their phones, and was confused when they did not ask her to go with them again. She understood that they had had a bad experience at that restaurant, but that certainly was not her fault. They just needed to go to a different restaurant where the service was better.

Self-Damaging Impulsivity

The impulsivity of borderline personality disorder also creates instability in behaviors. This instability seems to be due more to lower inhibitions and less thought before action. As the case study with Kelsey shows, behaviors can get out of hand very quickly and cause embarrassment or worse. Reactions occur before thought, yet this is not the only issue.

Many people who have borderline personality disorder are seen as the life of the party. They are fun-loving and ready for adventure. They might be up for bungee jumping or other daring feats that they hope will get others to like them. They are often giving and caring individuals who try to show this by buying things for others to impress them and try to make new friends. Unfortunately, this can get out of hand.

Daring Feats

People who have borderline personality disorder do not always think through different actions and are sometimes more likely to engage in thrill-seeking behaviors. They might be the first to accept a dare at a party or suggest a difficult or dangerous stunt. They often get caught up in the moment and go along with whatever seems fun and exciting. They are looking for ways to increase their self-esteem and see these daring feats as ways to show others they are strong and fearless. Unfortunately, they are susceptible to the suggestions of others in an effort to please them.

They do not think through what might happen as they are accepting these dares. They are only interested in making a good impression and having people like them. In addition to things like bungee jumping and skydiving, there are also impulsive acts that might be illegal or dangerous without any safety measures. They might try to walk along the railing of a high bridge, or steal something from a store. They might also drink too much and make themselves sick.

The impulsivity in high-risk behaviors is a temptation to them, and this can be spurred on when they are in a group of others who are just as impulsive. The impulsive behaviors tend to reflect the group. Thus, if the group is not an impulsive group, the impulsive behaviors might not be as radical at that time. If, on the other hand, the person is in a group that has been drinking and is out to find some fun, the chances of high-risk behaviors increase greatly.

Sexual Encounters

Another area of the impulsivity is in sexual encounters. People with borderline personality disorder often go through many relationships. They might also go through multiple sexual encounters. They are often looking for that perfect relationship, and their impulsive nature can nudge them into unwise decisions. They are particularly vulnerable to those who come on to them hard and heavy right from the start. Since they themselves often look for a quick relationship and tend to start out strong in the beginning, this appeals to them.

Unfortunately, this also leaves them open to being used for casual sexual encounters. They might think they are in the midst of a fantastic new relationship but are in actuality in a one-night stand. If they think someone likes them, they are less likely to think through what might be happening and proceed cautiously. With their impulsive nature, they tend to jump head-first into whatever relationship they perceive they are now in.

FACT

People with borderline personality disorder are 50 percent more likely to experience a physically abusive partner, being sexually assaulted, being sexually assaulted multiple times or at the same time by more than one person, being sexually assaulted by someone they do not know, and being both physically assaulted and sexually assaulted.

The impulsive sexual encounters provide a few different dangers. There is the risk of unsafe sex, especially if the partner talks them out of using any form of protection. There is also the risk of physical abuse. They do not know this person well, and have placed themselves in a vulnerable position with them. There is the risk of rape, sexually transmitted diseases, and physical injury. They might also find themselves the victims of theft in these encounters. Their need to be in a relationship, however, often propels them forward in spite of the risks. This can lead to pain and rejection.

Mood Instability

Mood instability can be intense and often results in angry outbursts. People with borderline personality disorder are normally highly reactive to environmental cues—both real and perceived. Borderline personality disorder has also been called emotional regulation disorder, which characterizes the strong emotional reactions that can occur. Angry outbursts can come up with little or no warning, and other moods can come up just as quickly. They can go from happy to angry to sad to happy in a short period of time. While they might seem repentant for an angry outburst, especially if someone got hurt, they will likely blame it on the target of their outburst.

Overlap of Borderline and Bipolar

Both borderline personality disorder and bipolar mood disorders are characterized by mood swings. The affect is unstable and can range from flat to exaggerated, swinging from one to the other. Both have a symptom of sensitivity to rejection, and can show mood swings in reaction to a perceived problem. In both disorders there is the potential for irritability and intense anger that can be projected without warning. In both cases, dysphoria can be present, as well as anxiety.

FACT

Dysphoria is a general feeling of psychological discomfort that might feel like a combination of depression, anxiety, and restlessness. It is a general sense that something is wrong without a sense of what exactly is causing it.

While these facts might speak of a similarity between the two disorders, bipolar mood swings are normally of longer duration and cyclical in nature. There is more of a transition from one symptom to the next. With borderline personality disorder there is more of a sudden jump from one mood to the next. The unpredictability of the mood changes in borderline personality disorder can cause violent reactions that threaten self and others, especially when affect is flat or negative.

Affect

Affect is the word used in diagnosis to describe an individual's presentation of feeling or emotion, especially as portrayed in facial expressions and/or body language. It is not necessarily an emotion, such as happy or sad, but encompasses emotions and behaviors as observed by another. Affect can be flat, which would indicate no emotion or lack of emotion in the person's behaviors and facial expressions, or labile, which indicates dramatic mood swings. Euphoric would be an exaggerated happiness.

Affect provides some indication of the mental and emotional state of the person being evaluated. When someone seems flat and unresponsive he could be in the midst of a depressive episode. A euphoric affect could indicate a manic episode. In each case, the affect can provide some clues as to what might occur next in mood swings. Swings in affect can indicate an inner agitation that might signal problems.

ESSENTIAL

Affect is recorded at each therapy session to determine the client's status. This can help indicate to the therapist how the person is coping and what might be happening both emotionally and biologically.

Finding Patterns

There are some patterns that might emerge when dealing with the emotions of someone with borderline personality disorder. Some things will tend to set the person off more than others. This will vary with the individual, but it often has something to do with pointing out something the person did wrong and pushing the issue. It might also pertain to abandonment.

When people with borderline personality disorder feel they have been boxed into a corner where they must admit they are wrong, they often become very angry. They cannot think through what they want to avoid, and react impulsively. They often deny that they have done something vehemently, and blame the other person. They might go into a rage in frustration and denial.

When people with borderline personality disorder fear abandonment, strong emotions result. They will begin with anger and/or fear and lash out at the person they think is going to leave them. This type of situation can run the gamut from anger to tearful begging. In each case the emotion will be vivid and will likely swing quickly.

QUESTION

Will everyone with borderline personality disorder react to fear of abandonment?
Yes, this is a large fear that is one of the main diagnostic criteria for this particular disorder. It is important to note, however, that each person will react differently, and will perceive the threat of abandonment differently. One situation might cause a reaction in one individual, but not in another. It will still come down to how each individual sees the situations they encounter.

Each individual will react to different situations. It is a good idea to make note of the situations that seem to cause the strongest reactions and prepare for those. This is not something that is easily accomplished without the help of a professional. The behaviors are impulsive and often irrational and need to be controlled so that everyone can be safe.

Self-Harm Thoughts and Behaviors

The need to protect the self makes it very hard to take criticism or accept blame. When someone with borderline personality disorder is agitated, she might do something that causes her pain in order to feel better. While this might sound confusing, it is actually how many who engage in some form of self-harm feel.

Forms of Self-Harm

Many people who engage in self-harming behaviors do so in order to feel better. There is a reported psychological release in cutting and burning for the person feeling the pain. This is not to say that those are the only two ways to engage in self-harm. Some have been known to pick at their fingernails or the cuticles around them, often leaving bloody fingers. They might also pull their hair, or simply act without caution.

The actions can be repetitive, becoming an automatic response to anxiety, or they can occur whenever the pressure or anger becomes too much. The self-harm can become addictive for those with BPD, as they rely on it to deal with problems and cope when they feel overwhelmed. Self-harm can also be the result of an explosive episode as a means of punishment, and sometimes manipulation.

Why Do It?

Self-harm, like using drugs or alcohol, is often an overt sign of pain underneath the facade. It is a way of communicating or showing that something is wrong. People with borderline personality disorder normally have low self-esteem and feel unloved and ignored. They might not know how to communicate their pain in a direct way

QUESTION

Do people who have borderline personality disorder always cut or hurt themselves physically in some way?
Not necessarily, they all feel pain and rejection, but some get down on themselves emotionally or psychologically rather than physically.

They also act to punish themselves based on their feelings of shame and guilt. They look at themselves as bad and deserving punishment. They might also use it to manipulate others, punishing them for lack of attention or thinking about leaving. Still others are simply continuing the patterns of abuse begun in early childhood. They might see it as what they deserve, or they might continue it simply as a matter of course.

Stopping Self-Harm

Self-harm is a complex problem that has multiple causes spurred by different thought processes. Some people are better able to resist the impulses than others. Some situations will send them to self-harm quicker than others, and will promote more harm than others. In each case there are things that can be done to help decrease this behavior.

Although people with borderline personality disorder are often impulsive, it is still possible to encourage thinking things through to reach a logical end. It is important to try to get them to stop before they act and think about what the result will be, for example scars or other permanent physical signs.

It sometimes helps to convince them to hold off for a set period of time—do not cut for ten minutes. Once ten minutes is up, if the urge remains, add another ten minutes. The point is to delay the harmful behavior as long as possible and try to get them to calm down and divert from the behaviors.

ESSENTIAL

Each delay in self-harm builds a coping strategy that can be used to go beyond the self-harm as the person learns to identify the situations that cause the urge, and works on self-esteem. Each delay is progress that can be used as a base for strength.

Another method is to try to divert the person to another behavior or activity that will eventually take her mind off of the issue that had her ready to commit self-harm. As her mind refocuses, the drive that pushes the self-harm lessens. She can begin to think rationally again about a different topic, especially if the object of refocus is something that utilizes other parts of the body in some activity. The more the person needs to think about and focus on this new activity, the harder it is to remain focused on the drive to self-harm.

This is also a good way to try to find other ways to cope with the problems that encourage the harmful behavior in the first place. New hobbies can form that are more productive and can occupy the person's mind. The thoughts of self-harm have trouble taking hold as other thoughts and behaviors move in.

Diverting to a new activity has a dual purpose as it refocuses thoughts away from self-harm and allows the person to begin to work on something that might help fill feelings of emptiness and unworthiness. Self-purpose and self-worth can increase during these other activities, but they should be monitored by a professional.

ALERT

Pick activities to refocus on carefully. The high impulsivity characteristic of borderline personality disorder can cause easy frustration or create a more dangerous version of the activity. Choose based on their interest and think about potential dangers beforehand.

Feeling Empty

People with borderline personality disorder often feel alone and empty. They do not like themselves and do not think others do either. They go through a lot of thoughts and self-doubts as they move through their lives. The problems with identity often cause ups and downs that leave them feeling empty and uncertain of their true self. Unfortunately, the empty feelings often lead to self-harm as a means of coping.

Self-Harm and Emptiness: The Connection

People with borderline personality disorder often report that they seek to avoid or ease the feelings of emptiness by causing self-harm. The emptiness is actually not as empty as it sounds. The feelings of emptiness are normally a means of retreating from the pain and feelings of loneliness they are experiencing. They retreat to a numbness that keeps them from having to cope.

Of course, this does not last, and the pain surfaces again. As it does, the compulsion to do self-harm can come up. The need for attention pushes them to do things they might not otherwise do, such as having a one-night stand or overspending. These behaviors make the emptiness go away for a very short time, but then they come back stronger as the realization of what they did hits them.

Dealing with Emptiness the Wrong Way

The relationships they are going in and out of often leave them feeling worse than when they began. They do things that they are not proud of, such as having sex with someone after just meeting them, or lying to them about marital status. This causes shame and guilt. When this happens, many self-medicate with drugs or alcohol, which reduces inhibitions and causes additional grief and pain.

People with borderline personality disorder often turn to drugs and alcohol to help them solve their problems, further reducing rational thought. They can often say and do things they later regret, causing pain to others. They are desperate for love and acceptance and cannot believe they already have it in some way. This is when they will agree to or put up with things they might not normally go along with. They are trying to get rid of the emptiness.

Absence and Emptiness

People with borderline personality disorder view even minor physical absences as painful, creating a strong feeling of emptiness. They cannot tolerate the separation and view it as abandonment, often thinking the other person will not return. There is an expectation that the other person will be there and available at all times. When this doesn't happen, the fear sets in and behaviors will begin that are designed to prevent the anticipated abandonment. Self-hate usually begins and many blame themselves for being alone. The low self-esteem prevents them from being able to tolerate even small absences without this fear in the ensuing emptiness.

CHAPTER 11

Borderline Personality Disorder and Reality

People with borderline personality disorder have problems with reality, and often they do not necessarily see situations as they truly are. For example, if you walk into a coffee shop and see two unfamiliar people speaking quietly to each other, you would probably assume they were simply having a private conversation. However, someone with BPD would observe the same situation and automatically think, "Those two people are making fun of me!" Trying to explain to them that those two people were probably just chatting to themselves won't help, as people with BPD often go to great lengths *to not be wrong* in order to preserve their self-esteem and mindset.

Self-Esteem Described

Self-esteem is how people think of themselves, and provides a measure of how valuable they perceive themselves to be. Self-esteem drives people to succeed if they believe in themselves and believe that they are capable of doing big things, or it causes them to create large defenses to protect themselves from their own negative self-image. Those who have low self-esteem do not believe they are capable of doing things, and often do not believe they are worthy of the love of others.

Development of Self-Esteem

Self-esteem is developed at a very young age, going back to how parents treat young children, and even infants. When parents raise their children with unconditional positive regard, and show them that it is okay to make mistakes and try again, they provide them with the basis for a healthy self-esteem.

Children who see that it is okay to not be completely right all the time are able to think through different situations and learn from them. Children who are put down in some way when they do something wrong tend to take on their mistake as part of their entirety. If they do poorly on a test, they don't dust themselves off and study harder next time, they think of themselves as just plain stupid. There is no in-between.

ESSENTIAL

While children move away from the direct influence of their parents as they get older, the words and reactions of the parents remain with them throughout life. It is not possible to take back hurtful words or "unsay" them, and the result can be years of self-doubt and pain.

Self-esteem develops through childhood in other ways, in addition to parenting. Children interacting with other children often learn from each other and can support each other, or they can cause other children to feel worse about themselves. Bullying is often perpetrated by people with low self-esteem to make themselves feel better, and is normally targeted at others with low self-esteem.

Children who form solid friendship groups and are able to explore and meet the approval of their friends can sometimes develop a healthy self-esteem, in spite of negative parenting at home. As children get older and approach adolescence, the influence of peers increases.

Teachers and other adults that children encounter on a regular basis also have an influence on how they develop self-esteem. Teachers who are encouraging and take the time to help the child succeed can help the child develop positive self-esteem that carries through to later life, whereas teachers who become impatient and irritated with a child who cannot get something can damage the child's self-esteem. The same holds true for coaches, child care workers, and other relatives who interact with the child. The more approval the child sees the better the self-esteem will be.

FACT

Self-efficacy is a person's estimation of how well she is able to complete a task. It is her measure of how capable she thinks she is at something. Self-esteem and self-efficacy are interrelated. As self-esteem rises, self-efficacy normally rises too. As one is reduced, the other is normally also reduced.

The Self-Esteem Thought Process

Positive attitudes normally go along with higher self-esteem, while children with negative attitudes often have lower self-esteem. Their outlook on life is based on what they think they are able to do and how they think they are able to navigate their circumstances. When children think they can do something, whether they have done this already or not, they are more likely to succeed. If, on the other hand, they do not feel capable of succeeding at some task, they have just reduced the likelihood of being able to do so. A child who practices a musical instrument every day gains the confidence to play at a recital, whereas a child who does not practice because he thinks he'll never play well anyway will not.

People with borderline personality disorder often feel they are flawed, defective, or damaged in some way. They look at themselves as bad and often process incoming information in a negative way. They think in extremes: things are either good or bad, with very, very little in between. Thus, they tend to see minor incidences as something much worse. This tends to crumble an already shaky self-esteem.

Think about our earlier example of the people talking in the coffee shop. Why would someone with BPD assume that two strangers are making fun of him? Because his self-esteem is so low, he assumes that everyone, including strangers, is criticizing him. If the pair of people briefly glanced up to see who entered the coffee shop, this action, however minor and benign, can be perceived as a slight. The person with BPD thinks he is being criticized, and his self-esteem drops further, causing him to view this situation for something it is not: an attack on him.

Case Study: Rick

Rick had worked hard all semester and was maintaining a "B" average. He had spent all night studying for his test and thought he had the material down rather well; he really wanted to get at least a "B" on this test and prove to himself and to his parents that he could excel academically. Rick had just recently been diagnosed with borderline personality disorder, a condition his mother had. His mother had called while he was studying and got into him about studying hard because he always seemed to mess up in school with final tests. This hurt because Rick had been doing well before she called.

This was not an uncommon conversation. As far back as Rick could remember, his mother had told him that he should study hard, because he had such trouble when it came to taking tests. He usually didn't have problems on the schoolwork and assignments, but he always had a difficult time with tests. He was determined get a good grade on this test to show that he was not stupid.

The test did not seem too bad at first, but the conversation with his mother kept creeping in, and he became angry when he encountered a question he was not sure of. Instead of moving on and finishing what he did know, he became stuck and started to call himself stupid. He started to think he was going to fail. His mother's words kept rolling over and over in his head and the answers to the questions just wouldn't come. He was completely unaware of the time, and before he knew it the time was up and he had to hand in his paper. He only got through two additional questions once the thoughts started to play in his mind.

Words That Hurt

As the case study shows, simple words meant to help can actually cause a great deal of pain and trouble for people with borderline personality disorder. They can become stuck in their mind and affect how they think of themselves. Even if the words are meant in a positive, helpful way, for those with borderline personality disorder, it is just another affirmation of how bad or unworthy they really are. They already have trouble feeling good about themselves and the negative feedback just confirms it. They are left storing this information in a deep pit inside until it erupts at a later date. This is often the only way they can assert themselves.

For example, in our coffee shop scenario, let's say that our person with BPD is named Anna. When Anna begins to get angry with these two strangers for their "gossip," her friend Cassie assures her that these two people were probably not talking about her, and then adds that perhaps Anna is being a little too sensitive. Now, Cassie's words are a constructive and useful criticism that, if taken to heart by Anna, could eliminate a lot of anger down the road—plus, Cassie adds that she wants Anna to enjoy their time together, not waste the entire day seething at something that didn't even happen. But Anna, who was often criticized for her sensitivity as a child by her mother, is devastated by this comment, takes this is a direct insult, and has a few choice words for Cassie before storming out—and believes almost everyone she sees on her way home is gossiping about her.

When those with BPD have low self-esteem, they are often unable to trust themselves or others. They lock themselves away in a sea of negative self-talk and turn inward, and they stop believing they are capable of succeeding at anything. Anna was unable to separate herself from her actions, so when Cassie commented that her behavior was a bit too sensitive, Anna felt insulted, and while she behaved with anger in retaliation, she was actually feeling very powerless and weak. Rather than stay and talk it out with her friend, Anna opted to turn inward and leave.

Identity Disturbance and What It Means

People with borderline personality disorder have identity issues, something that is evident as they struggle with self-esteem and do not have a clear sense of self. They lose sight of themselves, their wants, needs, and goals. Identity disturbance is one of the main criteria that distinguish borderline personality disorder from other disorders.

What Is Identity?

Identity is the sense of being that makes each person unique from every other individual. It is comprised of a person's beliefs, attitudes, abilities, personality traits, habits, goals, and all other things that make up a given person. Identity remains fairly consistent over time. It is a sum of what has happened, what is happening, and plans for the future.

A strong sense of identity helps in the development of self-esteem. The stronger the sense of identity, the more self-esteem develops and creates feelings of self-efficacy. In a home where a child is not encouraged to develop a strong separate identity, the child often becomes lost and enmeshed in the identity of his parents. This is especially true when the parent is overbearing and unstable. When this happens the identity remains fixed and unmovable. The person is unable to adapt to new situations without extensive outside help.

For example, when Ben was a child, his parents encouraged him to develop his own interests and goals. Ben really liked basketball, so his parents signed him up for a junior team, went to all his games, encouraged him when he played well, and consoled him when he didn't. They made it clear to him that his identity was not tied to being the best, but just enjoying his interests. Ben grew up knowing that hard work would help him do better at the things he enjoyed, but his parents would love him and he would be just as valued if he did not always win or come out on top. He was confident to try new activities and pursue many different interests, forming his own identity.

Tyler's parents signed him up for the same team, but were not so supportive. If Tyler played well, his parents praised him. If he did not, they criticized his performance to the point where Tyler believed that his parents only loved him when he succeeded. His identity became lost in pleasing his parents. Unlike Ben, Tyler grew up feeling like he was useless and unworthy of love unless he was the absolute best, something that plagued him personally and professionally into adulthood.

Adapting to Change

Although identity remains fairly consistent over time, change does occur, along with unexpected situations that require adaptation. People who have not developed their own separate and distinct identity become lost when this happens. They do not know how to change or adapt because they do not feel capable of working through change or special circumstances. When this happens to someone with borderline personality disorder, the reaction is often an angry explosion.

ESSENTIAL

Thought patterns for someone with borderline personality disorder are not necessarily based on true facts. They are often based on perceptions and misperceptions that can cause confusion and frustration, as others do not follow what they are thinking or saying.

If Ben and Tyler's coach told them one day that one of their teammates had fallen ill and he needed to switch up their typical positions for that game, Ben would probably be fine with this, even excited at the prospect of trying something new. But Tyler, used to playing in his own position, would not react well to this at all, and might even throw a fit. He is unable to cope with a new circumstance, and is terrified that he will not succeed in a new position.

Adaptation to changing circumstances takes a confidence in ability and self-efficacy that is high enough to help overcome new and different circumstances. When someone has little to no self-esteem, and does not see himself as capable of overcoming obstacles, an adaptation will not occur. Incoherent thoughts will increase, and logic will be less likely to hold sway. Instead the person will become inconsistent and unpredictable.

Inconsistency

Thoughts and behaviors for someone with borderline personality disorder can change rapidly and swing from one extreme to the other. One day the person could be overly solicitous to someone, and the next he could be talking behind the other's back. He might have a lot of energy one day, and barely drag himself from bed the next. Since the thoughts are not regulated by rational thought based on true facts, emotion often takes over.

The emotions of someone with borderline personality disorder might also seem inappropriate for the situation. He could become overly angry at something small, like a clerk forgetting to put ketchup in his fast food meal. This could set off an angry explosion at the clerk and the person in the car with him, as he blames the other person for wanting to stop there in the first place—even if he was in fact the one who wanted to stop there. On another outing, the same situation could present with no problem at all.

Plans for the future could switch numerous times. An outing planned for the following week could go through as many as twenty changes only to arrive back at the original plan, or be cancelled out of frustration. Sudden changes can occur in anything from opinions and goals to friends, hobbies, jobs, and living arrangements. This inconsistency can be the result of changes in the stability of identity, or identity disturbance.

What Is Identity Disturbance?

Identity disturbance is the disruption or alteration of self-image, or sense of self. As has already been discussed, people with borderline personality disorder often have low self-esteem and might not have formed their own clear identity. In most people, identity remains fairly consistent, yet able to adapt to new situations and needs. It is normal to feel some confusion when going off to college for the first time or enlisting in the army. These situations are new and require a new way of thinking and behaving.

But for people with borderline personality disorder, shifts of this magnitude could occur in familiar situations with little warning or reason. They might suddenly decide they do not want to be a lawyer right before they are about to graduate from law school. They might quit their job because they don't like their assignment on any given day. They might end a relationship with their significant other abruptly, and without offering a reason. They might also change from a needy role to a nurturing role.

FACT

Some research suggests that some components of identity disturbance can be linked to a history of sexual abuse, but not others. Thus, identity disturbance occurs in people with borderline personality disorder whether sexual abuse has occurred or not.

Types of Identity Disturbance

According to the American Psychiatric Association, some research suggests that there are four basic types of disturbance. The first is role is *absorption*, in which one single role defines the person. This can change as roles change. For example, a person who has borderline personality disorder who meets someone who bowls might throw himself into bowling and define his role with this. If this relationship ends, the role of bowler is likely to end too. This role defines the person's whole identity for the time he is enmeshed in it.

Another disturbance is *painful incoherence*, in which people create their own subjective experience on their identity. They often show distress or concern for how they view their identity. For example, the person above who identified with being a bowler because of a new relationship may express concern that his identity has no sense to it, no coherence. This factor seems to be most closely associated with identity disturbance in someone with borderline personality disorder.

A third disturbance is inconsistency in thoughts, feelings, and behaviors. This would include beliefs and behaviors that are completely contradictory. A person might believe that it is wrong to steal, and then turn around and steal. The bowler above may build his entire identity around bowling, but actually refuse to play at the alley, preferring to schmooze around with friends.

Finally, lack of commitment is associated with identity disturbance. Lack of commitment often comes in the form of difficulties in committing to goals or maintaining a constant set of values. It would also pertain to jobs or relationships. A man can say how much he prides himself on being a good husband, but is unfaithful to his wife every weekend.

These identity disturbance factors are used to distinguish borderline personality disorder from other personality disorders. Someone with borderline personality disorder would normally have higher scores on all four of these factors, indicating the severity of identity disturbance in this particular disorder.

Paranoia and Dissociation

In addition to identity disturbance, people with borderline personality disorder often encounter episodes of dissociation and paranoia. Dissociation consists of times when the person feels out of touch or out of body. People with BPD feel a separation from reality and might lose parts of their day. They might not have any idea what has happened. This often is a result of high stress. They might also experience an intense distrust of others and a fear that others are talking or thinking about some action against them.

Dissociation

Have you ever zoned out for a few minutes while performing a task, like cleaning your house, and then when you "woke up," you had either completed the task, or were still performing it? This is a very benign form of dissociation. *Dissociation* is a state in which a person loses some contact with current reality. It involves both physical and cognitive symptoms that take a person from current status. Most people do this from time to time; they think about other things while driving, or walking to work, focusing on something other than what is immediately occurring.

Dissociation is characterized by a couple of different issues. People experiencing dissociation often feel depersonalized, or separated from their body. They might feel like they are observing the actions of someone else rather than experiencing them themselves. It might seem like it is a dream rather than reality.

In addition to this "depersonalization," they might also feel *derealization*, a feeling of being detached from their body—and the world, too. They might almost think that they are floating or in some way apart from other people and things. Familiar objects might look strange or distorted. Depersonalization and derealization normally occur at the same time. In more extreme cases of dissociation, people might also experience episodes of amnesia, when they cannot remember what they did or where they were at a certain time.

Paranoia

Paranoia is a state of being in which the person is distrustful and suspicious of others, thinking that they are plotting against her or are out to get her in some way. This is based on little or no evidence and is often a product of the faulty thought processes and misperceptions characteristic of borderline personality disorder. She may see simple actions as signs of a conspiracy against her and take action herself. In our earlier example in the coffee shop, Anna was exhibiting symptoms of paranoia when she thought people were talking about her without evidence to support this idea.

Paranoid individuals often decide they must retaliate or defend themselves. They feel these actions are justified, and are confused when others do not see the same thing. They might even become angry as they realize others do not believe them. This type of behavior tends to alienate others and cause problems in relationships. If a person already feels alienated from others, which is common with borderline personality disorder, she is more likely to suspect others of having negative attitudes or intentions toward her. The additional mistrust inherent in borderline personality disorder adds fuel to the thought process.

Case Study: David

David has trouble walking down the street. He reported to his therapist that he believes the people he encounters are all somehow against him. If they look at him, he thinks they are plotting what they can do next. These are people he does not even know, but he has a fear that they are against him, and may even take some kind of action. He has begun to get in the habit of carrying a pocketknife with him for self-defense.

When his therapist asked him how he knows these people are plotting against him, he replied that he can see it in their eyes, the way they look at him, and he can feel it. When she asked whether or not anyone had actually approached him, he responded that they had not. He thinks they are wait-ing for an opportunity when they can take him unaware. When she asked why these people who do not know him would have designs on hurting him or humiliating him, he told his therapist that they just do, and became angry because he realized she did not believe him.

David went out from his home less, and when he did go out, he tried very hard to keep from turning his back to others. This meant that he often turned around or even went in circles. When people saw him doing these things they thought he was crazy and moved away from him, sometimes giv-ing him strange looks. These looks reinforced David's thoughts.

QUESTION

Is there any danger in the paranoid or dissociative thoughts?
There can be. Most of the time, these behaviors will result in a lapse in memory or some form of isolation on the part of the individual experi-encing these thoughts. In some cases, however, the extreme fear could cause the person to act defensively in some more dangerous manner. It is also possible that things will happen during these epi-sodes because the person is not thinking clearly.

How Common Are These Symptoms?

Unfortunately, lapses in reality are fairly common with borderline personality disorder. The identity disturbance is one of the main defining features for this disorder. The problems with self-esteem and formation of identity can often lead to problems with reality. The same issues within the brain that prevent a person with borderline personality disorder from recognizing proper social norms might also prevent her from recognizing real and imagined situations. Episodes of rage and extreme anger are more common, but the danger does exist and problems can occur during these breaks with reality.

Dangers

During these breaks with reality, the person might become completely separated from what she is doing and where she is. This could cause her to walk in front of a car, or wander away from where she should be. If she has children, it might also cause her to leave the children in a store or another area without realizing that she has done so.

This is also a time when danger of self-harm can be high. The break from reality might make the self-harm more likely as she perceives no real consequences, or as she uses the pain to bring her back to the present. It is also possible that she might seek to rid herself of the evil she thinks she has within her at a time like this.

When They Are More Common

Instances of disturbance can happen at any time, since misinterpretations can happen at any time. A simple statement or look can set one off. Yet there are normally strong stressors involved when the breaks with reality happen. The most common is again when the person perceives a threat of rejection or abandonment. Since relationships are often volatile and fleeting, abandonment does occur fairly often in some form. This can cause the person with borderline personality disorder to become overly stressed and lose track of reality.

People who have experienced some form of trauma might also be more likely to experience a break from reality. This is an area where posttraumatic stress disorder intersects with borderline personality disorder. The trauma that precipitates posttraumatic stress disorder also increases the stressors that can create a break in thought processes.

Case Study: Evelyn

Evelyn, a young woman with BPD, was devastated when her boyfriend broke up with her. He could not handle her BPD any longer, and ended the relationship, asking Evelyn to leave his house.

Somehow Evelyn had found her way home. She did not remember how she got there or when she left her boyfriend's home, only that she was in such agony over her relationship ending. She began cutting herself to ease the pain of what had happened and became lost in this sensation. Again, she did not know how long she was there, cutting. Her roommate came home and found her the next morning, her arms bruised and bloody, and immediately brought her to the emergency room.

Evelyn didn't respond when the admissions nurse asked questions. She felt like she was at home watching a movie. The doctor said that she would likely remain in this fog for a while longer and warned her roommate to keep an eye on her so she didn't hurt herself more.

What Might Happen?

Self-destructive acts are usually brought on through extreme stress associated with perceived abandonment, or during dissociative episodes. These breaks with reality might also cause more dangerous impulsive actions, or misuse of drugs and alcohol. They tend to produce strong reactions that could turn violent when the perceived threat is great enough.

Stress Reactions

Stress in someone with borderline personality disorder can cause severe reactions, especially if there is a break with reality in some way. The most common issue is identity disturbance. The person might lose track of who he is and what he is working on. He might switch quickly to something else, or his mood will swing from one extreme to the other.

Paranoia can result from stressors and the person can believe something is going on that is not. He might simply start a verbal altercation, but if he feels threatened enough, he might do something worse, such as carry a knife or take defensive actions. This is dangerous, as stressors often hit without warning. The instant reactions that come from misperceptions can set off a chemical chain reaction within the person. His adrenaline can start to pump quicker and the reactions within the body create a high alert status. This adrenaline needs to burn off in some way, and this often results in a strong emotional reaction.

Communication through these incidences is strained and is often characterized by anger and accusations. This tends to increase the likelihood that others will avoid the person with borderline personality disorder and treat him with suspicion. As this happens, fears of abandonment grow and the cycle feeds on itself.

CHAPTER 12

Communicating Through Borderline Personality Disorder

People with borderline personality disorder often have difficulty identifying their thoughts and feelings. Since they cannot identify them, they have trouble communicating them in a way others can understand. Remember that their thought processes can go different routes and they often come to erroneous or blown-up conclusions. People with borderline personality disorder often have their own unique perspective on what they see and hear, and it is often tuned to the potential negatives. There are times meanings get twisted or lost and cause larger misunderstandings. It is important to think about what might happen before communicating.

What to Expect

The person with borderline personality disorder often feels like no one understands her. She believes she is speaking clearly and explaining fully, and cannot understand why others have such a problem following what she is saying. She understands what they are saying and sees the communication problem as some fault or shortcoming of the others. She sees things from her perspective and her perspective alone.

The Borderline Perspective

People with borderline personality disorder often think they are explaining and describing their thoughts perfectly clearly. Unfortunately in many cases, they are not. They are looking at things from their own perspective with little thought of the perspectives of others. Thoughts are one-sided, and can be confusing to others.

They also have a hard time putting their feelings into words. There are times they cannot think them through or recognize them themselves, let alone put them into words so others can understand what they are feeling or trying to convey. The emotions could come upon them without warning or provocation.

QUESTION

How can we communicate if neither one of us know what we are talking about?
Communication takes time and effort, and most importantly patience. It is possible to learn some of the patterns that might emerge and be supportive rather than reacting.

From the Inside

People with borderline personality disorder have myriad thoughts and emotions that they have difficulty identifying. Some of these emotions come up so suddenly there is little opportunity to think them through before reacting. This is the nature of borderline personality disorder—the feelings come on quickly and the reaction is just as quick. This complicates the thought process, and as a result communication is challenging.

Their thought process is in black and white, so when they communicate it is from the confines of this rigid base. They do not see a situation with possible solutions; they see a situation that is either good or bad. This causes a block in understanding. They just see a large problem, whereas someone else might be assessing the situation for possible solutions. The person with borderline personality disorder gets caught in the emotion of the situation, especially if it is negative situation.

ESSENTIAL

People with borderline personality disorder process situations negatively, and they can get out of control when they perceive that a situation is bad. They then overreact and their form of communication is often a rage or fearful outburst.

From the Outside

The overreactions of people with borderline personality disorder can cause confusion, irritation, and sometimes fear. From the outside it looks like someone with borderline is incoherent and out of control. She might make no sense at all, and efforts to explain could be met with increased anger. There doesn't seem to be a way to get through to her and have a calm discussion.

People with borderline personality disorder also process based on how they see life. They are working from low self-esteem and fear of abandonment. This can cause misunderstandings that bring about rigid thinking and communication. They might remain fixed on one viewpoint no matter how hard someone else tries to reason with them. There are times when there is no reason, as they argue from a point of view that might seem to have nothing to do with the topic at hand. It often leaves others wondering what to do or say.

What to Do

It is important to remain calm and supportive even when it seems frustrating and endless. It is also important to try to be supportive and empathetic to the person's situation. This is not an easy thing to do when she is hurling insults and going into a rage. Remember that the words she is saying are normally not what she means. She is acting through her own perceptions.

The first thing to do is make sure there is no danger to anyone involved. Once this has been established, it might be best to try to simply listen without arguing and let her get it all out. She wants to be heard and understood. While understanding is not going to be easy, it is important that she feels she has been heard and her feelings acknowledged. When she sees that she has the undivided attention of another, it might calm her down and let her focus on what she is trying to say.

When the negative feelings start coming out, do not deny them or disagree with them. Saying "that isn't true" will not make things better, and might just create a larger episode. This will be seen as a discounting of her feelings, which causes increased anger and frustration. It is not necessary to agree with what is being said, but it is important to validate the feelings and acknowledge that they exist. The thoughts she is having might not be true, but she thinks they are and she needs to work through it. Once everyone is calm it is possible to try to get to the content of the message and feelings.

ALERT

Denying the thoughts and feelings that someone with borderline personality disorder is having can lead to a strong and sometimes violent reaction. The impulsivity combined with the frustration and negative thought processes can cause a dangerous situation.

Are We Talking about the Same Thing?

One reason the relationships do not last for people with borderline personality disorder is because they are unable to properly express themselves. They might be talking about something completely different from what someone else is. It is hard to determine meaning and get on the same page when two people do not know each other very well.

Mixing Messages Early On

Communication occurs both verbally and nonverbally. Early in a relationship nonverbal cues can give others a different message from the one that is meant. When the relationship is new, people with BPD might appear fun-loving and eager to take some risks. They could seem forward, which can be taken the wrong way. Others might think they are looking for a casual sexual interlude when in reality they are looking for a relationship.

The fun-loving attitude and impulsive behaviors also give the impression that they are confident and independent when they are really feeling unloved and unlovable. Verbal communication can confirm this, as they tell stories that make them seem successful and easygoing. The true message might be something entirely different—and is probably a plea for someone to like them. The person with borderline personality disorder might be trying to start a friendship when he moves close and smiles, yet it might seem to someone else that he is coming on to them.

QUESTION

How will I know what someone with BPD means when they communicate with me?
At first it will be very hard to understand what the person is trying to communicate to you. Remember that she is trying to establish a new relationship and is going to say and do things to get others to like her. As time goes on certain patterns will start to emerge to help provide clues to what she means.

As the Relationship Continues

When a relationship lasts for a period of time, the mixed messages can cause additional strife. People with borderline personality disorder are trying to keep up the image they think the other person wants to see while still trying to project wants and needs. This comes off as a confusing series of communication efforts. When they say they are worried about something that someone would not normally be worried about, or something that simply isn't true, they might really be trying to say something else. Since this is the main fear, it is also the main way they have learned to communicate. Thus, most of their communication has an element of this fear of rejection.

You might be talking about having to go on a business trip, yet the person with BPD is hearing "I am leaving," and her responses will be based on that. She might start accusing you of leaving her as you try to explain a legitimate business trip for one night.

Case Study: Lisa and Jeff

Lisa and Jeff were getting along great. They had been together for three months and saw each other every day. Jeff came home on Thursday and announced that he had to go away on an overnight trip Monday into Tuesday. Lisa began to panic. She just knew this would happen sooner or later. Jeff was leaving her just like everyone else did eventually. She began by begging him not to go. Jeff explained that he had to go for work. It didn't happen often, but when it did he needed to go.

Lisa accused him of lying about the trip so he could leave her. She asked him who the other woman was and began to get angry. Of course, that was it. There was another woman and Jeff was leaving her. She started screaming in a rage and threw her water bottle at him. When he tried to calm her down she kicked at him and punched him. She told him to just leave and never come back.

Jeff was completely puzzled by the whole scene. He didn't know what had happened. One minute he was talking about having to go out of town and then having a nice dinner when he got back, and the next minute he was trying to dodge a water bottle and defend himself from accusations that he was cheating. He tried to deny the accusations and it made her even angrier. He didn't know what to do, so he left.

Learning to Find the True Meaning Behind the Message

Meaning is an essential part of communication between people, and it is a bit more complicated when one of the individuals has borderline personality disorder. Meaning is often hard to determine from his words. When he gets upset, he normally becomes unreasonable and does not think clearly. As this happens, the words are emotion- rather than thought-based.

Where It Comes From

The emotions can be extreme, and they can cause the words that come out to come out wrong. The fear of abandonment and the feelings of low self-esteem and low self-worth bring out quick reactions that can cause painful words to come out directed at another person. Often, the words are really directed at themselves, but they are aimed at another person as they navigate the problems they see as insurmountable.

ALERT

It is important to watch for threats to self or others during these episodes. Threats can be used to gain attention and manipulate, but the high rate of suicide attempts and completions with this disorder make it a serious issue.

The natural anger that occurs in people with borderline personality disorder can boil forth whenever something seems to go wrong, or they think they have been wronged. When people with borderline personality disorder suppress parts of themselves in order to fit in and be liked, the parts they suppress or leave untended can lead to resentment. They might see that they have done all of the giving for another person and this other person does not even acknowledge the sacrifices. In truth, the other person normally doesn't even realize the sacrifices. The frustration and imagined slights build up. Then, when something happens to set them off, the anger comes out in an explosion that leaves the other person baffled.

Looking for Patterns

It can be very frustrating and nerve-racking when dealing with people with borderline personality disorder, especially when they are upset. They are unpredictable and might not make any sense. Additionally, they might be ranting about things without listening to a word someone is saying. If family members and loved ones are able to find patterns in what sets them off, they might be able to avert some of the miscommunication.

QUESTION

People with borderline personality disorder might show some signs of agitation that are similar from one extreme reaction to the next. Certain topics that are highly sensitive to them could start the agitation. They might pick at their nails or pull at their hair. They could start tapping their fingers or swinging their legs, indicating an increase in nervousness or anger. These reactions could indicate that whatever communication is occurring at that time is not going well.

What They Might Mean

The fear and anger reactions directed at others can be mean and insulting. People with borderline personality disorder can cause a lot of hurt with what they say. They lash out seemingly without thinking. In many cases they are not thinking before they react. Yet the reactions themselves are often a result of how they feel and might be directed inward rather than at someone else.

When they tell another person "I hate you," they could be speaking to themselves rather than the other person. The true meaning is often lost in the pain and anger of the message. When they say something like "I know that you are cheating on me," they are often trying to say they do not feel worthy of that person's love and attention.

The words are often an indication of what they are feeling inside, but they do not necessarily give a clear picture. The words do not always match the meaning. It is important to think before reacting. When others are aware of these facts and keeping an ear out to be in tune to what is going on in conjunction with what is being said, it is possible to distinguish meaning a little more closely. It will not prevent the mood swings, but it will help determine when some incidents might occur.

Dealing with the Swings in Thought and Word

The mood swings can hit at any time and can be severe. People with borderline personality disorder react on impulse, which means they do not always think through what they say or do before they act. The instability of self can cause happiness one minute and anger the next. Some stressors are likely to set off a bad reaction and can be identified and countered when they occur. Other factors, however, could be completely out of the ordinary.

What Is Normal?

Everyone experiences changes in mood from time to time. Different life circumstances and stressors can cause very happy and very sad periods. It is normal to go from feeling happy to hopeless when something bad happens. For someone with borderline personality disorder the extremes occur far more often.

When people with normal thought and reaction processes experience a mood swing, there is normally an event or issue that has come up to spur it on. It might last for a few minutes until reason steps in, and it does not normally result in danger to self or others. For someone with borderline personality disorder, the swings can occur within a matter of moments with little or no provocation or warning. The intense emotional shifts not only cause fear and frustration in others, they can also overwhelm the person experiencing them. This can cause the person to self-harm or engage in other impulsive and possibly dangerous behaviors.

ESSENTIAL

Certain triggers would also be more likely to pertain to borderline personality disorder. These triggers would include fear of abandonment and perceived rejection. People with borderline personality disorder are also sensitive to blame and being wrong and could swing in reaction to these events.

Mood swings for people who react in a normal manner might occur once in a while as a result of some circumstance that prompts it. It could occur once or twice in a week's time, depending upon the circumstance that prompts it. If someone is having trouble paying bills and loses her job, the swings might happen more often as she tries to deal with this strong stressor. When she gets another job and removes the stressor, the mood will swing upward in happiness, then level out and remain so until the next occurrence comes along. For someone with borderline personality disorder, the swings can occur multiple times in the course of each day. They would be severe regardless of circumstances, and could be dangerous.

What Helps

The identification of the potential triggers can help prepare for times when mood swings are more likely to occur. There is no guarantee because the instability inherent in borderline personality disorder can cause confusion and spur extreme swings over issues that are seemingly insignificant. It is also a good idea to try to understand where they might be coming from when they blow up. This understanding could help calm them down.

In all cases remain calm. The calmer everyone else is, the less likely the possibility that the situation will escalate. Use a steady voice and do not argue when the person with borderline personality disorder is in a rage or does not seem to be able to see reason. The misperceptions of rejection will override the ability to listen objectively and denials will only serve to create more anger.

QUESTION

Why is it a problem to tell my girlfriend that she is overreacting?
This invalidates her feelings and makes her feel like she has done something wrong. She thinks you are correcting her, which makes her feel stupid, and since her feelings are very real to her, it looks like you are minimizing her feelings.

Wait until the person settles down before trying to work things out. Once denials and responses begin, it often happens that the other is drawn into the delusions and fears of the one with borderline personality disorder. Once this happens you are on the defensive the entire time and anything you say will be misinterpreted in order to fit the imaginings of the person with borderline personality disorder. It is also important to acknowledge the pain, even if the message is untrue. Do not lie or promise anything that cannot be kept, and above all else maintain safety.

Case Study: Nina and Maria

Nina was having a conversation with her sister Maria about the end of her last relationship. She had been talking about him for over an hour and Maria needed to get to work soon. Maria was very concerned about her sister and did not want to hurt her feelings but she did have to get going. She tried to glance surreptitiously at her watch to see how much longer she had, but Nina saw her.

Nina became upset instantly and accused her sister of wanting to get rid of her just like everyone else. Maria had been through this before and knew enough to keep from denying and correcting Nina. She let Nina yell uninterrupted. When Nina stopped, Maria began by telling her sister how sorry she was that her boyfriend had left her, and told her she could see that Nina was still very upset and wanted Maria to listen to her.

Maria told her sister she needed to get to work and felt very bad about the fact that she needed to cut her sister short for now. She really wanted to be there to help Nina. Nina remained suspicious, but Maria asked her to wait until she got out of work and gave her a specific time when they would sit down and finish talking. Nina did not calm completely down, but the set time came and Maria was right there to listen.

Ensuring Your Own Safety—Above All Else

Communication with someone with borderline personality disorder takes patience and support. Yet it can sometimes be dangerous. A key feature of this disorder is the explosive anger and violent rage that can commence without notice. This violence could result in self-harm or harm to others. The person with borderline personality disorder might throw things or might start hitting or punching. There is a large portion of abusers in this population and much of it comes from the rage.

Rage

The rage that comes out in violent outbursts is an offshoot of the fear of rejection and low self-esteem. People with borderline personality disorder are often defensive and if they feel they are being threatened in some way they will respond quickly and impulsively. This response could come in the form of violence.

The rage can build up over a period of time as the person with borderline personality disorder misperceives social interactions and tries to please others. Once this pleasing period ends and the person sees some inequality in the relationship, resentment begins to build. This escalates as he perceives rejection and feels wronged. The person in a rage often does not know what he is saying or doing at the time. He is beyond reason and needs to get rid of the momentum and adrenaline. It can occur as a verbal assault or physical and can come up without warning.

ALERT

When these rages occur it is unlikely that people with BPD will listen to any reason. They are also unlikely to back down from a fight and the adrenaline will add to their strength. Physical restraint might be difficult and could cause greater danger to all in the struggle. Unless absolutely necessary, leave physical contact to professionals when a violent reaction occurs.

Warning

Since the person on the other end does not know that something is going wrong, the explosion often comes as a complete surprise. There is little warning involved in these rages. If the person with borderline personality disorder is known and patterns have been recognized to some extent, it is possible to determine situations that might cause a rage and thus anticipate the reaction before it occurs.

There might also be some physical signs that indicate an increase in agitation and possible explosion. The person might begin to show impatience in facial expressions, picking at his fingernails, pulling hair, clenching fists, or pacing. The general signs of agitation should be heeded as warnings that a rage could be building.

Staying Safe

The most important thing to remember is safety for all concerned. When things get out of control, safety is more important than anything else. There are times when the situation can become dangerous and harm can result. The best thing to do is avoid this whenever possible. If the situation is not completely out of control it might be possible to de-escalate by listening and empathizing. If the situation looks like it is going to get out of control it is time to get away until things calm down.

FACT

Empathy is the ability to put yourself in the place of another and see the other's experiences and feelings from his perspective. Sympathy is the act of feeling sorry for another's plight whether you understand it from his perspective or not.

When the rage starts and if it does not seem safe, it is time to get away and call professional help. If the person is threatening to commit self-harm, call the police and report the behavior immediately. If the person is threatening someone else, he needs to leave. If there is cause to believe that harm might come to someone during this time, call help immediately. The police are trained to assess the situation and get the person to the help they need.

It can be difficult to call the police on a loved one, but you must remember that your safety is paramount—and your loved one is compromising your safety when he flies into a rage, and it is very possible that he could seriously injure you, someone else, or even himself.

CHAPTER 13

Gender and Age

Borderline personality disorder has some distinctions based on gender and age. Females have a higher prevalence of this disorder (about 75 percent of people diagnosed with this disorder are female), although it might have more to do with which symptoms manifest. Males are more likely to be diagnosed with other personality disorders that have less to do with emotion regulation, but still aggression. Age is also important, as borderline personality disorder can only be diagnosed after a certain age and decreases rapidly in later life.

Females with Borderline Personality Disorder

Females are more prone to developing borderline personality disorder. There seem to be both biological and environmental circumstances that promote borderline symptoms in females as opposed to males. There are differences in how this disorder progresses with males and females.

General Information

Women are more likely to report histories of adult physical and sexual abuse. The physical abuse is often at the hands of primary caregivers, most notably the mother. Sexual abuse is most often at the hands of nonrelated people the child encounters through the caregivers. In some cases, the child is abandoned to someone who sexually or physically abuses her.

Females with borderline personality disorder are more likely to have co-occurring eating disorders. Eating disorders are often a response to a living environment where people do not see that they have any control in their lives. In women with borderline personality disorder it could be a means of establishing some form of identity.

Many females with borderline personality disorder also meet criteria for posttraumatic stress disorder. They might have encountered various forms of trauma in their lives, including prolonged abuse, sexual abuse, and abandonment. In some cases they have come from dysfunctional homes where violence is the norm.

Women are more likely to seek help for mental health issues. This makes it more likely that they will be diagnosed with borderline personality disorder more often than males.

Abuse and Trauma

Early lifetime trauma is largely associated with female borderline personality disorder, but is not unique to this personality disorder. The trauma does, however, affect how the disorder progresses. There is additional fear and patterns of victimization. These women often go on to find abusers in later relationships and continue to be abused. In a sense it is the only relationship dynamic they know. As they get old enough they might realize that something isn't quite right in their relationship choices, but they have become stuck in a pattern and are too fearful of being alone or abandoned to leave the person they are with.

They might also be abusers. Mothers with borderline personality disorder have a higher incidence of child abuse. Their rage and aggression is often targeted at their children in frustration, especially younger children who do things without knowing any better.

Sexuality

Females with borderline personality disorder might seem more seductive or sexual. Normal social boundaries are an issue that they do not recognize as completely as they should. Females have a tendency to dress suggestively and to be very forward with potential mates. They provide a very appealing initial impression.

The high impulsivity makes it more likely that they will be open to sexual intercourse very early in a relationship. They might even use it as a means of gaining a relationship. They might see sex as a way of pleasing their potential mate and keeping the person around. They might also see it as a means of manipulation to get what they want. The sexual interest of their potential mate provides them with a sense of control and increases their self-esteem at least for a short period of time.

Female Self-Esteem

Females often exhibit low self-esteem in more passive ways. They are likely to make announcements that are self-deprecating, they might cry and become upset when they do something wrong, or they might simply say they cannot do something. They are more overt in seeking approval from others, and will often ask friends for opinions or reassurance.

They are more likely to become angry with themselves and direct their violence at themselves rather than others. Suicide attempts are more passive in females, and less likely to be completed. They are more resistant to believing compliments than males, and they are often more willing to put themselves in compromising situations in order to gain approval. Gender roles seem to affect how borderline personality disorder develops in both males and females.

ALERT

It is important to note that the manipulation in borderline personality disorder is an offshoot of the symptoms of fear of rejection and abandonment. People who manipulate are not all diagnosed with borderline personality disorder. The manipulation is part of their reaction to what they perceive is happening in their lives.

Males with Borderline Personality Disorder

Males are diagnosed with borderline personality disorder in lower numbers than females. They are more likely to be diagnosed with substance abuse disorders, along with paranoid, passive-aggressive, narcissistic, sadistic, and antisocial personality disorders. Males with borderline personality disorder have a higher likelihood of incarceration or other restricted setting. Their behaviors are more aggressive and assertive.

Relationships

Males feel the drive to be in a relationship at all times, but are not as fearful of abandonment. They experience many short-term, unstable relationships that begin with intensity and then become problematic. They do see rejection as an issue, but are more concerned with what they are getting out of the relationship. Rather than using sex as an enticement into a relationship they seek sex as a main component in the relationship.

They are also more likely to have multiple relationships going at the same time. For men it is more about the chase and conquest that gives them a boost in self-esteem. They are addicted to the romance and the sex, but fear intimacy and commitment. They come on strong with attractive qualities such as romance and sensitivity, but these soon fade. Once they see that they have their intended mate hooked they begin to back off on romance and sensitivity and become more aloof. They are often beginning their search for another initial high with another person.

ESSENTIAL

The need for that initial burst of feeling at the start of a relationship is a driving force in both males and females with borderline personality disorder. In many cases, however, females seek to continue this high with the person they are with because they fear rejection and abandonment, while the males seek to find it in a series of relationships that begin before another ends so they have someone at all times.

Insecure Behaviors

Males with borderline personality disorder tend to turn to substance use and abuse to self-medicate. They, like females, have a high rate of comorbidity with abuse and dependence diagnoses. The substance is used as a quick way to take away the pain or escape from their problems with self-esteem and identity.

Males engage in suicidal thoughts and behaviors as often as females, but tend to make more lethal attempts. Some males follow the same patterns as females and try to cut themselves or overdose, while others might use a gun or other weapon. Males are more likely to use a gun than females.

Males are very sensitive to real or perceived criticism and can go into a rage quickly. While females can be aggressive and dangerous when they go into an angry rage, males tend to seek fights and prove strength and dominance to vent their rage. They are more likely to become violent and carry through with threats of physical harm to self and others.

Male Self-Esteem

Males are prone to reckless behaviors to prove their capabilities. They engage in many of the same behaviors as females, such as reckless driving and overspending. They are also more likely to seek promiscuous and deviant sexual encounters. They tend to be attracted to women who are needy in some way.

They tend to look for women who are in need of rescue, or who make them feel intelligent and strong. This often means finding women who have issues of their own and are not fully functioning. Women who seem whole or confident are a threat to them. They see confident women as more likely to abandon them, whereas the more needy women seem safer in this regard. This leaves them free to do the leaving and keep their fears at bay.

Other Diagnoses

There is some speculation that males are diagnosed less with border-line personality disorder because the symptoms they exhibit can seem more closely associated with narcissistic personality disorder, avoidant personality disorder, and antisocial personality disorder. Since this disorder is thought of mainly as a disorder for those who are overly emotional, there might be a bias in diagnosis from male to female.

ESSENTIAL

Males with borderline personality disorder might be mistakenly diagnosed with bipolar disorder, which is often treated with medication. This might take care of some of the symptoms, but it does not address all facets of the disorder.

Males might also react differently to parenting by someone with border-line personality disorder. Mothers of boys diagnosed with gender identity disorder have a higher likelihood of being diagnosed with borderline personality disorder. These boys might have had difficulty developing autonomy in the borderline parenting environment.

Case Study: Jake

Jake was in his early thirties and still lived at home with his parents. He got kicked out of college for making inappropriate sexual advances to girls on campus. He had a tendency to brush against their breasts whenever he could find an opportunity. He worked at a local mini-mart and spent a lot of his time at home smoking pot and looking at porn on the computer.

His girlfriend Amy was in treatment for anxiety disorders and was afraid to leave her house for long periods of time. Jake met her on the Internet. Jake often stalked her e-mail and Facebook accounts to see whom she was talking to. He got her to reveal her login information the first day they met. He was sure she was seeing someone else and constantly tested her by sending her requests posing as another man to see what she would do. He would fly into a rage if she responded to any of them in any way. Jake was also seeing two other girls at the same time and did not see a problem with expecting Amy to remain true to him while he went with others.

He didn't understand why his parents got on him so much about going back to school and making more money. It made him feel like he wasn't worth much and this sent him into a rage. His mother had to take his father to the hospital for a concussion after the last episode, and there was now a hole in the wall. Jake had been diagnosed with conduct disorder as a teen, but refused treatment beyond what he was required to attend and did not think he needed treatment now. He just needed everyone to get off his case.

What about Teenagers?

The general rule is that borderline personality disorder cannot be diagnosed until someone is at least eighteen years of age, has symptoms that are persistent, and has exhibited the symptoms for at least two years. Since this is a personality disorder, the belief was that an individual's personality needed to be fully developed before a diagnosis could be made. However, an exception has recently been made to diagnostic criteria. Borderline personality disorder can now be diagnosed in teenagers when the symptoms have been present for at least one year.

Symptoms of Adolescence

One of the reasons professionals are reluctant to diagnose adolescents with borderline personality disorder is the natural ups and downs associated with this life stage. Some individuals experience more extreme mood shifts during the teen years, which could be the result of greater hormonal shifts that occur at this time.

Adolescents can be more impulsive in nature during this stage. They do not have the benefit of experience to teach them that some of their actions can have negative consequences. The parts of the brain that normally promote abstract thinking and thought about potential consequences is not yet fully developed in the adolescent years. To put it simply, the natural impulsivity of teenagers is based on age and inexperience rather than a potential mental health disorder.

Adolescents are also still developing proper mood regulation skills. They are learning the proper social outline for different emotions but still have bouts of intense feelings. Adolescents are prone to tantrums and fits of anger, especially when things do not go their way.

Some research suggests that the prefrontal cortex does not completely develop until the age of twenty-five. This area of the brain is responsible for abstract thinking that can project and look at consequences for behaviors and connect the experiences of others with what that individual might choose to do.

Some adolescents can react more negatively to certain environmental events. A death or divorce could create more intense symptoms in some teenagers as they learn to work through the event. In each of these cases, the symptoms are normally hit and miss. They might come and go, or they might be the result of some external stimuli that causes a quick reaction. The reaction could mimic that of someone with borderline personality disorder. The key difference would be in persistence.

Persistent Symptoms

Symptoms in borderline personality disorder are persistent and pervasive. They continue across circumstances and across time. Adolescents who are going through different circumstances that are normal to that age group normally exhibit symptoms inconsistently and as a reaction to something that has happened or they have perceived in that particular time. Adolescents do not outgrow all of the symptoms of borderline personality disorder, but they do learn to deal better with the situations they face as teenagers.

If the symptoms persist beyond the course of one year, it is possible that they are the beginning of borderline personality disorder. An adolescent could fly into a rage when she finds out that her boyfriend is cheating on her and throw things around in her room. If she then gets into another relationship and they get into a fight, she might be angry at him, but not in a rage. If, on the other hand, she views this new relationship as yet another example of someone abandoning her and flies into another rage it would be important to check into what might be going on. In addition to borderline personality disorder there are other disorders that could lend themselves to anger outbursts of this nature.

ESSENTIAL

Symptoms of borderline personality disorder can overlap with symptoms of other disorders, especially disorders that are characteristic of adolescent years. These disorders could include oppositional defiant disorder, conduct disorder, and attention deficit hyperactivity disorder.

When to Seek Help

In general, any symptom that is persistent beyond an immediate stimulus is something to keep an eye on. When it remains for longer periods of time, it is something to have checked out. It would also be important to have the symptom checked out if it is a more severe symptom, such as self-harm or suicidal tendencies. When the symptoms persist beyond the person's ability to understand what she has done then they are likely driven by something that needs to be dealt with.

ALERT

Professionals are reluctant to provide a diagnosis of borderline personality too early, as they are afraid that the teen will be labeled with the disorder and stigmatized at a time when self-esteem is fragile to begin with. The worry is that the symptoms may change, indicating a different disorder, but the label will not.

Age can be another factor that can help with this determination. The older the adolescent, the more likely the symptoms could indicate borderline personality disorder. The younger the adolescent, the less likely the symptoms will be attributed to borderline personality disorder at that time. There are too many behaviors that can be attributed to normal developmental stages in childhood and adolescence that might mimic symptoms of borderline personality disorder. Yet, if the behaviors are present and remain persistent in some form, it is still important to seek help to determine what is going on.

Can a Child Be Diagnosed with BPD?

Children will not be diagnosed with borderline personality disorder. The personality is forming throughout childhood and adolescent years making it too difficult to determine this as a correct diagnosis. The misdiagnosis could cause stigma and prevent the true nature of the symptoms from being treated properly.

QUESTION

Does this mean children do not have borderline personality disorder? This is a question that is still under debate. It is possible that this disorder does not fully develop until after adolescence when hormone levels have changed. It is also possible that some children are developing the disorder but manifesting symptoms in a different way when they are younger.

Why Not Children?

The criteria set forth for diagnosis of borderline personality disorder often do not appear consistently in children in the quantity necessary for a clear diagnosis. In order to meet criteria, an individual must exhibit at least five of the nine characteristics listed in Appendix A for more than a year. In most cases, this is not found in children under the age of twelve.

ALERT

Since many disorders normally diagnosed in childhood can mimic the symptoms of borderline personality disorder, it is important for parents to ask the person diagnosing their child how the diagnosis was arrived at. Ask whether other disorders were considered too and request an explanation for why they were ruled out.

Children are often reacting to circumstances they do not understand, or mimicking what they see their parents doing. It is important to see how parents are handling their own emotions and determine whether the child is simply following what he sees the parents doing rather than independently exhibiting the symptoms.

Biological Component

The brain's limbic system is one of the areas of the brain most associated with development of borderline personality disorder. This system tends to go into overdrive during adolescence and puberty when hormonal changes occur. It is possible that early puberty could spur on early symptoms of borderline personality disorder.

The brain is not completely developed and personality is still progressing. It is possible that a diagnosis in childhood would change in adolescence or early adulthood after complete development has occurred. There is a danger in diagnosing this disorder too early and causing stigma to the child. The reactions of others could be traumatizing and spur on increased issues with self-esteem and self-harm.

ESSENTIAL

Children also exhibit symptoms differently from adults. They do not have the same understanding of what they are saying or doing and have not yet developed socially correct inhibitions to the extent an adult should.

Other Issues It Might Be

Children often exhibit symptoms similar to those in borderline personality disorder for different disorders. Symptoms such as inappropriate moodiness, self-destruction, high impulsivity, aggression, anger, and fear of rejection could be linked to other disorders that could include conduct disorder, attention deficit hyperactivity disorder, depression, anxiety, obsessive-compulsive disorder, and posttraumatic stress disorder.

They might also have problems with their environment that can cause adverse reactions. The death of a family member, a divorce, or a move to a different place could cause problems in adjustment. Adjustment disorder is often used to classify various symptoms that occur in times of change and stress, but then gradually disappear with time and return to normalcy. Children can have more than one disorder, and the symptoms of the combined disorders could mimic more of the symptoms of borderline personality disorder.

Borderline Personality Disorder and
Substance Abuse

CHAPTER 14

Borderline Personality Disorder Paired with Other Disorders

Borderline personality disorder is often paired with other disorders. Many times a person with borderline personality disorder will seek to self-medicate with alcohol or another substance. There is a high comorbidity with mood and anxiety disorders, and abuse is a common part of their history.

Borderline Personality Disorder and Substance Abuse

There is a high degree of substance abuse in people with borderline personality disorder. The symptoms they are experiencing with this disorder can often cause them to self-medicate in some way. They go through periods of agitation, anxiety, and depression and might become overwhelmed with the feelings. They become less able to handle pressure as pressure builds, which could cause them to turn to things that can help them block out the pain.

Appeal of Drugs and Alcohol

People who have borderline personality disorder often find themselves in situations they have no way to cope with. For them the pain they are feeling is very real and very consuming. They look for any escape or distraction they can find. The nature of the disorder often leads them to compulsive behaviors such as risky sexual behavior and overspending to distract them and make them feel better. Oftentimes these behaviors succeed in making matters worse, which leads to a need for other forms of compulsion.

Comorbidity is the presence of two different disorders at the same time. Each disorder requires treatment for that specific disorder, normally at the same time.

People with this disorder often have addictive traits to begin with that cause them to rely on and repeat behaviors in times of stress. Drugs and alcohol fall into place very easily, including prescription drugs. The euphoric feeling they initially experience promotes a need for more. They have a hard time regulating this need and tend to think more is better.

Prescription Medications

Prescription medications can become dangerous in the hands of people with borderline personality disorder. Their addictive personality causes them to overuse and rely on any medication to feel better. They do not want to experience any type of pain, and they need an instant fix to get rid of it. They will take the medicine as much as they need without regard to the instructions on the bottle.

Their symptoms of depression and anxiety could allow them to get a prescription to deal with these symptoms. Since these symptoms are only part of the problem, the rest of the issues with borderline personality disorder are left untreated and overmedication results as they try to feel better. In most cases the overmedication results in feeling worse, which prompts the need for additional substance use to counteract the negative results.

ALERT

People with borderline personality disorder often do not recognize the danger of prescription medications and might hoard them for use in suicide attempts. They might do this to manipulate someone or as a serious suicide attempt. If the medicines are from earlier injuries or are older, get rid of them after establishing that they are no longer needed for a legitimate condition, or if they are prescribed to someone else.

Relationships and Substance Abuse

People who have borderline personality disorder often have a hard time dealing with perceived rejection and abandonment. They do not like to be alone and experience intense emotions when they are in or ending a relationship. These feelings can cause them to turn to substances as a means of coping with the rejection and anxiety. Their choice of mates in relationships could present new opportunities for use.

They are more likely to be drawn to others with addictive personalities and will often associate with others who are substance and alcohol users. Together they might use the substance to enhance sexual experiences or to have fun and do things they wouldn't normally do. The substance might remove inhibitions, allowing them to be the life of the party. They can feel more comfortable in social situations.

While people with borderline personality disorder might seem happy and confident on the outside, they are often fearful and nervous on the inside. They suffer from low self-esteem and worry that others will not like them or will reject them. The substance use can make them feel braver and less anxious in social situations. They might think they need the substance in order to make friends or begin relationships.

FACT

People with both borderline personality disorder and substance abuse are more likely to maintain borderline symptoms after treatment. The substance abuse makes treatment harder and less effective and must be treated as an independent entity in order to produce positive results.

Treatment

Treatment needs to address both borderline personality disorder and substance abuse as two distinct disorders. When treatment focuses only on borderline issues the substance abuse symptoms can remain and cause relapse of borderline symptoms. The substance abuse is a means of maintaining an addictive lifestyle that clouds rational thought and keeps the person from dealing with the discomfort and unhappiness of the borderline symptoms. Treatment often works on both disorders at the same time. Some methods will overlap for both disorders, while others will be more specific for one or the other.

Borderline Personality Disorder and Mood Disorders

There is a high incidence of borderline personality disorder accompanied by mood disorders, which are often confused with bipolar disorder. Depressive symptoms are present as part of borderline personality disorder more often than not and is normally associated with feelings of anger, shame, loneliness, and emptiness in borderline patients.

Features

The symptoms of both disorders overlap, which makes it hard to determine which disorder is which. Borderline personality disorder is an emotional regulation disorder that has depressive episodes within the emotional swings. Mood disorders also have symptoms of mood swings and regulation issues. There are similarities in how these symptoms manifest, and there are some differences that can help distinguish which disorder it is.

People with both borderline personality disorder and substance abuse are more likely to maintain borderline symptoms after treatment. The substance abuse makes treatment harder and less effective and must be treated as an independent entity in order to produce positive results.

As many as 96 percent of people with borderline personality disorder meet criteria for mood disorders also. About 83 percent were comorbid with major depressive disorder, and around 39 percent were comorbid with dysthymic disorder.

Depressive disorders can have mood swings that go from elation and grandiosity to deep depression and feelings of hopelessness. Borderline mood swings can present the same range, although most swings are downward in reaction to fear of abandonment. Although both can come up rather quickly, depressive moods tend to remain steady for a period of time and cycle from one end of the mood spectrum to the other. This can distinguish one from the other, but when the two are together it might be a bit harder to determine.

Could It Be Both?

The comorbid rate between borderline personality disorder and mood disorders is high. This makes it harder to determine cases where a mood disorder is not present. The mood swings for borderline personality disorder comorbid with depression seem to be different. Depression is normally associated with feelings of sadness and guilt, while depression linked with borderline personality disorder seems to be associated more with anger and shame.

People with borderline personality disorder comorbid with a mood disorder might exhibit symptoms of boredom and restlessness. They are often intensely lonely when they have a depressive episode. The episodes in borderline personality disorder are normally the result of a relationship loss. People with mood disorders can experience symptoms of depression at any time. There does not need to be a trigger. The episodes in borderline personality disorder can last for hours rather than the typical days or weeks in mood disorder swings.

Treatment Issues

It is harder to treat patients with both borderline personality disorder and a mood disorder. The combined symptoms can also increase risk of self-harm and suicidality. As such, people with both disorders are harder to treat and have lower success rates. There are also indications that people who have both borderline personality disorder and a mood disorder are at higher risk for substance abuse disorders.

Treatment success seems to be one way. When the symptoms of depression in borderline personality disorder are treated they also seem to lift the symptoms of depression. Yet any substance abuse disorder issues would need to be treated as well.

ESSENTIAL

Studies indicate that children of parents with both borderline personality disorder and major depressive disorder are more likely to develop both disorders as they age. It is unclear whether the main issue is genetic or environmental due to parenting problems—or a combination of both.

Borderline Personality Disorder and Anxiety Disorders

People with borderline personality disorder are comorbid with anxiety disorders almost as often as mood disorders. Symptoms between the two are similar and can be confusing since the overriding fear for those with borderline personality disorder can produce panic reactions. The fear of abandonment can produce strong fear symptoms including increased heart rate and racing thoughts.

How Are They Different?

Anxiety disorders present with persistent anxiety that can interfere with the ability to lead a productive life, can produce constant fear, and can cause people to avoid certain social situations. Anxiety in borderline personality disorder is specific to the fears that underlie the disorder itself, mainly focused on abandonment and rejection.

ESSENTIAL

Separation anxiety disorder is a childhood anxiety disorder characterized by intense fear of abandonment by caregivers. The child will exhibit symptoms of panic when the caregiver leaves, and will show extreme symptoms in anticipation of the leave-taking. Children normally outgrow the disorder in later childhood.

The duration of the anxiety episodes with borderline personality disorder are related to the stimulus causing the fear. If the threat of abandonment is removed, the fear eases. Anxiety swings are quick. With an anxiety disorder the anxiety remains constant, excessive, and uncontrollable.

Stress

Stress is a catalyst in both disorders. As stress increases, symptoms in both disorders increase along with it. While borderline personality disorder will show stress through mood swings and anger reactions, the anxiety disorder will show symptoms of panic. The symptoms of borderline will have a tendency to burn out or be related to other aspects of the person's life, while the anxiety reaction will remain and show physical symptoms such as nausea and dizziness.

Borderline Personality Disorder and Abuse

Borderline personality disorder has a dual relationship with abuse. In some cases abuse has occurred in the past for many people diagnosed with borderline. The person with borderline might also be an abuser. Abuse can come in the form of verbal abuse, emotional abuse, psychological abuse, physical abuse, and/or sexual abuse. Incidences of domestic violence are high when one partner has borderline personality disorder.

Verbal Abuse

Verbal abuse is one of the most common forms of abuse in borderline personality disorder. Words can come out without thought and cause pain in an instant. Mothers with borderline could tell their children they hate them or that they are monsters. She might threaten to leave them—a potent threat since it is likely their biggest fear.

Children who experience this type of abuse or are subject to other forms of verbal abuse by nonborderline parents are likely to develop low self-esteem. They become fearful of social situations and have trouble attaching to others. They increase their risk of developing some form of mental health issue.

QUESTION

Why is verbal abuse so pervasive?
Verbal abuse can sit in a child's head for long periods of time, playing over and over again. There is nothing tangible to see and look at as abuse, so the child takes it as the truth and begins to believe they are the way they are described in the abuse. It is also a sign that they are unlovable by the very people they should be able to count on, removing more of their security.

People with borderline personality disorder are often in relationships that are abusive. They have low self-esteem and do not feel they deserve good things. As a result, they tend to place themselves into situations where others verify these thoughts. They accept it when others tell them they are no good or unlovable. They could go into a rage reaction, but will stay in the relationship and believe that what was said is true.

Physical Abuse

Borderline personality disorder often produces strong rage reactions that can produce violence in relation to the anger. Threat of abandonment can also promote abusive reactions. The self-doubt and pain can manifest in abuse of others. When someone with borderline lashes out at another, it could actually be aimed at himself.

People with borderline personality disorder are also more likely to be in abusive relationships. They are desperate to be in relationships and often choose unwisely. They tend to choose others with mental health issues themselves, causing more dysfunction in the relationship. If both partners have issues dealing with problems and working on relationships it is possible to have two people who are abusive toward each other in some way.

Unfortunately, self-esteem is so low in people with borderline personality disorder that they will choose to stay in a bad relationship rather than have no relationship. Abuse often escalates as a relationship continues, and the danger increases.

Abuse as a Child

One issue that has been shown in a number of borderline personality disorder cases is abuse as a child. Children who were abused or abandoned seem to have developed a form of arrested development attributed to the development of borderline personality disorder. It leaves them unable to interact in age-appropriate ways in social situations. This psychic pain is thought to be what the person relives when he is older and in his own abusive relationships.

There is a part of the child that does not develop appropriately in certain individuals. When this happens the inappropriate behaviors and misunderstandings of social norms seem to occur. It also sets up triggers that activate rage when they are older.

Wounds Carry Over

Children who experience abuse or abandonment carry this baggage within them. It remains throughout development and wears down their confidence and self-esteem. The fear and pain in childhood promote the fight-or-flight reactions in later life. The fears of childhood build and present them with the very real fears they experience as adults—even if these fears make no sense to others, or are unfounded. This is the ignition switch that sets off the anger reactions in many cases.

ESSENTIAL

An abused child's arrested development causes a lack of true understanding in how to relate to others. When she does relate to others, it is often an extension of the early abuse.

It is also the prompt that pushes them to enter into abusive relationships and remain there. The threat of abandonment and being alone is much greater than the threat of physical danger for them. They will put up with what they need to put up with in order to remain in the relationship.

Special Issues with BPD and Other Disorders

Borderline personality disorder encompasses a great variety of symptoms that can be related to other disorders as well. The symptoms in borderline are often intense and quick to come up and then leave. Symptoms of the other disorders are more specialized in one area and tend to remain whether there is an issue present to initiate them or not.

Treatment Problems

Treatment of both borderline personality disorder and another disorder can be challenging. The presence of another disorder can complicate treatment and decrease success rates. Borderline symptoms tend to decrease with age, yet the other disorders do not. Additionally, each of the disorders mentioned are highly comorbid with substance abuse.

Substance abuse is one of the stickiest issues to treat and has a high relapse rate. The substance abuse can mask other symptoms and create resistance to treatment. Substance abuse can cause a dependency that is hard to break because it helps ease the symptoms of borderline, even if it is only for a very short time.

Mood disorders cause additional problems that increase risk of harm and suicidality. They can enhance the feelings of hopelessness in borderline personality disorder. Yet symptoms of mood disorders seem to dissipate when the symptoms of borderline are dealt with.

Anxiety issues are interconnected. The anxieties caused by childhood abuse or the developed fears of abandonment add to the general anxiety of an anxiety disorder. Treatment using cognitive behavioral methods and therapies that deal with the mind/behavior connection seem to help with this connection.

Childhood

Mood and anxiety disorders often begin in childhood and can be linked to abuse issues in some cases as well. These disorders might precede the development of borderline personality disorder and the symptoms that occur might mask the additional disorder. These disorders are precursors to substance abuse disorders and can produce incidents of self-harm, such as cutting and burning.

By the time the individual has outgrown childhood and has entered into an age where borderline can be diagnosed, the other issues might already have been diagnosed. This could cause confusion for therapists as they might mistake symptoms of borderline as exacerbated symptoms of the mood or anxiety disorder. The symptoms could be excused as changes occurring as a part of aging and changes in circumstances. Early signs might not remain static. They could develop as the individual develops and interacts with others. It is important to look at the early signs as an initial warning, but recognize that they can evolve.

CHAPTER 15

Early Signs

Borderline personality disorder symptoms are often labeled as signs of other disorders, such as mood or anxiety disorders. But while many of the symptoms are similar, personality disorder symptoms are more pervasive and it often seems as though the person exhibiting the symptoms does not realize she is doing so. There is confusion, as this person believes her behaviors are normal and others are doing things to provoke her. It is a good idea to get professional help when personality characteristics are carried to an extreme, last over long periods of time, and interfere with normal daily function. A person who becomes angry when someone hits her car with a baseball would likely calm down over the course of the next day as she begins to deal with the aftermath. Someone who continues to express anger for weeks and mentions that the other person did it on purpose might have a problem.

Early Signs That Might Lead to BPD

While children cannot be diagnosed with borderline personality disorder, there are some signs in childhood that might carry through to that diagnosis. Borderline does not just appear one day; it often is the result of different diagnoses or problems at home and school that drive the family to the edge.

Other Diagnoses That Lead to Borderline Personality Disorder

While childhood diagnoses of mental health disorders do not doom a child to the development of borderline personality disorder, they might be the precursors in some situations. Children who experience mental health issues when they are young might be primed to continue these issues with borderline. The disorders themselves do not lead to borderline, but they could be the initial diagnoses for borderline symptoms that begin to appear in younger years.

Borderline personality disorder is often diagnosed after years of struggle with a child or adolescent who is defiant, overly emotional, prone to rages, and does not recognize that she has a problem. These children often perceive themselves as victims of the behaviors of others. Yet they might well have picked up another diagnosis or two along the way.

Professionals do not rush to diagnose children with mental health disorders. There are only a handful that are diagnosed in children, including mood disorders, anxiety disorders, oppositional defiant disorder, attention deficit hyperactivity disorder, and pervasive development disorders. Children with these diagnoses receive treatment, and in many cases the diagnosis can eventually be removed. In other cases, however, the diagnosis remains and as the child ages other diagnoses are added to the list.

Mood and Anxiety Disorders

More and more children are being diagnosed with mood and anxiety disorders. When children experience some type of trauma or abuse in early life they tend to develop mood and/or anxiety disorders rather quickly as a means of coping. They might have trouble in school and break down in tears when they get an answer wrong. They might not be able to participate in certain types of special events because they become too fearful.

One child could not go on nature walks because she was terrified of bees. Another child had to be removed from the classroom numerous times each day because she broke down in tears with her head on her desk. Children as young as seven or eight years old can exhibit these symptoms.

Mood and anxiety disorders can also develop without the presence of environmental trauma. There might be a genetic component that is activated early in the child's life, or the child could have problems perceiving situations correctly. When this type of thing happens, it is possible that deeper issues are at work and might continue. Children who have experienced some type of trauma or abuse and then receive treatment are often able to work through the issues and lose the diagnosis as the traumatic environment and stressors are removed. The child is taught to learn how to cope with stressful situations, and the environment around the child becomes more supportive.

ESSENTIAL

In many cases, children who do not do well in treatment and continue with the symptoms of the disorders of childhood often go on to develop substance abuse disorders as a means of coping with the psychological pain they are feeling and cannot get rid of. This could be the result of biological issues that are still malfunctioning combined with an environment that might still be dysfunctional. One or both of these factors can contribute to the continuance of the disorder.

In other cases, however, the mood or anxiety symptoms do not abate. When this happens, symptoms tend to grow and develop as the child gets older. The child might add a diagnosis in adolescence if behaviors continue to worsen. Some children are simply resistant to all treatment efforts.

Attention Deficit Hyperactivity Disorder

Attention deficit hyperactivity disorder (ADHD) has been a diagnosis of contention for years. Many children are accurately diagnosed with this disorder. There are some, however, who proposed that this disorder is overdiagnosed. The broad range of symptoms provided in this diagnosis can create a situation where children can be diagnosed with ADHD simply because the professional realizes there is a problem and cannot place it anywhere else. It allows for treatment and supervision in order to determine what is going on.

ADHD symptoms can run the gamut from trouble concentrating to trouble remaining still, to defiance to authority to problems understanding proper social norms. For some, the ADHD diagnosis is removed as the child ages and learns to cope better. They learn proper social skills and are able to function better in school. For others, however, the diagnosis remains.

QUESTION

Aren't there effective medications for ADHD?
Some medicines have been shown to help with some of the symptoms of ADHD, mainly the hyperactivity and attention elements. For people who have this disorder there is also a need to learn about proper social skills and anger control issues.

ADHD is often associated with oppositional defiant disorder, conduct disorder, and substance abuse disorders. Children who have a more lasting diagnosis tend to have trouble recognizing the proper way to behave in social situations and do not recognize social boundaries. They tend to get in trouble at school because they are disruptive and might have emotional outbursts. They also tend to get into fights due to uncontrollable anger and aggressive behaviors.

Oppositional Defiant Disorder and Conduct Disorder

Oppositional defiant disorder is a disorder characterized by opposition to authority, angry aggressive behaviors that are uncontrollable, and an inability to identify with the victims of their anger. Children who are diagnosed with this disorder are often also diagnosed with attention deficit hyperactivity disorder.

This disorder is normally diagnosed later in childhood, around eight or nine years of age. These children can be destructive and do not recognize authority. They will do things purposely to defy adults. If they perceive that someone has wronged them in some way, they are determined to get back at that person. The child often blows these perceived wrongs out of proportion and will go overboard in response. Any harm that comes to another will not bring about a sympathetic or guilty response by the child. The child will not recognize the pain of another.

In some children, oppositional defiant disorder ages out when they reach adolescent years and begin to follow social rules. For others, however, the disorder can become conduct disorder. Conduct disorder is a more extreme version of oppositional defiant disorder. The acts become more violent. The child tends to enjoy inflicting pain on others. There is no remorse, as the child sees the blame as belonging to the victim.

Into Adolescence

Each of the disorders described presents some symptoms that are also characteristic of borderline personality disorder. It is important to note that children exhibiting these symptoms are in early developmental stages where there is less ability to regulate emotions. Yet some children, as noted, do not grow out of the diagnosis. For these children the symptoms continue and become worse in adolescence.

In adolescence the symptoms can become more pronounced. In many cases the addition of some form of substance abuse diagnosis could also occur. Again, some of these disorders will age out as the adolescent continues to grow and develop and learns to respond properly. If this is not the case, and the content of the symptoms continue to grow, it is possible that they are resistant because the wrong disorder has been diagnosed, or another disorder is developing.

Confusion

As noted earlier, is hard to diagnose borderline personality disorder in younger adolescents because they are going through developmental stages where symptoms would mimic borderline as part of the natural progression. Symptoms that persist and are more pronounced than what would normally be expected of a teenager should be taken seriously. During this time, episodes of self-harm or even suicidality could come out. When this happens, it is important to be sure that the right diagnosis is in effect. Adolescents are often trying to find their way and figure out who they are. Their personality is still completing development and they are still learning how they feel most comfortable. Yet extremes are warning signs.

Some signs that a teen is having problems would include a drastic change in friends, becoming isolated, failing grades, and other unexplained behaviors. As a rule of thumb, if a parent feels something might be wrong, chances are something is wrong and it should be checked out. It might be something minor, but it is important to check as soon as things start to change and keep an eye on how the teen progresses. Contact teachers and friends and gather information.

Identity Problems

Older children and adolescents are trying to develop an identity. This identity is often developed as a result of early childhood experiences, parenting style, and the attachments that were formed as infants. As the young child progresses, peers and teachers also influence identity development. When children are raised in homes where there is abuse or neglect, identity problems can arise. Identity problems can also arise in loving and supportive households, yet these problems are often an indication of mental health issues to come.

In Abusive or Neglectful Homes

Homes in which abuse and neglect occur are homes that are normally dysfunctional, chaotic, and filled with anger. Children do not develop secure attachments to caregivers and do not see the world as a safe place to explore. They learn to be fearful and suspicious, and often have problems with self-esteem.

Children with a weak sense of trust have trouble believing in others or forming ideals. If they have not been encouraged to be autonomous they are reluctant to engage in exploration. They fail to become industrious or search for interests and skills.

Self-esteem is developed as children learn and grow through experimentation, making mistakes, and succeeding. When children fear to make mistakes, they learn to stop trying. They often receive negative feedback that gives them the impression it is their fault and that they cannot do things right. The child relies on the feedback of the caregivers and does not develop a proper sense of self. They fear to do anything other than what the caregivers have told them to do. They thus become an extension of the caregiver's identity.

In a Loving Household

As mentioned previously, while abuse is prevalent in reports of patients with borderline personality disorder it is not present in all cases. It is possible that the abusive household increases the risk of developing borderline personality disorder, but it is not a required cause. Some people develop borderline personality disorder in spite of everything their family does to help them.

In normal loving households, children are provided with support and unconditional love. They are encouraged to grow and explore. They are allowed to make mistakes and learn from them without penalty. Some children in this type of household, however, simply do not develop identity well. Their perceptions of their home situation could be off. There are cases where the child perceives the parents as more abusive and less supportive than they truly are and he reacts to these perceptions. He might have problems recognizing good and bad, and could develop black-and-white thinking. Efforts by parents and family members to help such children are often rebuffed, and problems are turned back on them. Nothing is ever good enough to make them feel better. They become stuck and show little autonomy or initiative.

Identity Diffusion

Identity achievement is a stage of development in which identity is in formation and as new concepts and experiences come about, new facets of identity begin to emerge in healthy development. During later adolescence and early childhood identity status is a large issue. The development of identity is based on the person's ability to explore, think, and resolve the similarity between the ideal self you would like to be and the real self you actually are. Identity diffusion is a status in which there is no firm commitment to values and goals and no active efforts to develop them.

Identity and personality tend to interact as they develop. For individuals with an open-minded approach this development goes much easier. A secure family base allows the adolescent to feel confident about expanding his world. For adolescents who have not developed a healthy separation from parents and who do not have warm, open communication at home, confidence is replaced with fear.

ALERT

It is important to realize that parents can do everything right and their child may still have problems with identity. The biological components of borderline personality disorder indicate that there are different issues within the brain that prevent this person from seeing things and understanding them correctly. While abuse is certainly a large factor in some cases of borderline personality disorder, other cases have no abuse whatsoever.

Identity Confusion

When the teen is unable to form a proper sense of identity, identity confusion can result. He might appear shallow and directionless and have a great deal of trouble forming and maintaining relationships, especially intimate relationships. These teens have no firm sense of self and tend to have problems resolving disputes and solving problems.

FACT

Females normally score lower than males when evaluating their sense of self-worth, and are more likely to report a decrease in self-esteem during teen years.

When identity confusion occurs, teens do not go through positive changes in self-esteem. They do not form solid friendships, and they see relationships as conditional. They fear support will be withheld unless they meet high standards and expectations set by others. They become what others expect them to be rather than progressing naturally to their true identity. This can lead to inner turmoil and emotional instability.

Emotional Instability

Emotional instability is a strong characteristic of borderline personality disorder. People are unable to regulate emotions properly and often unable to recognize proper emotions for proper situations. They become very upset at issues others might not even notice. The inability to form proper identity and positive self-esteem cause them to become quickly defensive. Yet emotional instability is not completely a result of environmental circumstances. The perceptions and the overreactions are often the result of brain processes.

Emotional Regulation and the Brain

Emotion is a brain function, but not a thinking function. It has a basis in the chemistry primarily of the limbic system of the brain. In most cases there are two different pathways that govern emotion. The first pathway goes through the amygdala, creating a stronger, quicker response. This quicker route is often used for fear or anger responses. The slower route goes through the neocortex, and here emotion is regulated by thought.

People with borderline personality disorder often have problems regulating emotions. Many of the emotions take the quick route through the amygdala. This bypasses normal regulation processes and creates reactions that might not be appropriate for the situation. The emotions might be out of proportion, or they might be different from what we would normally expect.

People with borderline personality disorder not only have trouble expressing or controlling the expression of their emotions, they also have trouble making sense of their own emotions. It is hard for them at times to distinguish between different types of emotions and to understand which would be appropriate for the situation at hand. Thus, someone with borderline personality disorder might express anger instead of disappointment when she finds out that her favorite team did not win. This anger would probably be out of proportion for the situation. It would also likely occur more frequently than one game by one team at one time. While there would likely not be a predictable pattern, there would be situations that would be more likely to provoke stronger emotions than the situation warrants.

Negative Processing

Negative emotions seem more dominant, with sadness and crying also occurring in an uncontrolled manner. Since the amygdala is normally responsible for fight-or-flight reactions, it is also more closely associated with negative emotions. The quick processing and impulsive responses are characteristic of borderline personality disorder. This negative processing can often be traced back to early childhood. In some cases it is the result of abandonment or abuse, while in other cases it is simply a part of the forming personality.

In either case, negative information is processed much quicker, leaving little time for thoughts. Reactions are almost instantaneous due to the impulsive nature of borderline. The person involved often does not realize or admit to fault in any overreaction, normally blaming it on someone else. Someone else caused her to react that way.

It Is Not My Fault

People with borderline personality disorder have a very hard time recognizing when they have done something wrong, as they normally process it as someone else doing something to them. They are often playing the role of victim. When they are the victim, they feel that they have every right to be upset. Their low self-esteem and the trouble they have recognizing proper social norms cause them to place blame in others.

This often causes great confusion and frustration on the part of others. They cannot defend themselves, because when they do it escalates the situation. Even if they choose to defend themselves, they are met with a brick wall. The person with borderline personality disorder will not recognize that she has done anything wrong and will become angry when others push the point.

Situations That Explode

Certain situations are likely to cause emotional reactions. Any situation that has to do with fear of abandonment or rejection will almost always cause an instant overreaction. Emotions will run the gamut from fear to anger to desperation. In each case blame will be placed on the other person. As that person tries to defend himself, the situation escalates.

People are placed in a lose-lose situation. They cannot defend themselves or point out that the other person is wrong because it will escalate the situation, yet they are accused of doing things they did not do. When this happens they naturally become frustrated and often decide to leave. This escalates the situation even further because the fear of abandonment has been realized. At this point things are likely to get out of hand and the emotional reaction either results in some form of self-harm or words or actions designed to hurt the other person.

The person with borderline personality disorder often does not have a clear sense of self, and identity is not formed correctly. Since this is the case, any situation that might put into question her identity or further damage her self-esteem will cause heavy reactions. People with borderline personality disorder do not realize that they have not formed proper identity. One area where this confusion seems to become evident is in sexual orientation and sexual identity.

Conflict with Sexual Orientation

The inability to form a proper identity can translate to gender identity too. As children age into adolescence, they tend to encounter more gender stereotyping. Puberty causes differences in appearance and body function. Sexual drives begin to become more of an issue. Thoughts about gender and gender identity become more prevalent.

Gender Stereotypes

Gender stereotypes are attitudes and behaviors that are formed in a given society. They are reinforced throughout childhood by parents, other caregivers, teachers, and peers. Some of the stereotypes can be overemphasized by parents. A man might want his boy to grow up to be strong and dominant, discouraging sensitivity and warmth. A woman might overemphasize looks and passivity in a daughter. In some cases, the media creates a larger influence on how gender identity develops in these children.

Television shows often portray distinct roles for males and females. Males are normally shown as strong, aggressive, and capable. Females, on the other hand, are seen as nurturing caretakers. In some shows, they are seen as sex objects. Sex itself might be seen as casual enjoyment with no strings or pain attached.

FACT

Homosexuality is ten times more common in males with borderline personality disorder, and six times more common in females with borderline as compared to those in the general population.

In each case, the stereotypes and impressions presented tend to lock teens into certain identity paths. If they do not feel comfortable on these paths, it becomes a problem. For people with borderline personality disorder, identity is already an issue, and the additional pressure to conform to certain gender stereotypes can cause confusion and dissonance. Thus, development of problems with gender identity can begin.

Gender Identity Disorder

Gender identity disorder occurs when a person believes that he or she is actually a member of the opposite sex trapped in the wrong body. The person does not feel comfortable with the sex he or she was born with. This issue has been linked to borderline personality disorder. While the reason is not yet clear, there is a higher incidence of gender identity issues in people diagnosed with borderline personality disorder. In some cases, people who believe they are living as the wrong sex lost some of this belief as they were treated for borderline.

ALERT

It is important to be sure that borderline personality symptoms are not the cause of gender discomfort before taking permanent steps to alter gender.

Sexual Addictions

People with borderline disorder also have a high incidence of sexual addictions. They are more likely to engage in abnormal sexual activity and promiscuity and seek varied means of sexual gratification. They are often sexually assertive, are more preoccupied with sex, and experience more depression and dissatisfaction in relation to sexual encounters or the lack thereof.

QUESTION

Why does my friend with BPD take so many risks with sex and multiple partners?
Sex is often used to fill empty parts of her life and keep her busy. It might be used as a way to calm suffering. And since most of these encounters end poorly, it might also be a form of self-punishment comparable to cutting or burning.

Sex can often be used as a means of relieving some of the pain associated with borderline. It can be like a drug for the person involved in it. It might be a means of preventing abandonment and maintaining involvement. Unfortunately, it can lead to some dangerous consequences, such as sexually transmitted diseases, unwanted pregnancy, rape, and physical abuse.

Alarming Behaviors

People with borderline personality disorder are highly impulsive and often exhibit dangerous behaviors. They can become very violent, posing a threat to both themselves and to others through intense physical contact or throwing things. They do not have a normal sense of inhibition and social regulation, so they tend to go to extremes in their behaviors, such as overspending, overuse of substances, reckless driving, and other thrill-seeking behaviors.

Overspending

Overspending can occur for a couple of different reasons. People with borderline personality disorder might spend money in an effort to gain enjoyment for a period of time. They might do this by gaining objects, normally clothing, accessories, and expensive foods. When they start to feel bad about themselves, this spending gives them a chance to boost their self-esteem. They feel better in new clothes or with a new purse, or might feel like they are someone more important if they have expensive wine or food. For a short period of time these new possessions might ease some of the loneliness they are feeling.

They might also overspend in an effort to gain friendships and romantic relationships. When the relationships first began they normally become overattentive and might shower their new friend with gifts. These gifts can be costly in order to impress. They might see this as the way relationships are conducted.

ESSENTIAL

Overspending often leads to further complications, debt, and poor credit. This, in turn, leads to additional feelings of low self-esteem and anger with themselves. They then go out and spend money on things to feel better again—which causes more debt and more stress.

Substance Use

Substance use is common in people with a personality disorder. They often use this means to escape the pain and loneliness they are feeling. They might also use it as a way of increasing self-esteem and feeling more comfortable and effective in social settings. The problem is that use often gets out of control.

They often do not know when to stop, and if a little helps, they figure a lot will help more. People with borderline personality disorder have been known to continuously overuse drugs and alcohol. They then do things that are dangerous or place themselves in situations that are dangerous while under the influence of the substance. They might become more violent, or might become the subject of violence themselves.

Reckless Driving and Other High-Risk Behaviors

People with borderline personality disorder often engage in high-risk behaviors. They might drive recklessly, exceed the speed limit, weave back and forth between lanes to pass other vehicles, or drive while intoxicated. In each of these situations they place themselves, their passengers, and others on the road at risk. They might do this to show off for friends, or they might do it if they are in the midst of a fit of rage. They are not normally patient people and do not like to sit behind slow drivers.

FACT

Chaos manufacture is a term used to describe when someone with borderline personality disorder promotes unnecessary chaos by creating or maintaining an environment of risk, destruction, confusion, or mess.

Other high-risk behaviors might include skydiving, bungee jumping, skateboarding, or other extreme sports that could cause physical danger. They are often thrill seekers who like to live life on the edge. Their impulsivity prevents them from thinking through the potential consequences of these behaviors, and their need to be liked prompts them to do things that gain attention. They might also engage in these behaviors in order to produce expressions of concern from others or to create confusion and chaos. These behaviors often leave loved ones wondering what to do.

CHAPTER 16

If Someone You Know Has Borderline Personality Disorder

Borderline personality disorder symptoms need to be taken seriously. While some symptoms can create confusion and frustration, others are more serious and pose a threat to health and even life. Roughly 4 percent of people in the United States have borderline personality disorder, and about 20 percent of the clinical psychiatric population has been diagnosed with this disorder. This means that about one in five people that have been diagnosed with a clinical mental health disorder have been diagnosed with borderline personality disorder. There also is a high morbidity rate, especially when symptoms of self-harm and suicide ideation or attempts are evident.

When to Intervene

Some behaviors and issues will be more important or more pressing than others. There will be times when it would be better to pick battles rather than try to fight on every front. Some issues will obviously be in need of intervention. If the person with borderline personality disorder is showing signs of self-harm, that would be a definite time to bring in professional help.

Problems Recognizing the Need for Intervention

It is not always easy to deal with someone who has borderline personality disorder on a daily basis. There are usually mood swings and impulsive acts that leave you wondering what to do. Relationships are not the only area where someone can become hot then cold. Someone with borderline personality disorder might also be prone to changing jobs often or even changing where he lives on a regular basis. People with BPD often have a hard time staying in one place and dealing with things when that initial perfect image goes away.

QUESTION

My son has not ever been able to hold down a job, punches holes in our walls when he gets angry, and goes out all night drinking. He does not think he has a problem, but I do. How can I be sure?
In most cases when a parent feels something is wrong with the child, there is something wrong. Trust your instincts and begin to write down all of the behaviors that concern you. Consult with a family physician, showing this person all of your concerns. An issue to consider is your child's age—if he is a legal adult, your options may be limited as to what you can do.

Sometimes people with borderline personality disorder have a need to hide behind a created public image that they might think leaves a good impression of them. This persona is hard to uphold for any length of time. When issues become more apparent and others begin to question it, it is often easier to leave than to stay and work things out. This creates situations where the person with borderline personality disorder moves from place to place or person to person. Those with a permanent relationship of some sort with the person often find themselves trying to play catch-up.

Self-Harm

Some forms of self-harm seem simply irritating, such as picking at or biting nails, scratching at scabs, or pulling hair. These behaviors do not seem dangerous to begin with, but if they increase in intensity or happen more often, they could become a problem. Fingers will start to show signs of pulled cuticles and scabs and open sores appear around the base of each nail. Minor cuts might keep coming back or fail to heal because the scabs are picked off before the wound is completely healed. Excessive hair pulling will become evident as some spots on the scalp might become thinner or even bald.

Self-harm can come in many different forms. It can be as individual as the person. It is not limited to cutting, burning, pulling hair, and other behaviors mentioned in this book. Anything that can cause any form of injury or discomfort could be considered self-harm.

In each case the behaviors are becoming more harmful and consistent. This is usually an outward symptom of internal thoughts and compulsions that are becoming stronger. If these thoughts continue to progress the behaviors could become worse and more harmful to self or others. The insecurities and low self-esteem begin to wear down the ability to think rationally. Minor mistakes become big deals that cause the person to overreact. In some way the forms of self-harm become a release. As the need for release escalates the form of self-harm could escalate too. Other forms of self-harm are either more severe right from the start or progress to that point. Cutting and burning are two of the most common methods people with borderline personality disorder use as a form of psychological release.

Problems with Intervention

People with borderline personality disorder often do not see a need for intervention. They do not recognize that they are doing anything wrong and become angry and defensive when others point it out. They often proceed to lay the blame on the other person. This tends to lead to a confrontation that completely sidetracks the conversation.

The distrustful nature of borderline personality disorder makes them less likely to believe what others are saying and trust that they are trying to help. They often treat attempts to help them suspiciously. They are also often paranoid and might feel that others are actually trying to hurt them or lock them up.

Finally, in most cases, they do not recognize that something is wrong and they do not want to stop their behaviors. They do not see that any of their behaviors are dangerous, and they are enjoying them. For them, some of these behaviors are a means of numbing some of the pain they feel. This makes it very hard for someone to express their concerns.

Expressing Your Concerns

Expressing concern about the behaviors is often a difficult task. People with borderline personality disorder do not think they are doing anything wrong and will not necessarily understand what is being said to them. Their first reaction is to protect their self-esteem and put the blame back on the other person. The next reaction is to become angry and defensive, which could lead to an episode of rage. By the time this episode is over, no one feels like expressing their concerns anymore. People are often too emotionally drained and intimidated by the reaction they received.

What to Do

The highly explosive nature of borderline personality disorder makes unpleasant conversations risky. They should be well thought out and delivered calmly. It is a good idea to have a plan in place and think about what problems might arise. Prepare for what might happen ahead of time.

It might be a good idea to express concerns as a family or with friends present. The person with borderline will likely try to put the speaker on the defensive through accusations, blame, and angry denials. When more than one person is present the others can offer support, so while one person is deflected another might not be pushed off track or bullied.

ESSENTIAL

Bullying is a common defense used by people with borderline personality disorder in order to get what they want or take control of the situation. It is a systematic behavior designed to assert physical, social, economic, or emotional control over another.

Timing

Once the plan is in place, wait for as good a time as possible to implement it and broach the subject. Timing is important. If the person is already agitated, the first words will likely set her off more and create more agitation. The situation could escalate before it begins.

A good time to plan it would be a time when others can be present and everyone is normally relaxed, like a family dinner or a night when everyone is home with no place to go. If someone seems rushed or begins to watch the clock the person will pick up on this and divert the conversation.

If the person is in the midst of regret after an episode of bad behavior, a conversation might begin as suggestions on things that might help with the issue of regret. If the person is actually in the hospital or jail as a result of some behavior, it would be a good time to enlist professional help in the conversation and proceed while she is still feeling the negative effects of her actions.

Getting a Professional to Help

In some cases the best plan of action is to enlist professional help right from the start. The professional will direct everyone involved in what to say and do and will become the focal point for the anger and denial that will come out. This person will be more likely to be able to identify the risk situations before they occur and head them off.

It is also helpful for family members and friends to have the help of a professional to learn how their own words and actions might contribute to the problems that are occurring and provide suggestions for ways to respond and cope with the issues, especially denial and confusion.

Dealing with Denial and Confusion

People with borderline personality disorder often retreat deep into denial when they are confronted with situations they do not know how to deal with or do not want to deal with. This denial is a defense mechanism that helps them avoid truths they do not want to face. When in denial, the person allows himself to believe that some fact, experience, or circumstance does not exist.

Getting to the Roots

Denial is very hard to cut through. This defense is often built up over a long period of time and works to prevent psychological pain. It is often the result of deep-seated fear and pain, often from childhood and stages of child development. Children who have experienced abuse or traumatic experiences at home often have many issues relating to self-esteem that they bury in order to survive. They might secretly blame themselves for whatever has occurred and hide from that fact in an effort to preserve what little self-esteem they might have.

People with borderline personality disorder have breaks with reality and do not see their own hand in a situation. They manipulate situations so that they look like the victim. Memories can be distorted based on perceptions that are focused on this thought process. It is important to leave accusations of abuse to professionals and withhold judgment.

Others who have not been abused have perceptions of pain that has occurred as a result of what others have done to them. Something does not necessarily have to be done to a person in order to present deep-seated issues that bring about denial. In some cases, the person realizes at some level that he has done something wrong and seeks to bury that.

Self-Esteem and Self-Image

In many cases, the issues of denial are designed to protect a person from damage to self-esteem or self-image. People with borderline personality disorder have a hard time with self-esteem and do not have a firm self-identity. Denial keeps them from realizing these facts.

When people are in denial they are able to ignore what they do not want to deal with. When these issues are a threat to their self-esteem, the denial keeps them from feeling worse about themselves and their reality. Getting to the root of this allows people to work on building back up their self-esteem by facing the issues that keep holding them back. In most cases, the person has a problem facing reality. She has built up many walls to keep her from having to face the fear that she is unlovable and unworthy. In reality, the denial acts to push others away.

People with BPD do not wish to see their self-image tarnished in any way, because it is too fragile. When someone challenges their issues of denial, they see this as a direct attack on their self-image. They might secretly believe that the image they present to others is real yet suspect deep down inside that it is not. They do not want this exposed. They think they are able to fool others and often try to fool themselves.

Cutting Through Confusion

The conflict between true self and public image often creates confusion, as people with borderline personality disorder react in erratic ways. They do not see things as others do and have a distorted view of self. People who are trying to help them often become confused, as the disharmony between real self and ideal self conflict with each other. The person with BPD can become so completely absorbed in the public self that she is portraying to each person that the other people have little knowledge of her real self.

This can create distortions in thinking and reactions as concerns are discussed. It is important to remain patient and supportive throughout any conversation. It is likely that confusion will result as the responses come back from both the real self and the public self. There is no solid base for the person to work from, and the responses are based on her defenses and her perceptions of what is occurring.

Breaks in reality can occur, especially when people with BPD are stressed. When they are confronted with another's concerns it often causes stress. These breaks can cause what seems like a split personality.

Case Study: Carl

Carl went through a series of angry episodes that resulted in hospitalization for deep lacerations caused by slicing his arms and wrists. His parents were on heightened alert when he came home from the hospital and jumped at any sign of possible danger. The police did not believe the parents at first, and actually thought that abuse was going on. This changed when they were called to the residence and saw what Carl had done to himself. They were now ready to support the parents if more calls came in.

Carl's parents thought it might be a good idea to get away and take a vacation to let Carl settle down and have some relaxation. They decided to go to Florida and spend a week at the beach. The first couple of days went very well. After that, however, Carl became bored with hanging out with his parents and decided to go off on his own. He disappeared for two days. When he returned, his parents were distraught and angry. They had called the police to check on him, but the police were reluctant to file a missing persons report since Carl was eighteen years old.

Carl and his parents argued. He accused his parents of trying to put him in jail and get rid of him. They vehemently denied this and tried to convince him that it was just not true. These denials set Carl off even more. He went into the bathroom and slammed the door and locked it. They were not able to get in.

ESSENTIAL

Gaslighting is a common occurrence with people who have borderline personality disorder. It is a method of convincing people who have a grasp on reality that their understanding is actually false.

Fearful that he was again slicing his arms and wrists, they called the police. Carl was in the bathroom raging and hitting the walls. They could hear the banging and became even more frantic. When the police got there, however, Carl settled down. He walked calmly out of the bathroom and said he went in there to get away from his parents because they would not stop yelling at him. He said he was afraid they were going to hit him. Carl's parents spent the next few hours at the police station trying to explain the true situation.

What Should You Say?

It is not easy to think about what to say when dealing with someone with borderline personality disorder. Truth sets the person off more often than not, and lies are definitely out. The person is already mistrustful and expects to be lied to. There are times it is tempting to simply say nothing and avoid the person altogether.

Say Nothing

The behaviors of people with borderline personality disorder can be intimidating. They might bully and their fits of rage can be dangerous. Trying to speak with them often only brings negative consequences no one wants to repeat. This can cause some people to say nothing in order to avoid an uncomfortable scene.

However, doing nothing causes more guilt and pain as the worry of harm increases. There is a feeling of helplessness associated with this decision. Control has been given over to the borderline person, who is behaving badly.

Try to Reason

It is hard to explain behaviors to people with borderline personality disorder. They have trouble understanding what is being said and often become quickly defensive. Explanations can be interpreted as lies and reaffirm the borderline person's general attitude of mistrust. Reasoning also leaves the door open for debate, which allows the borderline person to twist information around and switch focus.

Once the door opens for them to provide a rebuttal the original message and intent can get lost. The accusations can start, and the communication pattern begun numerous times before will repeat itself.

Direct and Supportive Approach

The direct approach, if handled supportively, might be the best method to use with borderline personality disorder people. It is very important to make sure everything said is the truth. If something is unknown, it is better to acknowledge that it is unknown rather than guess wrong and have it look like a lie. The honesty of admitting this might set them back a little bit and give them pause to think. It might also cause them to go off on a rant. If that is the case, do not get angry or upset. Remain calm and supportive. Do not apologize for not knowing something, but do tell them you are sorry they feel bad. Remind them that you are trying to help.

Be supportive throughout the conversation and do not try to defend or deny. Acknowledge their feelings and allow them to speak. Be supportive and do not tell them they are wrong. Do not agree with anything that is false or wrong in some way. This would again be lying. Empathize, but do not say you understand something you do not. Ask for clarification and explanation in order to better understand.

QUESTION

My husband always starts yelling at me and telling me I don't know what I am talking about. How do I get around this?
The best way to get through a pattern that keeps repeating itself is to switch your responses. If you normally try to defend yourself or argue back, stop. It continues the pattern. Tell him you love him no matter what he says and be supportive of his feelings. Ask him questions. Do something to change your part in the pattern.

What Should You Do?

It is difficult to think clearly in the midst of the conversation, as it is often emotionally charged and jumping from one accusation to another. The format of the conversation usually follows a similar pattern from one conversation to the next. In each case the message is lost in the ensuing verbal exchange. The best thing to do is find ways to break this pattern.

The Pattern

Each relationship is unique, and each pattern of interaction is based on this relationship. As two people get used to speaking with one another they begin to form particular ways of talking and choosing words. This is the pattern of communication used. It becomes predictable and takes over the true message and intent. It takes on a life of its own.

Responses become automatic. When this happens, each party stops actually paying attention to what they say and what they hear. Actual listening and attending to the meaning of the message ceases. This means the communication is simply a repeat of a previous communication.

If the communication normally starts with someone expressing concern and a desire to help and then deteriorates to questions about getting a job and quitting drinking, it forms a pattern the borderline is ready for. Responses become automatic and they learn what to say and how to say it in order to divert attention.

Breaking the Pattern

It is important to break the communication pattern in order to bring about a different outcome. This is not as easy as it sounds. The concerns on one end are not the same as the concerns on the other. The meanings of the other person are lost in the need to get the message out.

ALERT

Avoid making accusations. People with borderline personality disorder will become defensive and communication will break down. Once their defenses are activated they are less willing to talk and compromise.

One way to break the pattern is to begin with a different message and refuse to be drawn into that same pattern. Let the points normally focused on go. It might be very important for them to stop drinking, but if that is the focus of each previous message and each previous message has resulted in a mess, leave it alone for now. Learn to establish a new relationship pattern before tackling this issue again from a different standpoint.

Develop a support system of people who love the person with borderline personality disorder and project love and support. Do not react to the painful words that are spoken, and do not fall back on old responses.

Seek Help

One way to learn how to break these patterns is by consulting a professional beforehand. Write down all of the information pertinent to the symptoms and go over it step-by-step with someone who can guide and advise. If possible, have a professional available when the conversation takes place.

Discuss all concerns ahead of time and role-play to prepare for the responses. Learn to work together with the help of a professional. Ask questions and listen to the answers with an open mind. The main focus is on getting treatment and increasing function.

CHAPTER 17

Treatment

People with borderline personality disorder are often difficult to treat, as they do not always respond well or willingly in treatment. Treatment also tends to be troubling,
and sometimes a little frustrating for the client's therapist
and other members of the treatment team. These clients
are more likely to be reluctant to begin therapy, resistant to
therapeutic methods, or downright belligerent and unco-
operative throughout the treatment process. The general
symptoms and issues they face as a natural progression of
the disorder make it harder for them to follow along with
what they are supposed to do, much less why they should
do it.

When Is Treatment Necessary?

With borderline personality disorder treatment is a must. The symptoms are severe and can cause additional problems when left untreated. Borderline personality disorder is often accompanied by other disorders that need treatment as well, especially substance abuse disorders. This is not a disorder that will go away on its own. It does need treatment in order to remove the threat of the harmful symptoms. There are different options that can be taken in treatment, depending on how severe symptoms are.

Seeking Diagnosis

Before seeking a specific treatment, a diagnosis should be made. Help should be sought when symptoms become a large part of the person's life. If there is a possibility of danger, professional help should be contacted immediately. If the symptoms cause a great deal of pain and confusion within the home, then something is wrong and should be dealt with. Always assess risk of danger and pain—both physical and psychological. It is better to seek help and find that it is something simple than to not seek help and suffer tragedy.

ESSENTIAL

Some therapists are reluctant to treat borderline personality disorder either because they do not feel they have enough training or because it requires more time and effort than they have available to them at a particular time. If you suspect that the therapist you have chosen is at all hesitant, discuss the matter openly.

The symptoms of borderline are so severe and notable that it would be hard not to notice them. Yet when someone is involved in trying to deal with these symptoms in a loved one, it is hard to think clearly. If the person with borderline personality disorder will not seek help, do it without him and learn what options are available from a professional. A proper diagnosis cannot be made until the person with borderline goes in person, but the professional can give the loved ones some helpful information that will help them plan out their next steps.

Adolescence

It is important to recognize the signs in an adolescent. Whenever possible, it helps to get treatment for this disorder as it begins. If the disorder is caught and treated in adolescence, it might avert some of the negative consequences that often occur in young adulthood, such as substance abuse issues, incarceration, heavy debt, and loss of relationships with family. It is also beneficial to seek treatment and get control of the disorder before moving on to college.

Diagnosis of adolescents younger than eighteen is on the increase. As more is known about borderline personality disorder in its progression, physicians are better able to make an earlier diagnosis. Signs in adolescents are often very visible at home, but parents do not necessarily know what to do to help them. In many cases, the school system initiates some form of restrictions in the learning environment or mandates treatment of some sort in order to allow the child to continue at the school. Adolescents with borderline personality disorder are often found in alternative education schools, which are able to provide both mental health counseling and supervision and education.

In some cases, the symptoms are so severe that the adolescent needs additional help, such as when the adolescent is prone to self-harm and suicidality, he has been hospitalized at least once, or has visited the emergency room. If this type of thing happens enough, the adolescent will likely need to be put into some type of residential housing designed to help with mental health issues. If the adolescent has not shown symptoms of self-harm, and has not posed a threat to others physically, then it is likely treatment could be in the form of outpatient therapy.

Adults

It is a little trickier seeking treatment for adults, especially if they do not believe they have a problem and do not want treatment. Unless they do something that involves law enforcement in some way or lands them in the hospital there is little to be done to force them to seek treatment. On the other hand, if loved ones are willing, there are ways of setting up penalties for not seeking treatment. If the person with borderline personality disorder lives at home, the parents could threaten to kick him out if he does not seek treatment. Someone who has financial ties might cut those off. Loss of contact is actually a large threat for someone with borderline personality disorder, so it is one to use carefully, since it might set off a rage reaction.

It is also important to remember to refrain from making any threats that will not be kept. This only reinforces to people with borderline that they can do what they want to do without consequence. It makes them less likely to heed this person again, as they do not believe there will be any consequences. This type of scenario is normally harder on the people who must carry through with the threats than the person who will suffer from them.

QUESTION

What should you do if you think someone is planning to commit suicide?
If you think there is a possibility of suicide, get help immediately. If the threat is imminent, call 911 and try to keep the person where you can see him until help arrives as long as it is safe for you to do so.

Where to Go for Help

Help is not as hard to find as it might seem. There are plenty of people out there who will be able to help with the various components of the borderline treatment process. The severity of current symptoms and the status of the person with borderline personality disorder will dictate who should be contacted first.

Primary Care Physician

If the person with borderline personality disorder has a regular physician that he normally sees, this should be the first phone call. Make an appointment to see the physician either separately or with the person with borderline personality disorder. Unless there is an authorization, doctors cannot say much to anyone other than their patients, but they can provide some information on who to contact next.

Ideally, the borderline patient will be present too. This will allow the physician to do a general medical exam and rule out other potential physical causes for some of the symptoms. This is important, as some symptoms of mental health disorders are actually brought upon by medical conditions that need to be treated with medication. Once medical causes are ruled out, the doctor will normally refer the borderline patient to a mental health clinic or private professional.

Most clinics and private therapists need a referral from a medical doctor or another agency, such as the courts or social services organizations. The primary care physician should have some idea of who is around the area and who might be best to contact.

QUESTION

Why can't my daughter's primary care physician just treat her for this?
Some symptoms of borderline personality disorder can be treated to some extent with medication; however, most of the symptoms need to be treated by a mental health professional.

Choosing a Therapist

When a primary care physician has issued a referral, this should be the first mental health contact. It might not be the only contact that needs to be made, but it is the starting point. This is where an actual diagnosis will be made. Ask around with friends and family and see if anyone else has heard about the person the doctor made a referral to.

When the therapist is initially contacted, you will need to have important information on hand. Write down any symptoms and behaviors that have been observed by others. Have medical insurance information available. If the borderline patient is willing to make this appointment, it is best if she does it herself. Privacy regulations do require that she make her own contacts once she turns eighteen years old. If she is not willing, however, and the contact is being made to determine what can be done about this person, it is important to have as much information as possible.

Relevance of Information

Some information will be especially relevant. Information directly related to the symptoms will be relevant. If the person with possible borderline personality disorder is cutting, that is important and could be directly related to the disorder. If she is buying a new TV this might only be relevant if it is part of chronic overspending.

By the same token, some information might seem irrelevant but have some significance. If parents are planning on getting a divorce, or the borderline patient avoids crowds, the information is relevant and necessary. Be open to what the questions are and think of any information that would go along with what the therapist is looking for.

Questions to Ask

When choosing a therapist, or acting on a referral, it is important to have some questions ready to ask. The first question would be what credentials the therapist has. How long has the therapist been counseling others? How much training does he have? Does he have experience with borderline personality disorder?

Since borderline personality disorder has so many complicated symptoms, it would be important to find a therapist with experience working with this population. He would already have specialized training and knowledge on the course of the disorder, and would not be easily swayed by manipulation. It would be good to ask him how much experience he has with borderline personality disorder specifically and see what he says. It would also be a good idea to ask him if he has the time available that is necessary to devote to someone with borderline.

Mental Health Clinic

For some, the county department of health will have a mental health clinic that will provide these services at a reduced cost. This is beneficial for those who do not have a primary care physician to make a referral. It is also good for people who do not have health insurance or have a low income.

Clinics such as these might also be substance abuse clinics, or might have licensed substance abuse counselors on hand to help with substance abuse issues if these issues have developed. A county mental health clinic is often the first choice for the court system when treatment is mandated for an individual.

Making Decisions

Treatment options can be confusing and sometimes intimidating to work through. At first it seems time-consuming looking for all of the required information and filling out page after page of paperwork. This process is lengthy initially and it sometimes seems like there is more paperwork than therapy. It sometimes seems that way to the therapists too.

ESSENTIAL

It is important to research health insurance to see what information they will need in order to approve a certain provider. There might be some services they will not cover, or they might have specific providers they will expect to be used.

Once the paperwork is done the process becomes more humanized and therapeutic. People will be there to help explain options that will aid in informed decision making. It is a good idea to enter into the process with as much information as possible beforehand.

Finding Information

Finding information can be an interesting process. There are various means of doing so. Information can be found on the Internet, at local hospitals, in the newspaper, through a physician, and through local human service and county agencies.

Hospitals, Physician Offices, and Newspapers

Hospitals often have a list of information on psychiatrists and psychologists who work with that hospital. They can provide contact information and information on specializations if available. Hospitals also often have support group meetings and information on support groups in other locations.

Physician offices might have information on support groups, especially human service agencies that have organized systems in place and hand out fliers. They would have information on area clinics and some of the therapists they have referred people to in the past.

The local newspaper will often list days, times, and locations for various support group meetings. They are usually in a calendar section and are in there a few times a week. These listings would be for support groups for the person with borderline personality disorder and friends and family. These groups are not meant to replace therapy.

ESSENTIAL

A helpful activity would be to create a medical file. This file should include signs and symptoms by age, especially instances of self-harm. It should have information on any previous mental health treatment for this or another disorder or condition, including clinician name, diagnoses, and any other information on the treatment that is noteworthy. Any medications the borderline patient is on should be listed, along with dosages, how often and when taken, and any side effects they have suffered from taking them.

The Internet

The Internet has a wealth of information. The trick is to sift through all of it for information that is true and pertains to the topic at hand. The first sites to look at are government and educational sites, as they are often the most credible. They are sites whose web addresses end in either .gov or .edu. Some very credible sites end in .org, such as the American Psychological Association, the American Psychiatric Association, and various medical associations. Some .com sites have good information that is specific to borderline personality disorder. There is a list at the end of this book of helpful sites and web addresses.

Independent Search

Sometimes an independent search of the phone book and Internet will yield people in the area who are able to help with borderline personality disorder. Local newsmagazines and fliers might have some information or advertisements that will offer some information.

Local religious clergy are another source of information. They might have knowledge of various practitioners in the area who are good, and perhaps which ones to avoid. They sometimes work with their parishioners and learn about the various professionals through them.

A college or university will also likely have a counseling center with contacts to outside sources and agencies in the area. They are not normally equipped to handle deeper psychological issues like borderline and will have a list of referrals ready for student needs. The college or university might also have a psychology department with professional psychologists on hand in teaching and research roles. They often keep in touch with others in the area and might have a good idea of who to turn to and what might be available.

FACT

The National Alliance for the Mentally Ill (NAMI) has both state and local branches, and often has knowledge of other mental health organizations in a given area.

Human Service Agencies

Human service agencies often have their own networks. They encounter clients who need more than one service from more than one agency, so they need to know what is in the area and what each agency offers. They might be able to help find a good therapist, and other referrals as needed. They are often able to help someone apply for health insurance, food stamps, and other social services. They can usually find programs that help with employment and budgeting. They might also be able to refer legal services for low income, and help find housing if necessary.

Gathering Information

It is a good idea to have a pad of paper and a pen ready for each search. Write down all pertinent information and gather a list to go back through. This information can be categorized according to need: therapist, medical insurance, social services, and so on. List websites with notes on what they contain. Once the information is gathered it is time to sift through it to see what is there.

Shouldn't I bring every bit of information I have to the therapist?
Not necessarily. Some information is not necessary and will cause a delay, as the therapist needs to sift through it. Grades and incidences of violence or other stand-out instances at school are important, but it would only be important to talk about not eating lunch at school or being late if these behaviors were recurrent and the result of some chronic inability or fear. Be thorough so the therapist has enough to go by, but leave out gossip and suspect information.

Sifting Through Information

Not all of the information found will be useful, and some might be false or misleading. Sift through it to find information relevant to the desired goals and look for information that might be an opinion rather than fact. It is also important to try to find information that is not biased.

False or Misleading Information

Some of the information found in the search will be false, or it will create the wrong impression. Borderline personality disorder is a highly stigmatized disorder and much of the information out there is geared toward arguing that point. Some websites tend to blame parents for the development of the disorder, while others are designed to debunk the idea that all people who develop borderline personality disorder were abused as children.

Some of the warning signs would include presenting a one-sided set of opinions on the topic. If the information all points in one direction and one direction only, it is a site to avoid. Sites that are trying to sell something should be treated warily at best. They are going to present information in a way that makes their product seem necessary and desirable.

What to Look For

Sites that are produced by actual mental health organizations are going to be more credible and more factual than sites that are designed for blogging or selling something. These sites normally have access to the latest research and update site information accordingly. They are fact based rather than opinion based and provide balanced information rather than information that seeks to persuade or direct.

ALERT

Websites can put out any number of misleading forms of information. Just because a name has a PhD behind it does not mean it should be relied upon as dispensing the truth. Look through the site and be sure it is offering factual information. Is there access to professional journal articles? What type of information is it providing?

Look for authors on websites. Are they professionals in the field? There are many general information sites on the Internet with material written by anyone who can look up and write information. This information could contain errors. Sites with authors who have a professional license, a PhD, or an MD are more likely to have credible, useful information that can be relied upon.

When in Doubt

Question everything and see what passes the test. When there is information that is still questionable, but has some information that seems to answer some questions, ask a professional. Call the primary care physician or a therapist if one has been located. Call a local mental health agency or the county health offices. Someone should be able to explain the information.

The bottom line is to ask questions. Ask as many questions as necessary to provide the answers needed to make decisions. Do not stop asking questions or rely on others to provide all of the information. Oftentimes people will fail to mention certain issues or symptoms. Therapists are not mind readers and cannot make judgment calls on things they do not know about. Do not assume they know what is going on. Ask questions and clarify answers.

Is It Working?

In many cases the proper treatment can help someone with borderline personality disorder ease symptoms within the first year or two. Most symptoms tend to go away as the person gets older. In some cases, however, the symptoms remain. In these cases, there is often the presence of continued abuse or the remission of co-occurring disorders. Different factors can influence how long symptoms continue, such as the client-therapist relationship and treatment objectives.

Treatment Components

It is important to determine how treatment is progressing once it begins. The client-therapist relationship is very important and needs to create mutual trust and respect in order to work. A therapist might not work well or might not want to work with a person who has borderline personality disorder. When this happens the therapist should refer the client to someone who would be better suited for the task.

Most treatment plans are designed around the specific needs and symptoms exhibited by each individual client. While progress should be shown in at least a couple of objectives, it is not expected that all objectives will be successfully completed in that time period.

There should also be treatment plans that outline the objectives they will be covering and provide measurable outcomes that will show progress throughout treatment. Once a diagnosis is developed, a treatment plan is constructed to work on the issues that need attention. Most treatment plans are about three months in length and are updated at the end of each three-month period. Each treatment plan has a carryover of old objectives that still need to be completed and new objectives to begin work on.

Client-Therapist Relationship

A client-therapist relationship should be established over the course of time. It is not instant, which is cause for concern in someone with borderline. People with borderline personality disorder are often quick to enter into relationships and often subconsciously try to place the therapist in a caretaker role, making him responsible for happiness and well-being. The attempts for quick bonding can overwhelm the therapist and throw him off from his objectivity.

The therapist must be able to slow the relationship down and establish firm boundaries in order to be effective and avoid getting caught up in the emotional baggage and manipulation that are characteristic of initial meetings. This is an area that would be covered in the treatment plan.

Treatment Plan

A treatment plan is an outline of what will be covered in therapy. In some situations the therapist creates the treatment plan after the initial evaluation and consultation with the client. In other cases the therapist will sit down with the client and construct the objectives for the plan together after the evaluation and diagnosis.

QUESTION

What happens in an initial evaluation?
An initial evaluation often lasts at least a couple of hours and is sometimes spread out over two or more days. There is a medical evaluation to ensure that biological issues are covered. This can be done by a family physician and provided to the therapist. The therapist will then ask a series of questions designed to get an idea of the client's life history, family history, and behaviors and problems that have occurred throughout her life. The questions and the way the client acts in the evaluation is all taken into account when making final determinations.

The plan shows the goals, the time frame for each goal, and what the client must do to complete it. It covers each issue that is determined during the evaluation in a separate goal. Goals can be continued from one plan to the next and some might never be successfully completed.

Measurable Outcomes

The treatment plan provides objectives that are measurable in some way. This allows reviewers to see that progress has been made on the objective. It also allows the therapist to see how the methods being used so far are working. If the outcomes are showing no progress or if the issue is worsening, it might be time to switch to a different approach.

Insurance agencies often look at treatment plans to determine whether or not the treatments are acceptable for the symptoms and to see how progress is going. If they feel the progress is not moving along, or the objective is not valid, they will refuse to pay for that particular activity. It is important to use a number of therapy options and ensure that they are options acceptable in the therapeutic community. If the therapist is using a method that no information can be found on, question this. Many therapeutic options are available that have been tested through scientific research.

Origin in Psychoanalysis

CHAPTER 18

Therapy Options

Treatment options could include a combination of psycho-therapy, prescribed medication, and forms of behavior therapy. Psychotherapy could be conducted on an individual basis, in groups, and with family members. Since social norms are an issue and there is a high incidence of impulsivity, the client in treatment could be at odds with the treatment team, especially in the beginning before trust is established in the therapeutic relationship. As discussed earlier, development of trust is an issue in clients with borderline personality disorder as a natural result of the thought processes present with the disorder itself.

Origin in Psychoanalysis

Psychoanalysis was the original method of treatment. The initial line of thinking was that the inability to properly develop an independent identity due to a fluctuation between loving and hateful affective states was due to unresolved issues within the psyche. People's lives remain contradictory and chaotic in this flux and severe identity problems form. They are unable to integrate proper perceptions of others and remain in a constant state of conflict. The unresolved issues needed to be identified and explored.

Trust issues create an impediment to treatment that makes choosing the right options of prime importance. People who come into the office with trust issues need to work through those first before getting to the problems that sent them into the office in the first place. This takes time, which means shorter-term treatment methods are not as well suited to this particular disorder. There are often simply too many issues to work through before progress can begin.

The psychoanalytic approach was initially discredited in the treatment of borderline personality disorder due to its lengthy process and lack of measurable results. This approach has recently seen a resurgence in use and potential success, especially in disorders that need a longer period of treatment time to work through multiple issues. This is an option that has seen some solid success in prisons, where inmates have the time to work on and explore feelings and past experiences. While it is becoming a more popular option outside of the prison setting, most health insurance agencies would like to see some form of results in a shorter period of time. Many clinics opt for forms of cognitive-behavioral therapies, in addition to drug therapy and group and individual psychotherapy.

Drug Therapy

The chemical imbalances and areas of that brain that do not seem to be activating properly often need a pharmaceutical nudge. Medication is also helpful in working on other, comorbid issues such as depression, impulsivity, and anxiety. Medications can help ease acute symptoms so the client is able to settle down and concentrate on treatment. There is no magic pill, especially with borderline personality disorder. Medicine can help, but just so far. Certain medications are used, including antidepressant, antianxiety and antipsychotic medications.

Used for Core Symptoms

Drug therapy is not effective in treating the overall disorder. It is, however, somewhat successful in treating the core symptoms and psychotic aspects of the disorder. Medications are therefore targeted at specific symptoms. They are also targeted at comorbid disorders. As noted earlier, borderline personality disorder is often comorbid with other disorders, including mood and anxiety disorders.

Unfortunately, these medications are much less effective for mood and anxiety symptoms in borderline personality disorder clients. Some of them carry some danger of abuse. This can be an issue with borderline clients since they tend to overuse what they have and sometimes stockpile medications for later use and suicide attempts. There is a tendency to prescribe medications that are not addictive for people with this disorder.

ALERT

The high risk of self-harm and suicide attempts, along with the tendency to form dependencies on people and substances, increases risk of overuse of some substances. It is important to remain aware of prescribed medications and ensure that other, illicit drugs that might interact with the prescribed medicines are not in use at the same time. Let the prescribing doctor know if there are drug issues.

Balancing the Brain

The essential goal of the medications is to increase the brain's biological ability to function properly. As discussed earlier in the book, certain brain chemicals seem to be off in people with borderline personality disorder. These chemicals need to be returned to a normal balance in order to increase the proper function of the brain and the reactions it stimulates. Certain medicines are designed to work on different brain activities and restore normal function.

Dosage is another issue that will be taken into account. The dosage must be high enough to be effective, but not so high that the patient is unable to function or engage in normal daily activities. The treatment needs to take any other issues into account also, such as mood and anxiety disorder. Determining the proper medication to prescribe and its dosage will benefit greatly from the medical history chart previously suggested. If this information is available, the doctor can determine potential side effects and how large a dosage is needed to work on that particular person.

QUESTION

My wife has diabetes and is on insulin for it. Will any of these medications cause problems?
It is possible for some drugs to interact with already prescribed medications. It is important to let the doctor know what other drugs she is on and why, and the doctor can advise you. *Do not start or stop taking any drug without first consulting your doctor.*

Dangers

The large variety and number of symptoms characteristic of borderline personality disorder, along with the high rate of comorbid disorders, causes a need for relief of many different types of symptoms. People with borderline often feel the need to take the edge off all of the symptoms, and some medical providers go along with this. Since any one medication will not ease all symptoms, there is a tendency to overprescribe. The result is a person who is prescribed four or five different drugs to deal with multiple symptoms. Each of these drugs has side effects and could interfere with another drug.

Drug therapy loses its effectiveness over time. Some people with borderline personality disorder might respond well for an extended period of time, but most do not. They might respond favorably to begin with, but the underlying issues associated with borderline often make this a short-lived experience, as they seem to override the positive effects of the medicine.

Additionally, the quick-fix mentality of people with borderline often leads them to get as many prescriptions as possible and avoid any kind of psychotherapy. This does little to help and increases addictive thought processes, preventing the person from actually working through the issues and realigning thoughts for a more permanent easing of symptoms. Therapy in some form is necessary.

Cognitive Behavior Therapy

Cognitive behavior therapy (CBT) is one of the most widely used approaches to treatment of borderline personality disorder. It works to help people with borderline personality disorder recognize the inner conflicts that are contributing to or causing some of their symptoms. They learn to see how these unconscious conflicts and faulty thought processes affect how they react to situations and daily stressors. The point in all forms of cognitive behavior therapy is to help people learn how to properly perceive and work through the issues everyone comes into contact with on a daily basis and prevent thoughts and behaviors from becoming extreme and outside of normally recognized reactions.

What Is CBT?

CBT is a form of psychotherapy that works on maladaptive thought processes and the resulting behaviors. One of the main goals is to change reactions and behaviors by changing the way thoughts and perceptions are processed. This form of therapy is focused on the here and now. It is behaviorally driven, so it does not look as much at past experiences as much as it does the current thought and behavior patterns and how to change them.

The therapist is more actively involved in CBT as opposed to other forms of therapy, such as psychoanalytic, where the therapist takes a passive role and listens. With CBT the therapist is more involved in directing the client, helping the client identify the issues that are causing faulty thoughts and working with the client to alter these thoughts and the resulting behavior.

Illogical Beliefs

People with borderline personality disorder often experience distorted or illogical beliefs. These beliefs often coincide with the black-and-white thought process they exhibit: "I have to do all of my work completely right and be perfect and agreeable or I will be rejected." This type of all-or-nothing thinking leads to defensive behaviors designed to meet these high expectations. When they are not met, poor behaviors result.

ESSENTIAL

Most people with borderline personality disorder create faulty belief systems as they go through their lives. They have trouble recognizing true social situations and often misinterpret what they hear and see. The CBT processes are designed to alter this pattern.

When cognitions match the event, reactions are normally adaptive and healthy. When they do not, reactions can become problematic. Thus, fixing the thoughts can help fix the behaviors. This is done in a three-step process: things happen, we interpret those things, and those interpretations directly affect our resulting feelings and behaviors. This theory assumes that it is the way a situation is interpreted that causes the problems rather than the situation itself.

Revising Cognitions

CBT seeks to help people work toward a clearer thought process that allows interpretation of an event that is logical and correctly corresponds to the event. In many cases thoughts go on overload and get carried away. A person then catastrophizes and cannot function beyond that point because his anxiety level has raised and he is not thinking clearly. For someone with borderline personality disorder this often takes place when a threat of abandonment occurs.

With CBT the illogical thoughts are identified. They are then challenged and eventually replaced with more logical thoughts. Thoughts can become automatic, especially responses to negative situations. They become so routine and habitual that they are hard to identify because the process of bringing up these thoughts is so instantaneous.

Once the thoughts are identified they are challenged. One way to challenge them is to have the client try to think through his maladaptive thought to its conclusion. In many cases the thought has a catastrophic end that makes little sense, or has no real end because the thought/reaction has taken over. The belief is then revised. This is the most difficult step, as the thought process has become so entrenched that it needs to be redirected and the automatic reactions need to be halted.

Therapist Role

This is where the therapist must often take the lead. The therapist acts as an educator as well as a therapist, providing information and direction as well as therapy. This can take the form of mini-lectures on the dynamics of thought and behavior, handouts, readings, and even homework. The therapist provides instruction on the thought process, offering information on how the brain works and why perceptions are so important.

The therapist might have the client read through various articles and examples of how this process works and then have him create his own chart with examples of a situation, the instant thoughts on the situation, and how these thoughts affect subsequent behaviors. Therapist and client then go through and identify thoughts that closely identify with reality and others that deviate from normal expectations and create problems.

Clients often have homework with CBT to continue to reinforce what is learned in the sessions. Once a client leaves the office, the thoughts have a tendency to revert back to their original pattern. The homework is designed to keep the client focused and working on the issues at hand.

FACT

A way for someone with BPD to control his anger is to work on self-control. Ask your loved one to carry an egg timer for a day, and when he gets angry, use it as a visual focus for delaying his reaction a certain period of time. Ask him to set it for five minutes to begin with and then longer periods of time after each incident.

Various forms of CBT are used in treatment of someone with borderline personality disorder. These include dialectical behavior therapy and schema therapy. Each of these forms of CBT is a bit more specialized on how it addresses thought processes.

Dialectical Behavior Therapy and Mindfulness

Dialectical behavior therapy (DBT) is a newer approach that is designed specifically for people with borderline personality disorder. It is a form of cognitive behavioral therapy that works on the affective instability and impulsivity in either a group or one-on-one setting. The inability to regulate emotions is the key element addressed by this therapeutic option. It focuses on teaching individuals different skills that work with emotional regulation, mindfulness, distress tolerance, and interpersonal skill development for identification and regulation of social skills.

Emotional Regulation

DBT helps people with borderline personality disorder explore how they react to situations and how these reactions affect their lives and the world around them. It theorizes that everything in life is connected in some form, and behavioral reactions both affect and are affected by the behavioral reactions of others.

ESSENTIAL

DBT sees self-destructive behaviors as learned coping techniques designed to reduce the intense and negative emotions that occur. This leads to emotional vulnerability, which creates quick, intense, and overwhelming emotional reactions that cause the ups and downs in thought and feeling.

This form of therapy often uses role playing to help the client identify situations that normally initiate fear and stress for them. These fears are explored and misconceptions are discovered. The client then works with the therapist/group to look for solutions that help with self-image and negative processing. This therapy validates and accepts clients as they are and acknowledges that even the self-damaging behaviors make sense in some way.

This validation bypasses the quick anger reactions that often come when someone tries to explain why a behavior or fear did not make sense. To people with borderline personality disorder it does make sense; they are genuinely feeling what they say they are feeling. So the first step in helping them deal with the emotions is to acknowledge them.

FACT

DBT does not try to remove emotion. It helps clients learn to experience feelings without having to shut down or overreact. They are taught to experience the emotions without allowing the emotions to be in control.

Strength-Based Change

DBT emphasizes that people with borderline personality disorder are capable of making sound decisions and trusting in their abilities. They can learn to make good judgments and determine how and when to trust themselves. This does not preclude the need for change. Clients are also taught that they must change in order to create a better quality of life.

The therapies are designed to help clients become unstuck from rigid patterns of thought and behavior, especially when emotions become stronger and threaten to overwhelm them. The clients are taught to create new patterns that bypass the thought processes that lead them to become stuck in arguments, extreme positions, and constantly changing polarized positions on issues. They learn that they have the ability to take control of their lives.

Functions of DBT

DBT seeks to achieve particular goals, which include increasing the client's motivation to change, identifying and enhancing the client's capabilities, properly matching these capabilities with areas in need, and creating a solid therapeutic environment. The therapist meets these objectives by using group skills training, phone coaching, one-on-one therapy, and homework assignments.

Therapists maintain their own skills and motivation through weekly team meetings for consultation. These meetings help the therapist work through issues that are causing problems and keep them fresh and focused. Others are able to see areas or options that might escape them.

The therapist will also meet and work with family members to ensure that everyone is on the same page. Family members often reinforce the negative thoughts and behaviors of their loved one without even realizing it. Working with the therapist, they learn how to reinforce the positive behaviors in the home. This is important because the therapist only sees the client a couple times a week, and the home environment is often where many of the maladaptive behaviors began.

ESSENTIAL

Dialectics is a concept that proposes that everything is connected to everything else in some way, change is constant and inevitable, and opposites can be integrated to form a closer approximation of truth.

Stages and Targets

There is a strict order in which problems are addressed in DBT. The treatment is organized into stages and targets in order to avoid getting caught up in the successive crises of the moment that normally occur. The logical progression begins with the most severe behaviors, such as self-harm and suicidality. The second goal would be to keep the client in therapy, and the third would be to begin to build a better quality of life by promoting new thoughts and behavior skills. This then leads to a sense of fulfillment and connectedness that replaces the emptiness and aimlessness.

Schema Therapy

Schema therapy is a form of CBT that looks at the formation of thought patterns based on how people process and categorize information as it comes in. Schema therapy focuses on ongoing problems that are normally enduring in nature. They are based on the schemas that are produced as an individual interacts with society.

Schemas

Schemas are the mental frameworks people use to organize the information taken in from their social world. People form frameworks for each social situation they encounter. They know what to expect in situations they have encountered before because they have been through those or similar circumstances. They form guidelines for how to act based on what they experience and perceive as the social rules for that situation.

ESSENTIAL

People cannot attend to everything they encounter. As such, they develop mental shortcuts. Schemas are mental shortcuts that attempt to reduce the effort expended on attending to and processing various social stimuli.

The more a situation is encountered, the more firmly fixed the schema for that situation becomes. Also, the stronger the reinforcement behind the expected behavior, the more likely it will be heeded. For example, students form solid schema for how to take tests. They must behave in a certain way when they take tests. This is strongly reinforced by the strict monitoring by teachers and the threat of failure if caught cheating or doing something outside of what is expected in this situation.

Forming Maladaptive Schema

People with borderline personality disorder often have trouble understanding social rules and do not necessarily form correct schema to help them along. These schema are formed in childhood and repeated throughout life. This causes problems as they misinterpret situations around them. They are so fearful of abandonment that they often react harshly when they perceive they are about to be abandoned. Their beliefs often create behaviors that produce the result they are trying to avoid.

As beliefs are altered, behaviors go with them and tend to increase function. If someone believes she is going to be abandoned she forms maladaptive coping styles. If she does not believe she will be abandoned she might be able to function and interact in more acceptable forms.

Coping Styles

Coping styles are the ways people react to the schemas they have formed. Everyone reacts to stressful situations in his or her own unique style, but there are three general modes that most coping styles fall under: surrender, avoidance, and overcompensation. With surrender the person basically feels helpless to change the situation and lets it continue as is. With avoidance the person avoids thinking about or dealing with the situation and lets it continue to develop without trying to stop it as she denies its existence. With overcompensation the person goes above and beyond dealing satisfactorily with the situation. She might deal with the problem and continue to dwell on it in a hypervigilant state.

FACT

The schema therapy approach tends to allow a closer relationship between therapist and client. There is an emphasis on this relationship that is different from other therapies designed to have the therapist remain a safe, objective distance from the client.

Schema Therapy Goals

Schema therapy is designed to work on the schema modes of the person with borderline personality disorder. Schema modes are the emotional states and coping responses people use. Schema therapy seeks to end the maladaptive coping styles, heal the early maladaptive schema, learn to identify and stop the self-defeating schema modes as they come up, and find ways to positively get emotional needs met. The three stages of treatment include bonding and emotional regulation, schema mode change, and autonomy.

Stages

In the first stage the therapist works on bonding with the patient and teaching affect regulation and coping skills. The therapist works to empathize with the current problems the client is having and convey support. The client and therapist discuss the client's life history and childhood experiences. They work on affect regulation and distress tolerance skills through meditation, creating a schema diary, writing up flashcards, and listing pleasurable activities.

In the second stage, they work on setting limits and handling crises. They explore the client's safety and support network and establish client rights. Communication patterns are explored to work on punitive and rigid patterns in need of change. Specific consequences are outlined for violation of limits in the relationship.

In the third stage, the client and therapist work on developing healthy relationships. The client learns individuation to help form identity and follow natural inclinations. There is a gradual termination of the therapy and a plan for aftercare that includes contact after termination.

Counseling/Psychotherapy

Psychotherapy is designed to help people learn to deal with the identification and regulation of emotions that have gotten out of control. It is the overall term used for various approaches to counseling, including the psychodynamic approach, the behavioral approach, the humanistic approach, the cognitive approach, and the cognitive-behavioral approach.

Single Approach

Each different counseling approach concentrates on certain aspects of the issue. They come at the problem in a different way specific to the concepts behind the approach and the theories on how these approaches will help. Different approaches tend to have different outcomes based on the problems the client is experiencing and the diagnosis.

In many cases one single approach is not able to take care of the entire problem. The variety of symptoms in borderline personality disorder can make it difficult for one approach to cover all of the symptoms. Yet it is important to provide a consistent approach. Therapists cannot simply move from one approach to the next, as this will confuse clients and perhaps cause a loss of trust in the process. Yet it is possible to combine aspects of more than one approach into the treatment process.

Integrative

Many therapists have moved to a more integrative approach to counseling, combining elements of more than one approach to the process. The DBT approach tries to present a strength-based approach to cognition that fills in gaps created by using just cognitive approaches. The cognitive behavior approaches work on both thoughts and behaviors but do not cover past issues that are affecting current functioning. Psychodynamic approaches explore the past issues that might be affecting current function. Schema approaches look at how to work with these past issues to realign current thought and behavior.

Each approach has some parts that together can create a whole. This allows the therapist some flexibility that can be tailored to the individual client. A client is taken as he presents himself in psychotherapy, and each presentation could require a different combination of therapeutic options.

Types of Delivery

Therapy can be conducted in a variety of formats and settings. People with borderline personality disorder will likely face more than one form of treatment, possibly in more than one setting. Many borderline clients begin with a hospital visit.

The hospital is usually the first stop when self-harm issues get out of hand or suicide attempts occur. If the issue is severe enough, the borderline patient will remain in a behavioral health or mental health wing of the hospital to be stabilized and assessed. This is a short-term stay, however, and alternate means will be discussed before discharge. If conditions are severe and there are breaks with reality, the patient might be moved to a psychiatric hospital for an extended period of time.

Most clients engage in psychotherapy one-on-one with a therapist in individual counseling sessions. They might meet one or more times a week in private therapy to go through individual issues. Clients might also be placed in group therapy sessions to learn to interact and work with others. This is good practice for those with borderline personality disorder, as they can show their interaction issues for the therapist to see.

Some psychotherapy has begun to come up online. This is normally in the form of chat rooms that allow people with borderline personality disorder to meet and talk to each other. Some sites might have a therapist on-call to help provide support and talk to someone who is having problems at that moment. There are also some options for home visits to help the family learn to function with their loved one and comply with the treatment themselves.

ALERT

Online forms of therapy cannot replace face-to-face counseling. Although they can be used as a source of contact for additional information and support when the loneliness is overwhelming, personal contact is necessary to determine how the client is doing. Tone of voice, affect, and body motions cannot be assessed over the Internet.

Group Support

In addition to formal forms of therapy, support groups provide help in learning to cope with life with borderline personality disorder. Groups are available for both the people diagnosed with borderline and family and loved ones. Groups can be conducted in person or online.

Purpose

Groups are used to complement formal therapeutic options. Others who have experience with the same issue often conduct groups. They often provide information and support. Some groups provide a place to vent and express concerns to people who are able to understand and empathize.

ESSENTIAL

To find a good support group, ask around to get information on groups in your area. Speak with your doctor and therapist to see what they recommend. Churches often host group meetings for various support groups and might have some information on where to go. Call the local hospital and substance abuse clinic as both of these places might have some information.

Groups fulfill a social purpose. They are a means of getting out and about in an environment where others understand the issues an individual is facing. People can feel safe talking about experiences and can develop a support network.

Support Network

People face issues on a daily basis. Some issues are larger than others, yet one thing is fairly consistent. The stronger a person's support network is, the more likely it is they will successfully get through the issues they face. People who face terrible issues but have a good support network are more likely to get through positively than people who face minor stressors daily with no support network.

A support network offers a place to fall back on unconditional positive regard and acknowledgment. It provides people a place to turn when symptoms become problematic and there is a need to find help. People who are supportive can take up the slack and help others function when they cannot.

Problems with Groups

While groups can provide great support for individuals dealing with borderline personality disorder, they also have some downsides. Most of the people in the group are there because they have similar issues. This does not mean they are doing well working on these issues. If the group is not moderated well, unhealthy behaviors will be mixing with healthy behaviors. There are likely to be problems with anger and misunderstandings.

For family members, old patterns of coping can interfere with group progress. Many family members ultimately begin to focus and define their lives based on the problems with the member with borderline personality disorder. When they get into a group, their communication often revolves around complaining about that person. If the other group members are on the same level, they will probably be doing the same thing. Support groups are not designed for complaining but for growth.

How Serious Is BPD?

Many people with borderline personality disorder receive their diagnosis in a hospital setting. The symptoms for this issue often result in attempts at self-harm, suicide, or aggressive behaviors that result in injury. Borderline personality disorder is a serious mental health issue that needs professional treatment. While research indicates that people can age out of it as they move into middle age, there are often comorbid issues that are not prone to

CHAPTER 19

Evolving Knowledge of Borderline Personality Disorder

Borderline personality disorder began its existence as an issue that bordered on schizophrenia, and was met with puzzlement and impatience. The pervading attitude caused many to feel even worse than they did before they went in for treatment. Fortunately, research and the evolution of new treatment options have provided more knowledge and hope in working with someone with this issue.

How Serious Is BPD?

Many people with borderline personality disorder receive their diagnosis in a hospital setting. The symptoms for this issue often result in attempts at self-harm, suicide, or aggressive behaviors that result in injury. Borderline personality disorder is a serious mental health issue that needs professional treatment. While research indicates that people can age out of it as they move into middle age, there are often comorbid issues that are not prone to the aging process. Poor coping habits are formed throughout life that remain and continue to affect daily function. It is important to get help when dealing with this disorder.

Handling It on Your Own

This is not an issue that is easily handled alone, or without professional guidance. Many of the symptoms the person exhibits can be severe and even dangerous. The instability of the symptoms and the explosiveness of the anger can create poor coping skills in those around them. Anxiety and fear can activate defense mechanisms in those around the person with borderline.

QUESTION

My daughter has a lot of symptoms of borderline personality disorder and I would like to get her help, but I am afraid she will be put in a mental hospital. What can I do?
Most people who are diagnosed with borderline personality disorder outside of a forced setting remain at home or are placed in a supervised setting. It is also important how old your daughter is—if she is a legal adult and her symptoms have not posed a danger to herself or others, you may have a more difficult time securing help for her.

Family members and loved ones tend to isolate themselves from others. They are too busy worrying about and taking care of the person with borderline. They do not take care of themselves and allow for fun—this causes guilt. They are easily manipulated when they are run down, and they tend to give in and allow behaviors they wouldn't normally because they are afraid of the reactions.

Guilt

Guilt can manifest in many ways. The loved one with borderline does not necessarily mean to hurt. They are often hurting themselves and much of what they lash out about is a product of their own psychological pain and anger at themselves. They go from denial and blame of others to self-hate. This roller coaster can trip others up and produce thoughts and reactions they might regret later—or feel guilty about.

This guilt can cause poor decision making and add to the problem structure within the home or relationship. When the person with borderline feels guilty he might decide to harm himself or make a suicide attempt. He might also engage in attention-seeking behavior to make sure others are still with him and concerned. All of this translates to additional confusion and pain for others.

ESSENTIAL

Additional guilt is often placed on family members based on research findings that cite child abuse and neglect as a cause of borderline personality disorder in some cases. Unfortunately, this seems to be an issue that creates assumptions of abuse when there is none.

When loved ones feel guilty, it is often a result of thoughts of resentment or anger, or words or behaviors that seem to have hurt the person with borderline personality disorder. They then become more attentive and abandon their own lives more. They might not think making time for themselves is a good thing. They often look at it as selfish, especially when the person with borderline tends to blame them for the state they are in.

Stress

The stress of living with or interacting with someone with borderline personality disorder is daunting at best. The stress can make it difficult to function and go about daily life, especially when the person with borderline is actively rolling through emotions and engaging in self-harm. Stress reactions can make a situation worse, as the adrenaline begins to pump and prompts action.

Stress can also cause health problems related to how people cope with it, and how they let it affect the rest of their normal lives. Poor eating and sleeping patterns can add weight, increase blood pressure, and produce a general feeling of malaise.

Impact

Borderline personality disorder is a serious issue that can prompt additional serious issues in those who have it and those who are dealing with someone who has it. New forms of treatment and discoveries of biological connections have created hope for greater function and a stronger chance of recovery from many of the symptoms. Yet this does not happen without professional help. The risks associated with the behaviors of the person with borderline can be life-threatening.

The stress of these risks and the strong emotional reactions can catch everyone else up and harm the family unit and quality of life for all. Words are often twisted and used against family members; they find themselves constantly on the defensive and are often manipulated and lied to. The disorder robs the family of normal function and this can cause resentment and pain. There is help for this, and support for those who are dealing with it.

Support for You

Family members and loved ones often get lost in the shuffle of this issue. Most of the energy and attention is focused on the person with borderline and what she is doing. Is she going to hurt herself? Is she going to blow up? What comes next? Guilt and fear are often common feelings of people who have to deal with someone with borderline personality disorder. Constant suicide threats can cause others to become hypervigilant in order to try to prevent tragedy.

Hypervigilance

Hypervigilance is an extended state of vigilance that causes an extreme awareness of surroundings searching for potential danger. When people are bombarded with constant stressors they become overly attentive to anything that might be viewed as a potential threat and react ahead of time. It creates a constant state of stress and fear.

This is a condition that primes people to overreact and overanalyze situations. People become mistrustful and anticipate negative circumstances. They process incoming information based on this suspicion and anticipation of disaster. It is like living in a battle zone with no relief.

Taking Away Blame

Family members struggle with feeling responsible for the development of borderline. Parents tend to look back and think about what they might have done wrong. They can usually find something they think they did to cause problems for the person with borderline. If abuse was an issue, chances are there is additional guilt. Guilt, however, does nothing to help the situation, and those who are dealing with the many issues inherent in borderline need some relief from the stress or they will have trouble too.

QUESTION

What do I do when my daughter insults me and tells me I'm hurting her even though I'm not?
Try to ignore personal attacks and keep in mind that the words themselves are often more manipulative in nature rather than heartfelt accusations. Disengage with your daughter and tell her you will speak with her when she calms down.

New research provides a clear link between borderline personality disorder and biological causes that do not necessarily stem from childhood abuse, neglect, or abandonment. For families that have generations of mental illness, the need for support and professional help is even greater. Blame and guilt do not help with the problems that are occurring, and they do not help everyone move forward.

Turning to Others

People who deal with someone with borderline personality disorder often shut themselves away from others in an attempt to avoid judgment and blame. They do not want to try to explain a situation that is treated with such stigma. They want to avoid the label for their family, especially younger family members. The stigma can carry over to them based on the small amount of information that is out there for the general public to access.

The feelings of helplessness can threaten to overwhelm, especially when there is a fear of turning to others. In some cases, loved ones do turn to friends and more distant family members. These people often mean well and might be able to offer some emotional support. Yet they likely do not have a great deal of knowledge on the subject of borderline personality disorder and might not want to delve too deeply into the matter.

Friends and family can offer love and unconditional acceptance, which certainly helps provide a needed boost and some reassurance that life will continue to go on. They might be able to help with chores or run errands. They can listen with a sympathetic ear. They can be there, but they probably can't completely empathize or understand what is going on from the inside.

Turning to Others with the Same Problem

Support can also come from support groups where others with the same issues come together to seek solace and tell their stories. These are not professionals, but they do have similar experiences and might have some tips or resources to exchange that will help others in the same circumstances. The information that they can provide can give some help in finding counselors, working with anger, and dealing with agencies that can help when circumstances come up.

The stories and camaraderie help family members learn that they are not alone and have others to turn to. This is important as they try to cope with severe symptoms that threaten to tear the family structure apart. It is a place to get out and be with others who understand what might be going on without judging. They also understand the fear of judgment and potential guilt, and how things can be turned back on them. Some of the members who have been there for a period of time might have learned important information, like how to feel without guilt.

Allowing Yourself to Feel

The guilt of dealing with someone with borderline personality disorder can cause a shutdown of emotions. When people get hurt enough, they tend to withdraw and avoid the situations that hurt them. In the process, they shut off feelings in order to deal with the problems that keep coming at them.

Are You Feeling Anything?

Many deny that they are feeling anything in an effort to minimize the situation they are dealing with. They do not want to feel anything because the feelings are often negative and painful. In other cases, they might be so numb and desensitized that they do not recognize that they are feeling anything.

The numbness can set in and reduce the ability to assess and react to the situations as they come up. There are so many situations to fear and dread that it is easier to not feel. The hurt that is caused by the accusations can cause people to begin to isolate themselves so they do not have to deal with them. They retreat rather than face what they fear might be true—even if it is not. They begin to doubt themselves.

Doubt

The material available on borderline personality disorder often focuses on the connection between child abuse and development of borderline. This is not always the case, yet there are many who see this as a fact. Children with borderline might also perceive abuse where there was none.

It is hard to argue with people with borderline, as they can become very angry and manipulate others to get them to take their side. When people are confronted with this type of situation they can begin to doubt their own memory of what happened. They start to buy in to the manipulation and stop trying to press an issue. They let the borderline person get away with something because they are not sure they didn't cause it.

Giving In

It is not uncommon to simply give in when the issue gets too heated or the accusations begin to fly. The manipulation causes self-doubt and the words that come out often cause pain. Each time a person gives in to something he knows is wrong, or that makes him feel bad, he causes more pain for himself. This pain causes him to retreat further.

If he gives in and something bad happens he feels guilty, like he could have headed it off if he had remained steadfast. This is normally not the case, but it seems that way, and might well come out that way from the person with borderline personality disorder. People with BPD always seek to avoid blame for whatever went wrong. There is little to validate what their loved ones are going through.

FACT

There are strict rights to privacy for the client, based on the Health Insurance Portability and Accountability Act (HIPAA). When parents or other family members are paying for the therapy, however, they do have some rights as far as attendance, motivation, and benefits of therapy. They cannot have access to what is talked about in sessions, but they can have some say in what types of treatment are being used and whether or not it should continue based on their financing.

Validation

Validation is an important element of recovery for family members. The constant need of the person with borderline personality disorder to blame others can leave her loved ones with no recourse in a discussion. The person with borderline takes center stage in therapy and often gets away with things because it is just too overwhelming to keep her from doing what she wants to do when she wants to do it. This leaves other family members feeling left out and unimportant.

They are going through strong emotions themselves, but cannot express them because it causes a larger issue with the person with borderline. They are the target of false accusations that are either the result of manipulation or false perceptions, forcing them to defend themselves when they have not done anything wrong. They also see the person with borderline enlist aid and sympathy from others, making them seem like the bad guy in yet another incident.

Each family member needs to feel that he or she is heard and believed. They need to feel they are just as important as the person with borderline.

They want to be able to function peacefully and cannot. This causes pain and resentment. When they cannot voice this pain, or when their pain is minimized by the issues of the person with borderline, problems can occur. They can become angry and feel guilty for their anger.

Getting Angry

People coping with someone with borderline personality disorder often experience some anger. They are angry that their family is in a constant state of alarm and uncertainty. They are angry that they have to cope with something they do not know how to handle. They are angry for any number of reasons. This is natural, and the accompanying thoughts are natural too.

Resentment

Family members and loved ones can grow to resent the person with borderline. The constant instability and emotional volatility of borderline personality disorder can completely disrupt a family situation. People get tired of the issues they must cope with as a result of the thoughts and behaviors of another. They might begin to think that if they could just get rid of that person they could have a normal life. Then, they might worry that if something happens to the person with borderline, they will be responsible, especially if it is a son or daughter.

Loved ones might also harbor resentment at past hurts that have never been addressed. The person with borderline often gets away with hurtful statements and behaviors in his quest to ease his own symptoms. Others can get so caught up in surviving the drama that they are too relieved when it is over to bring it back up again—or they might be on to the next dramatic incident.

Manipulation

People with borderline personality disorder often manipulate others to keep from being alone and prevent being blamed for their disruptions. They are very good at looking like they are the victim and gaining sympathy from others. They might also manipulate for money or favors.

Manipulation often happens when people with borderline personality disorder fear impending rejection or abandonment. They will do and/or say anything to keep the object of their affection with them. They might threaten or cajole, or both. They could say they are going to kill themselves if that person leaves. They might go so far as to try to do something to show that they mean it. They might plead and make promises based on what they know the other person wants to hear.

Manipulation also occurs when people with borderline want something and see a way to get it. They might seem coldhearted when they do this. They might try for money or some types of services like driving them somewhere or cooking and cleaning for them.

Taking Sides

One of the main forms of manipulation has to do with getting people to take sides. They want others to affirm for them that they are good and others are to blame for their problems. They do this by providing the other person with lies and half truths. They tell stories designed to get the other person to feel and believe the way they want them to.

ESSENTIAL

Explain the issues associated with borderline personality disorder to other family members and friends so they have an idea of what they might encounter. Remember, however, that people with borderline often act dramatically different when they are around others, causing some to doubt the descriptions they have been given.

This is a danger with therapists, as the person with borderline works to elicit sympathy and emotion. Once therapists lose objectivity and work to help the poor person in front of them they become ineffective. They end up serving the ends of the person with borderline.

When people with borderline think they are being attacked by another, or that they are being rejected, they tend to try to get others to go against that person. They want people to take sides: theirs. They will say and do what they need to ensure that this happens.

Betrayal

The manipulation and taking sides can cause increased anger and pain. A person who is dealing with someone with borderline personality disorder might feel betrayed by the move against him. He could lose friends and see family members turn against him as the person with borderline acts to make him the focus of everyone else's anger and blame.

He might also feel betrayed as this person with borderline reveals secrets or confidences to others in an effort to manipulate a situation. He feels betrayed by other family members if they believe the information, or if they ignore his pain. These feelings can cause anger to continue to grow.

Becoming Too Invested in Someone Else

It is important for friends and family members to be involved and supportive. The person with borderline personality disorder needs this affirmation and security. There does come a point, however, where others can become too invested. They can get caught up in the symptoms and manipulation and lose their own identity to the illness.

Living for Them

Family members, especially parents and spouses, can become so wrapped up in what is happening to their loved one that they build their entire lives around dealing with the disorder. The disorder does require a set of behaviors and coping skills that are utilized on a daily basis. It also requires some changes to lifestyle and interactions within the home and without.

Yet it does not require that others give up their lives and interests in order to care for this one individual. They will be little good if they do not have their own ways of maintaining their own identity. There needs to be some separation.

Separating

Everyone needs to live his or her own life and form personal interests and work on those interests. The interests should be outside of the home and have nothing to do with the person with borderline personality disorder.

This provides people with the opportunity to continue to develop their own separate interests and identity. If they do not do this, they can easily become enmeshed in the person with borderline personality disorder. Their interests and goals will be put on a back burner and they will deal only with the needs of the person with borderline. They might feel guilty about pursuing their own interests, but in actuality it is more helpful.

It is impossible to help others when there are issues that need to be worked on personally. When people become too enmeshed in the problems of another person and do not continue to develop their own identity, they cannot help because they cannot think or see beyond what they are experiencing. They are more likely to burn out because they are focused only on the needs and wants and demands of another. They can become resentful of the fact that they are stuck doing these things when there are other things they would rather do, causing them to create a victim mentality themselves. If they do not maintain the boundaries and separate themselves in some way they get lost in the disorder itself.

The Struggle

When working with someone with borderline personality disorder it is common to become so wrapped up in that person's needs and wants that personal needs and wants are forgotten. It is also common to feel that the needs of the person with the disorder are more important and must be taken care of first. People might feel like they are not doing enough to help the person if they do not sacrifice their time and energy to help and care for the other.

Borderline personality disorder people often manipulate others into taking care of them and being responsible for them in some way. They want to be taken care of and nurtured to try to get rid of the feelings of abandonment and low self-worth. These needs, however, often override the needs of others. They will accuse others of selfishness often as a means of controlling them and guilting them into taking care of their own needs.

Be Selfish

There are times when everyone needs to be selfish. It is not really being selfish, but it seems that way, especially if the person with borderline personality disorder encourages this thought process. Self-care is as important as care of others. If a person does not take care of his own needs and wants, he will burn out and become resentful. He will not be effective at caring for others.

ALERT

Signs of burnout could include constant feelings of sadness or doom, frequent bouts of crying, being quick to anger, lack of desire or energy to do anything, feeling worthless and guilty, feeling like nothing you do is good enough, anxiety, and feeling overwhelmed.

This might mean going away for a couple of days. The trip will likely cause a strong reaction, but that is for the person with borderline to work out with her therapist—another area where professional help is necessary. If there is no one to go over this with, it is likely the trip will not occur. Seek professional help and be selfish. It is important to the entire family/relationship structure for each individual in the structure to have time to him- or herself and a personal life. Create a strong sense of boundaries and distance when necessary.

Making Their Problem Your Problem

People with borderline personality disorder often seek to have others be responsible for their problems and misdeeds. They are quick to point fingers and assign blame. They are also quick to delegate problems to others through manipulation. There is a Dr. Jekyll and Mr. Hyde behavior pattern that can emerge when someone with borderline needs to create a good impression.

The Outside Face

People with borderline can create a wonderful first impression. They can come across as very caring and calm. They also tend to present themselves as victims in some way. They normally tell elaborate stories to others about what is going on in their lives. These stories might include a list of wrongs done to them by others, especially family members.

They do this in order to enlist the aid of others and have them take sides in this issue. In many cases the issue is minor, or is completely justified on the part of the other person. They might say they are very brave about what is going on and begin to cry to manipulate others and convince them something more is going on than has been revealed.

Case Study: Joan

Joan is a sixteen-year-old girl who lives with her mother. Her mother tends to go out with her boyfriend a lot and is not the most attentive parent. Joan is able to go out and do what she wants most of the time. When she runs out of money she just goes into her brother's room and takes some of his change. She doesn't normally take enough for him to notice. One day, however, Joan wanted to go with her friends and her mother told her that she could not go. Joan became very angry and decided she would go anyway. She went into her brother's room and cleaned out all of his change so she could call a cab and go.

When she got home she found out she was grounded. She could not understand why what she did was a problem and blamed her mother for her behaviors, telling her that if she had let her go in the first place there wouldn't have been any problems. Her mother remained firm. Joan called all of her friends and organized a "Team Joan" campaign against her mother. She told the parents of these girls that her mother stayed out overnight each night and didn't keep any food in the house. She said she was hungry and went out to get food because she couldn't think of anything else to do. Her mother had told her she couldn't go get anything and would have to wait until later that night after she went out to eat with her boyfriend before she would get anything.

The incidents Joan related to others were done through tears and moaning that her mother didn't like her and was always mean to her. Joan claimed that she tried very hard all of the time to please her mother but just couldn't do it. Some of the mothers believed this and gave Joan special treats as a result. They also made sure to invite her to special events and bring her along when they went shopping or out to eat.

Getting Sucked In

As Joan's case shows, there is a charisma to the stories and behaviors of people with borderline personality disorder when they are trying to convince someone of something. They are adept at switching their emotions on and off when they are manipulating others to get what they want. At home Joan was punching walls and throwing dishes at her mother, screaming in a rage about how much she hated her. With the mothers of her friends she was sitting meekly in a chair trying unsuccessfully to hold back tears while she told of how her mother would get angry and threaten her, telling her she hated her. Joan would look hurt and confused by it and explain that she did everything she could to make her mother love her.

QUESTION

My daughter is telling everyone that I am a bad mother. How do I get them to believe me when I say I didn't do the things she said I did?
This is always a hard area to navigate and sometimes the best thing to do is just let it be and keep going as you have been. Your daughter will fool them for a while, but it is unlikely that she will be able to maintain the image and stories she is putting out there and others will begin to see the truth for themselves. Sometimes if you protest, others become more convinced that you actually did something.

This type of scenario often tugs at the heartstrings of others and they form instant opinions without investigating the facts. They get sucked in and begin to do things for the person with borderline. They become responsible and begin the pattern of caretaker. As familiarity sets in, the people who have been manipulated begin to see changes and run into difficulty. If they have become too enmeshed they have problems disentangling themselves. If they have not become too enmeshed they often try to quietly withdraw from the situation and might become the target of verbal attacks or manipulation.

CHAPTER 20

Where Do You Go from Here?

Borderline personality disorder can be treated and people can learn to improve and enjoy life again. The more people learn about borderline personality disorder, the more they are able to understand and anticipate the issues that can arise. They are also better able to deal with them, as they learn what works and what doesn't. They key word is "work." The symptoms that are present with this disorder can cause confusion and quick misperceptions that need to be identified and dealt with before actions occur. There is a need for awareness and attention.

Ending the Unstable Pattern

The patterns created when dealing with someone with borderline personality disorder are often firmly entrenched in the family system. Diagnoses normally do not occur until the symptoms have been present and able to wreak havoc for a while. The family normally has to go through quite a bit of pain before they realize they need to get help. This often causes the family members to develop unhealthy patterns of behavior to compensate and deal with the person causing so much instability.

Harmful Patterns

In many cases, the person with borderline controls the interactions, either purposely or subconsciously. Her thoughts and behaviors can keep people who are dealing with her off balance. There is fear of harm and other unwanted consequences from her impulsive and unwise behaviors. And the intense, uncontrolled outbursts of anger can be scary and stressful, intimidating others. This intimidation sets up harmful patterns in all those who are in contact with her.

The person with borderline reinforces these patterns with her own behaviors, rewarding others when they do not get in her way or when they do what she wants them to do. If they do not comply with her wishes, the person with borderline may respond with anger and vindictiveness. The others then return to patterns that they have used before to cope and keep things calm. As these patterns continue, they act to entrench all parties in an endless cycle of dysfunctional behaviors.

What Might Happen

Family members might seek refuge in denial or try to overcompensate for past perceived wrongs by becoming overly attentive and solicitous to the person with borderline. These behaviors do not help. They lend themselves to the instability of the situation and allow the person with borderline to continue to manipulate and engage in harmful behaviors unchecked.

These harmful behaviors, rather than alleviating the person's low self-worth and concerns about abandonment, actually reinforce her symptoms. She is engaging in self-destructive behaviors and is bringing others down with her. Instead of helping, the cycle just becomes more entrenched.

Trying to Break Out

The destructive patterns can be broken with work and awareness. Again, this is not a disorder that can be handled alone. It takes professional help and a support network to learn to deal with and decrease the symptoms. As family members and loved ones become enmeshed in the issues, they form their own poor coping and behavior patterns. These need to be dealt with too. It does little to work on just the person with borderline, as she then goes home and interacts with people who are used to interacting with her in certain ways. She falls right back into these patterns.

Some friends and family might have trouble with the new behaviors of the person with borderline as they are not used to interacting with her in this new way. They have formed expectations, and while the patterns are maladaptive and unpleasant, they are known. People tend to gravitate toward what they know rather than taking chances. If abusive behaviors stop, they are unsure of what is happening and become uncomfortable.

Thus, friends and family might unconsciously act to prevent the person with borderline from breaking out of these patterns of harmful behaviors. They might push the person back into her old behaviors and roles. Someone new to treatment will be more susceptible to this until she forms new relationships and everyone learns the new rules of interacting.

ESSENTIAL

Some friends and loved ones receive constant text messages or phone calls in the middle of the night that threaten self-harm if they leave the borderline person.

Learning New Patterns

It is important for those who are in constant contact with the person with borderline personality disorder to get professional help too. They need to take back their own lives and learn to behave in new ways in order to help the person with borderline—and themselves. In order to do this they need help recognizing what they are doing and how it is affecting everyone.

All the family members need to learn what they have been thinking and doing that contributes to the symptoms and the problematic interactions.

Once these patterns are recognized they can be dealt with. Everyone needs to learn why his or her reactions are the way they are, and how they can be changed. For those who experienced abuse as children, or at the hands of the person with borderline personality disorder, there is a need to heal.

Easing the Destructive Impact

The pain and confusion caused by borderline personality disorder of course affects the person diagnosed with it as well as friends and family. Hurtful words are said, impulsive acts cause others financial hardship, angry episodes lead to fear and dread, and self-harm keeps everyone on high alert. Words cannot be unsaid, and people who have formed negative opinions as a result are not likely to change them. There are plenty of issues to cope with.

Getting Past the Words

The damage done by the angry tirades, accusations, and put-downs can affect loved ones. Their self-esteem and ability to trust in themselves is eroded and they question their own motives. They have likely been the targets of direct attacks that put them down and blame them. They have also been the targets of smear campaigns designed to elicit sympathy.

It is hard to get past the words that hurt, yet it can be done. In most cases it takes the form of therapy. Family therapy is often used to try to heal wounds in all members and teach everyone a new approach to family interactions. The dynamics are assessed and restructured to help everyone move beyond the pain.

Working on New Communication

Pain might be forgiven but is usually not forgotten. Family members need to work through and learn to find new ways to communicate what they are really feeling. Someone with borderline personality disorder learns to recognize and properly give voice to his thoughts and emotions without the attacks or rages. Family members and loved ones learn how to communicate their own feelings without activating the fear responses or rage.

The new communication patterns will be used to convey true meaning without manipulation or defense mechanisms. Each member will learn how he or she speaks to others and how this affects what the others think and feel. Everyone will also learn to ask for clarification rather than assuming what the other person meant was something negative.

Dealing with Damages

People with borderline personality disorder often have other issues that cause them problems. They might have legal issues or problems with finances. Their high impulsivity can cause them to overspend, lose jobs, and get into accidents that result in damages to the property of others. All of these issues need to be taken care of.

Different resources are available to help, including legal services organizations for legal representation, consumer credit agencies, and other forms of aid that can help the person with borderline deal with the issues he created. This is an important and often shaky step because he is more likely to try to get away from responsibility than face the problems confronting him.

Substance Abuse Issues

Substance abuse issues can keep the person with borderline personality disorder from succeeding in dealing with his illness. The ability to retreat and avoid pain through substance use can cause some of the symptoms to remain. There is a loss of inhibitions that promotes the overemotional reactions and highly impulsive behaviors. The drugs might also work to stimulate areas of the brain that exacerbate borderline symptoms.

Substance abuse issues can lead to illegal activities and less money. They cause the person using to become dependent, and increase symptoms of other disorders that are present, including borderline. These issues need professional counseling and assessment in order to deal with both diagnoses at the same time.

Letting It Go

In most cases the best thing to do is let go of the pain. It does no good to hold on to grudges or resentment that sit inside and continue to cause unhappiness. The anger at the person with borderline is based on past issues and behaviors. The hurt is very real, but it needs to be explored and accepted. If it is not, it will remain a sore point in the relationship.

Trust is another issue that does not recover easily, and in many cases it does not recover fully. There is usually a little sliver of distrust that remains no matter how good therapy is. If the person with borderline does not get on board with accepting responsibility it might be best to limit contact and move away from the interactions that have characterized the relationship. They are damaging and if the person does not want to work on them, the process will be one-sided and responsibility will remain with the family members and loved ones.

There is no clear reason why many people with borderline personality disorder improve with age. Some speculate that impulsivity naturally decreases with age, and people learn over time and experience how to avoid the situations that give them the most trouble.

Stepping Away from Over-Responsibility

One goal of therapy is to increase the client's ability to recognize and work with emotions and dysfunctional thoughts. People with borderline personality disorder also need to learn to accept responsibility for their actions. This is an area where they will show reluctance. They do not want to deal with responsibility and will try to avoid it. They have spent many years in this pattern and are fearful of what it entails.

Avoiding Responsibility

This is one of the last issues to go for all parties because it is a pattern of interaction that is one of the hardest to change. It is hard to let go of responsibility and let people with borderline personality disorder fall and face consequences on their own. Some of the consequences will be severe. One mother had to watch her son be led off to jail for a hit-and-run accident that caused damage to three cars. He yelled at her that it was her fault he was going to jail because she wouldn't give him more money to run away. A sister who normally did her brother's science papers stopped doing them and listened as he screamed at her because he failed the course.

People with borderline try to switch the responsibility to someone else, and often they succeed, because they let things go and others get them done so they do not suffer either. When one woman's husband refused to do the dishes for three nights in a row she finally gave in because mold was beginning to grow on them. He knew this would happen and set the situation up so it would.

Consequences for Others

It is hard for loved ones to let things go and let the consequences follow. They feel this way because they love the borderline person and do not want her to feel more pain. They recognize on some level that a great deal of pain is involved in borderline personality disorder. Another reason is because the issue will cause additional consequences for them too.

They might be financially responsible for some aspect of what the person with borderline has done. They do not want to be penalized and might act to keep the person with borderline from feeling consequences so they do not either. These behaviors reinforce the borderline person's avoidance of responsibility, but it is almost impossible to keep her from eventually suffering penalties for her deeds. It is important for loved ones to be careful about what they rely on a person with borderline for, because they must be willing to continue relying on her in order to keep from taking on the responsibility themselves. In cases like a car loan, be prepared to let her lose the car. Sometimes chances need to be taken in order to keep responsibility where it belongs.

Taking Chances

When loved ones remove themselves from over-responsibility they do not normally feel very good about it. They are often nervous about how the person with borderline will deal with the issues, and they worry that it will be too much for the person. They might fear that the person with borderline will fail to meet the demands and fall.

They might also fear that by walking away from over-responsibility they will lose their relationship with that person. They might think the person with borderline will hate them and never speak to them again. This might be encouraged by the person's words presented in anger. The person with borderline often accuses and blames, then threatens.

Threats

The person with borderline personality disorder might make threats in order to get loved ones to take responsibility. They might say they cannot do something themselves and will hurt themselves if they are left to deal with it. Loved ones have already been through this type of situation before and will be fearful of the damage that could be done if they do not help ease the problem.

ALERT

Threats are usually for manipulation, but people with borderline personality disorder have a higher-than-average rate of carrying out threats. Take threats seriously and be on the lookout for signs such as loss of hope, stockpiling medicine, withdrawing from others, talking about when they are gone, and talking about hurting themselves.

The person with borderline might threaten that she will have to leave and find someone who cares. This can cause pain in loved ones as they do care and do not feel validated or recognized by the person with borderline. In each case taking responsibility for the issues of others does not help them. People with BPD need to learn to deal with problems on their own so they can feel better about themselves and learn new ways of coping with the issues they face.

Learning to Cope

It is important to realize that everyone will need to learn to cope with the symptoms and the aftermath. Many people with borderline also have other mental health issues that might or might not respond well to treatment. Some of these issues could remain even if the borderline symptoms are relieved. If the person does not seek treatment, there are many symptoms and situations to learn to cope with in some way.

If No Treatment Is Sought

This is the hardest situation to work with as the symptoms will remain active and unchecked and loved ones and family members have to try to deal with the behaviors that come out. People who do not seek treatment have a high risk of substance abuse in order to mitigate some of the pain. They self-medicate and retreat further into the faulty thinking that drives their behaviors.

They can become so wrapped up in what is happening to them that they are not able to think clearly. The outbursts could increase and become more violent. This is not a problem that goes away, and they need to find more and more ways to cope. Since they do not opt for treatment, coping methods normally impact on others. They become more dependent on others and more manipulative. They will not listen when others try to point out there is a problem, and their reactions might become so severe that other people stop trying for fear of the reaction.

For the Family

When no treatment is sought family members need to learn to cope with the issues that come about. They can still seek treatment and support for themselves. They can also look to other family members and form their own support network. Treatment is highly recommended, as it will help them learn what they should and should not do to keep from becoming too enmeshed in the onslaught of emotions and unstable behaviors.

Family members and friends can join support groups and learn different coping methods from people there. Professionals can help them work through the pain and confusion they are facing. Through all of this it is important to maintain a sense of self and construct boundaries they are not willing to let others cross. They must take time for themselves even if it means calling someone to babysit the person with borderline personality disorder.

Relax

Loved ones need to learn what relaxes them and how to effectively use these activities to have a way to relieve stress during the demanding and often chaotic episodes. This could include exercise, deep breathing, meditation, taking a walk, or even taking a bubble bath. The choice of method is as individual as the person seeking it.

Schedule this time and stick with it. Many things will come up to derail plans, but it is important to do it anyhow. The person with borderline often might have other plans. He might be angry if you take time for yourself. He might play on guilt or try to threaten you. But it is important to relax and take time away.

Build a Support Network

Building a support network is one of the most important coping methods around. People in a support network can help with the roller coaster of emotions and the feelings of guilt. They can also help present a united front to the person with borderline. There will be times when it might seem that there is too much going wrong and no one will understand. This is not true, and a support network keeps the isolation from overwhelming everyone.

QUESTION

How do I go about forming a support network for myself?
Most of the time there are already some people readily available: friends and other family members, for example. If there are no friends or family members who will provide positive support, seek spiritual organizations, support groups for people affected by borderline personality disorder, mental health professionals, and community organizations. There are many people who are trained to help and who want to help; it is just a matter of finding the right fit.

People in the support network do not need to do anything other than be there. They can listen and provide a comforting shoulder to lean on. If members are knowledgeable about borderline, they might also have some suggestions that will help. They can become a lifeline when things get too rough or a place to go when someone needs to step away for a bit and relax. The psychological boost of feeling like you belong and have someone in your life who is on your side can help you get through some of the most difficult times.

Breathe

It is important to take a moment and breathe. Have confidence in your ability to overcome the issues that are presented and believe in the treatment processes that have come to show progress and hope. Take each day as it comes and rely on others for love and support. No one is alone in this, and others are often willing to help and be there to lean on. Let them.

Believe in your ability to get through this and become stronger. Believe in your ability to learn and grow with the guidance and support of professionals who can help. Do not try to deal with this alone. It is a severe issue that needs to be taken very seriously. People who work with borderline personality disorder spend years in school learning about mental health issues, and then more time working under other professionals to be sure they know what they are doing. They do help. If one doesn't seem to, do not give up. Some therapeutic relationships are not a good fit. Keep looking until your find the right person and then get to work.

There is life during and after borderline personality disorder. The trick is to find the right treatment process for all concerned and develop new thought and behavior patterns. There is a lot of work and pain involved, but there is also love and hope.

APPENDIX A

Symptoms Checklist

Borderline personality disorder is characterized by strong, pervasive symptoms that are diagnosed in late adolescence through early adulthood and should include five or more of the following:

1. Extreme fear of abandonment. This fear is beyond normal fears of being alone and is often accompanied by desperate behaviors designed to prevent it.
2. Trouble maintaining relationships due to extremes of devotion and devaluation. Relationships begin quickly and become intensely close very quickly. They then go the other way just as quickly.
3. Very poor and unstable sense of self. Low ability to form independent identity.
4. High impulsivity in at least two of the following areas:

   - Spending money
   - Sexual encounters
   - Substance abuse
   - Reckless driving
   - Binge eating

5. Recurrent suicidal thoughts and behaviors, threats, or use of forms of self-harm, such as cutting, burning, hair pulling, etc.
6. Emotional instability and strong mood swings that often include depression, irritability, or anxiety. These swings can be extreme and normally short in length, lasting hours rather than days in most cases.
7. Chronic feelings of emptiness.
8. Intense anger that is inappropriate for the situation. Also difficulty controlling anger.
9. Brief periods of time where there is a disconnection with reality or paranoia. These periods are often stress related and are not enduring.

Additional Resources

American Psychiatric Association

Offers information about borderline personality disorder, the latest research, its symptoms, causes, and treatments.

↪ *www.psych.org*

American Psychological Association

Offers information about borderline personality disorder, the latest research, its symptoms, causes, and treatments.

↪ *www.apa.org*

BPDCentral.com

Site specific to borderline personality disorder. General information is provided, along with some chat boards for questions and interaction with others dealing with this disorder either personally or through a loved one.

↪ *http://bpdcentral.com/resources/therapist/main.php*

Borderline Personality Disorder

This site is part of the National Education Alliance for Borderline Personality Disorder. It lists different events and information for families and professionals.

↪ *www.borderlinepersonalitydisorder.com*

Borderline Personality Today

Offers information about borderline personality disorder, its symptoms, causes, and treatments.

↪ *www.borderlinepersonalitytoday.com*

DBT Therapists

Provides information on providers using dialectical behavior therapy.

☞ *www.behavioraltech.com/resources/crd.cfm*

Mayo Clinic

Medical website that provides information on the disorder, causes, symptoms, and treatment.

☞ *www.mayoclinic.com/health/borderline-personality-disorder/ DS00442*

National Center for Biotechnology Information

Offers information on current research on borderline personality disorder.

☞ *www.ncbi.nlm.nih.gov/pubmedhealth/PMH0001931/*

National Institute of Mental Health

Offers information about mental illness and treatment.

☞ *www.nimh.nih.gov*

U.S. Department of Health and Human Services

Child abuse and maltreatment statistics.

☞ *www.childwelfare.gov/systemwide/statistics/can/stat_natl_ state.cfm*

WebMD

Provides information on medical aspects of borderline personality disorder, options for treatment, risks, and related disorders.

☞ *www.webmd.com/mental-health/tc/ borderline-personality-disorder-topic-overview*

Index

We Have
EVERYTHING
on Anything!

With more than 19 million copies sold, the Everything® series has become one of America's favorite resources for solving problems, learning new skills, and organizing lives. Our brand is not only recognizable—it's also welcomed.

The series is a hand-in-hand partner for people who are ready to tackle new subjects—like you!

For more information on the Everything® series, please visit www.adamsmedia.com

The Everything® list spans a wide range of subjects, with more than 500 titles covering 25 different categories:

Business	History	Reference
Careers	Home Improvement	Religion
Children's Storybooks	Everything Kids	Self-Help
Computers	Languages	Sports & Fitness
Cooking	Music	Travel
Crafts and Hobbies	New Age	Wedding
Education/Schools	Parenting	Writing
Games and Puzzles	Personal Finance	
Health	Pets	